Love and Kisses
and a Halo
of Truffles

Other books by James Beard

Love and Kisses and a Halo of Truffles

LETTERS TO HELEN EVANS BROWN
EDITED BY JOHN FERRONE

James Beard

ARCADE PUBLISHING · NEW YORK

FIRST EDITION

The letters of James Beard are published with the permission of Reed College and the executors of his Will. Quotations from the letters of Helen Evans Brown are published with the permission of Philip S. Brown.

The frontispiece, showing James Beard and Helen Evans Brown, is used by permission of Dorothy M. Conway.

James Beard's comments on restaurants, food producers and their products should not be construed as endorsements for or criticisms of those institutions and products as they exist today.

Library of Congress Cataloging-in-Publication Data

Beard, James, 1903–1985
 Love and kisses and a halo of truffles : letters to Helen Evans Brown / edited by John Ferrone. — 1st ed.
  p. cm.
 Includes index.
 ISBN 1-55970-264-8
 1. Beard, James, 1903–1985 — Correspondence. 2. Brown, Helen Evans — Correspondence. 3. Cooks — United States — Correspondence. 4. Cookery. I. Brown, Helen Evans. II. Ferrone, John. III. Title.
 TX649.B43B43 1994
 641.5′092 — dc20   94-9548

Published in the United States by Arcade Publishing, Inc., New York
Distributed by Little, Brown, and Company

10 9 8 7 6 5 4 3 2 1

BP

Designed by API

PRINTED IN THE UNITED STATES OF AMERICA

Contents

Introduction

One day in October 1985, the year James Beard died, I had an urgent phone call from Clay Triplette, his loyal houseman. He had been ordered to clear Jim's 12th Street apartment of every sign of human habitation so the house could be put up for sale. The contents had been auctioned off a few weeks before, financial records were in the hands of the executors, and the legendary kitchen was already a ghostly place, but there were bulging file cabinets in the basement destined for a Dumpster. After consulting one of the executors I went to the rescue. An hour later I carried away several shopping bags of files and assorted papers, which I stuffed under my bed, the only available storage space in my apartment. It was more than a year before I could sift through the cache, and when I did I struck gold. There in my hands in a tightly packed box of letters was James Beard's love affair with food and with Helen Evans Brown.

In 1952, when they began to correspond, James Beard was stretching toward his full height as "a titan of the table art," as the *New York Times* food editor had dubbed him, and Helen Evans Brown was the reigning authority on the West Coast. They had been introduced earlier by the food editor of *McCall's* when Helen was in New York lining up magazine assignments, but she really didn't catch Jim's eye until publication of her *West Coast Cook Book*. Well-researched and charmingly written — Jim thought she was as good as M. F. K. Fisher — it collected and documented the best recipes of the Pacific states. Razor clams and salmon cheeks may have reminded him of boyhood summers at the beach in his native Oregon, but, more important, Helen was carrying the flag for American cuisine, an idea dear to Jim's heart. The book would become a model twenty years later for his own opus, *American*

Cookery. He wrote her a fan letter. She wrote him one back. All four of his cookbooks were waiting for autographs, she told him, and she was looking forward to his fifth, *Paris Cuisine,* to be published that year. "Thanks for the dope about the shrimp," she went on to say. "I really knew they shouldn't be cooked over three to five minutes but I didn't have the guts to say so." This is how their dialogue on food began, and it never stopped until Helen's death, twelve years later.

Helen and her husband, Philip, an antiquarian bookseller and accomplished cook, lived in Pasadena; Jim was based in New York. He paid the Browns a first visit in the spring of 1953, escalating friendship into love. Thereafter he could be sure of an affectionate welcome and an extra-long, extra-wide mattress. He could sit on the patio in a kimono with his morning tea, bird-watching. The Browns were as close to family as anything he would have in the years ahead. He was crazy about both of them — a number of these letters are addressed to Philip or to "Dear Browns" — but it was Helen he adored.

She was attractive, smart, outspoken, one of a series of strong-minded women who played a part in Jim's life, but the one for whom he felt the deepest attachment. Although they were born just a year apart, Helen filled the role of a chiding and protective older sister. She was unfailingly supportive and gave him backbone when he fretted about his next move, but she also scolded when he overworked or soaked up too much butter and cream. On two or three occasions she lashed out at him in justifiable anger. He didn't accept criticism from many other people in his life. Helen's unequivocal good sense was just what his wobbling psyche needed.

Like Jim, she had originated on one coast and migrated to the other. She spent her early years in Brooklyn and then studied at Connecticut College for Women and at Hunter College, in New York. It was during her first marriage, in New Haven, that she became interested in food; she ran a catering service, the Epicurean, with a friend and then a restaurant, named Brownstone House. She soon met Philip Brown, pulled up stakes, and moved to Los Angeles, by way of Reno. In 1940 she began writing a monthly mailing piece, "Balzer's Bulletin," for an upscale grocery store, and the following year, a food column for a new fashion magazine, *The Californian.* She published a small cookbook, *Some Shrimp Recipes*, in 1946 and a full-length cookbook, *Chafing Dish Book*, in 1950. By then she was writing for the West Coast magazine *Sunset* and for national magazines, including *McCall's* and *House and Garden.* She was well known enough to be approached by a major publisher, Little, Brown, for her next book, *West Coast Cook Book.*

Jim also made his debut in the food profession through a catering service, after failed careers in singing and acting. While looking for theatre work in New York in the late thirties, he met a German-born brother and sister with as deep an interest in food as his own. Together they started Hors d'Oeuvre, Inc., as a way of revitalizing cocktail-party food. It came to an end with the onset of World War II and publication of Jim's first cookbook, *Hors d'Oeuvre and Canapés* (still in print), in which he neglected to credit his partners. During the war, after stints as cryptographer and farmhand, he was hired by the United Seamen's Service to manage service clubs in Rio de Janeiro, Panama, and Marseille. By the time he returned to New York, at the end of 1945, two more of his cookbooks, *Cook It Outdoors* and *Fowl and Game Cookery*, had been published, which led to his being hired by NBC for a weekly TV show sponsored by Borden. His food demonstrations were the first ever on network television and helped to promote his image as an outsize pinup for good eating. But it was his next book, *The Fireside Cook Book* (1949), energetically promoted by his publisher, that made him famous and extended the repertory of American kitchens. He spent most of the following year living in Paris, where he met Alexander Watt, a Scottish journalist. They collaborated in writing *Paris Cuisine*, the book Helen was waiting for when she and Jim started to correspond.

As two evangelic cooks in an age of convenience foods, they had a lot to say about the sorry state of American cooking. Among their frequent targets were writers of quick-and-easy cookbooks and home economists, many of whom worked for big food packagers and some of whom were good friends. The rigidly practical approach of "the home ec gals" often clashed with Jim's and Helen's sensuous philosophy of food. She wasn't even allowed to call a dish "lovely," Helen complained, and Jim got apoplectic in his bouts with a home ec mustard queen. Their recipes were routinely blue-penciled to eliminate anything that might strain the resources or wits of the average "homemaker." (Men didn't count; they cooked outdoors.) How could the level of cooking be improved, Jim argued, if you aimed for the lowest common denominator? He and Helen believed with all their hearts that American cooks could be led to a promised land beyond tuna casseroles.

They felt pretty much alone in their mission. The only food authority of any stature on the scene was Dione Lucas, British exponent of the Cordon Bleu creed, whom Jim sometimes criticized while acknowledging her technical virtuosity. The most influential food critics were Clementine Paddleford of the *New York Herald Tribune*, Jane Nickerson of the *New York Times*, and Sheila Hibben of *The New Yorker*. Craig Claiborne, with a culinary schooling at the École Hotelière in Lausanne, was about to bring a classic, Continental touch to the food columns of the *Times*. Julia Child and Simone Beck were ready to turn ordinary citizens into French chefs.

America's world of food was young, and today's gastronomic clichés were just appearing on the horizon. Spaghetti Carbonara had become the most exciting pasta discovery in Jim's repertoire. His signature dishes were lobster à l'Américaine, Chicken with Forty Pieces of Garlic, and Choucroute Garnie. He was perfecting potatoes Anna and the soufflé. The Waring Blendor was a new toy in his kitchen, and the croissant, something of a mystery. The guru was learning, and each visit to the restaurants and vineyards of Europe made him a little wiser.

In the 1950s there was airmail service between the coasts, and overnight delivery was taken for granted. Jim and Helen wrote to each other two and three times a week, dating their letters simply "Tuesday" or "Friday." Even during their trips abroad, they scarcely drew breath, and one of Helen's letters from Pasadena reached Jim in Paris in three days flat.

He needed abalone recipes for his next book. She asked his advice on wines to serve with ham. Tamales flew east. Truffles flew west. He sent her utensils from the shops of Europe. She tracked down the Chinese bowls he couldn't find in New York. They swapped views on dieting and better ways to make money. "I too am poor and fat," Helen announced after a despairing letter from Jim.

He was often more concerned about his income than his weight and had a lifelong fear of going broke. It drove him to take on too many assignments and into consorting with the enemy — the producers of the cake mixes and boil-in-bag vegetables he once scorned. Critics continue to fulminate over his commercial ties — and a few vigilantes, who forget that food is business as well as art, would like to see him entirely discredited — but magazine articles and books didn't even pay the grocery bills. Try as he might to hew to the gospel of honest cookery, he was forced to concede that maybe he and Helen would have to compromise a little about quick-and-easy recipes. Maybe their mission, after all, was to make convenience foods more palatable.

In a profession increasingly shaken by rivalries and squabbles, Jim's and Helen's partnership was without parallel. They could be envious of colleagues who grabbed lucrative assignments from under their noses, but they never fought with each other over territorial rights. Helen had the West Coast, with extensions into Mexico, the Southwest, and the Far East. Jim had the rest of the world. Only rarely did they find themselves on the same turf. "I do hope, Jim, that our cheese articles won't conflict," Helen once wrote sweetly. They donated recipes to each other's articles and books, passed along assignments, sang each other's praises in public and private. They agreed, without modesty, that they were the best in the business. She was a better writer. He knew more. Helen proclaimed that he was "*the* foremost authority on cooking in the country."

Their efforts to team up produced a string of schemes. Helen suggested a syndicated column and a coast-to-coast radio conversation that would allow them to go on living as they were. Jim hoped to uproot the Browns and hug them closer. One favorite seduction plan was to run a restaurant together, a longing that grew after he managed a fast-food place on Nantucket in the summer of 1953. He may have been following in the footsteps of his mother, who ran a residence hotel with a good dining room in Portland, Oregon, before he was born. But he also saw it as an agreeable way to make money, with time off for travel. In January 1954 he wrote that they could have the services of the *Maasdam*'s head chef if they could get a restaurant going, and at the beginning of 1957 he came close to acquiring a Greenwich Village landmark, Grand Ticino. When there were no further prospects at home, he was ready to move to the West Coast, if Helen would join him in a restaurant somewhere near the ocean between Monterey and the Mexican border, with the enticing prophecy that "it could be the Pyramide of this country, with both of us." In 1958 he thought he had found the perfect spot, on the Eastern Shore of Maryland, and with his friends Bettina and Henry McNulty considered buying a large Victorian house to turn into an inn and restaurant. Later in the year his pupil Clare Boothe Luce turned his gaze to New Mexico as a possible paradise. It all came to nothing, and he had to content himself with designing menus for other people's restaurants — Chillingsworth Inn on Cape Cod, Helen Sigel Wilson's restaurants in Philadelphia, and the spectacular series of restaurants under the aegis of Joe Baum and Restaurant Associates.

Jim had further ideas for Beard and Brown. In 1955 he and his friend Agnes White rented space on lower Fifth Avenue for a shop that would offer food specialties, antiques, and cookbooks. They hoped the Browns would move east so Philip could run the shop while Jim and Helen cooked up delicacies. When the Browns wisely declined, the lease for the shop was terminated and the inventory sold off.

The same year, Jim tried his hand at a cooking class, soon to become an important part of his career, and this opened another opportunity to woo Helen, either by having her as a guest teacher in New York or running a session with her each year on the West Coast. She taught one class in New York in the fall of 1962 but confessed she would rather create new dishes and write.

As it turned out, their only major collaboration was a cookbook, *The Complete Book of Outdoor Cookery*, published by Doubleday in 1955. Jim had already produced an outdoor book for Barrows in 1941, and, as Californians, the Browns had had years of experience over the grill. Philip was an expert on the subject and became a silent partner. The correspondence of 1953–1954 is dominated by reports of their food tests on various types of grills and smokers.

Before the book was finished, they were casting about for their next subject. Jim proposed "Historic Menus," "Favorite Dishes," "An Alphabet of Food," "The Best of Beard and Brown," "Short Cuts to Entertaining," "Classic Recipes and Their Variations," and "Recipes and Recollections" — a foretaste of his *Delights and Prejudices*. A last proposal came from Helen, in 1961, for a book on wine and cheese. It is a mystery why none of these ideas materialized. True, both authors had trouble enough meeting deadlines for their own assignments without doing another book together long-distance, but they may have been reticent for other reasons. Twice Helen had to reproach Jim for misusing material from their outdoor cookbook, which might have made her wary of further collaboration; and could Jim's steady rise to Titanship have made him less eager to share the limelight? In any case, his next book was done with his Portland friend Isabel Callvert, while Helen worked with Philip.

Almost from the beginning of their friendship Jim and Helen talked of turning their letters into a book — a double autobiography with commentary on food — and they set about rewriting some of their recent letters as samples. "I am doing a letter which answers your questions on brioche, on French names, and on sugar peas," Jim wrote. "Then I am criticizing Dione [Lucas]'s dinner. . . . I have spoken about a couple of books and may talk a little about a restaurant." Their agent took the idea to Alfred and Blanche Knopf, who liked it and asked for a full proposal. Helen felt that such a book could not be hurried, too many other projects intervened, and the plan was put on the back burner, to be stirred from time to time. Ten years after it was first suggested, Jim gave it a final stir.

The chief benefit of keeping the scheme alive was preservation of both sets of letters. Helen might have saved Jim's anyway, but Jim was not a keeper of scrapbooks or memorabilia, and he had a reputation for hurling photographs and anything else of interest to posterity into the garbage, from which they were sometimes retrieved by his staff. Despite Helen's care, his letters to her twice came close to being destroyed — not only when Jim's house was being spiffed up for the real estate market in 1985, but also five years earlier, when a fire at the Browns' house consumed Helen's journals and other documents.

Apart from what they reveal about his personal life and his relationship with Helen Evans Brown, James Beard's letters are worth having for his passionate pursuit of good food, whether at home, aboard ship, or in the starriest restaurants of France. After rereading these letters a few months before he died, he summed them up succinctly for Philip Brown: "We sure ate a lot." Their diets were doomed to fail.

It must have been shattering to Jim when his friend Helen died in December 1964. She was sixty. The rare kidney disease that first surfaced in 1961 had developed into cancer. She was too ill to work through most of her final year, and Philip took over her writing assignments. Jim's last surviving letter to her was written in August from Provence. He was able to pay her a visit in November, two weeks before she died.

This volume is in part the book they often talked of doing. If Helen's voice is largely absent, her presence can be felt on every page. "God, it's been a long time since we had a good chat," Jim wrote to her in his next-to-last letter. After twelve years, there was still a lot more to be said.

John Ferrone

Editor's Note

Early in their correspondence, Helen Evans Brown told James Beard she was saving his letters so he could remember all the wonderful food he had eaten. Approximately 450 were in Philip Brown's safekeeping after her death. In 1984 he sent them to Jim to reread before donating them to an archive, and they were still in Jim's possession when he died. Excerpts from 300 of them appear in this collection.

With few exceptions, the letters were typewritten, averting the challenge of transcribing the world's most inscrutable handwriting. Unfortunately, ninety percent of them were undated. Nearly two years were spent attempting to date them from references to Jim's published work and to various social events before the discovery of a cache of his engagement books made the task a good deal easier. The dates given here, in brackets, are reasonably accurate.

It was not possible to present the letters in their entirety. I have selected excerpts that focus largely on food, but they also give some idea of the convivial life Jim led, professionally and socially, despite the poor health and depression that plagued him throughout these years. Much of the deleted material concerns travel arrangements, routine discussions of writing assignments, and gossip about friends and colleagues whose names would be meaningless to most readers. For the sake of a more readable book, deletions are not indicated.

I silently edited the letters in other ways, correcting language and facts, supplying a name, word, or phrase where needed, and making an occasional transposition, taking my cue from Jim's and Helen's declared intention to edit their letters for publication.

The recipes given at the end of the book are inspired by references in the letters (indicated with an asterisk). Unless otherwise attributed, they are either adapted from Jim's own recipes or are reconstructed from directions in the text.

I am grateful to a number of people who in various ways have helped this project along:

Morris Galen and Reed College, for permission to publish the letters; Philip Brown, for allowing me to retain the letters during the preparation of this volume and for supplying dates, facts, and encouragement; Clayton Triplette, for saving the letters from oblivion; The University of Wyoming Heritage Center, for providing Helen Evans Brown's correspondence, and Jeremy Johnston, for the arduous copying of Beard's engagement books; the Oregon Historical Society, for access to their James Beard archives; Cecily Brownstone, for the generous use of her library and her memory and for many happy hours of reminiscence. For plumbing their memories, files, and albums I also thank (in no order) Mary Hamblet, Henry and Bettina McNulty, Naomi Barry, Denise Otis, Jane Nickerson, Mateo Lettunich, Caroline Stuart, Mary Lyon, Sam and Florence Aaron, Joe Baum, Julie Dannenbaum, Frederick Rufe, Chuck Williams, and Van der Veer Varner. I am indebted to Evan Jones and Robert Clark for their informative biographies of James Beard; and to Roberta Leighton for fine-combing the manuscript. I was especially fortunate to work with Jeannette Seaver, a fine cook as well as a fine editor.

1952   1953

Both James Beard and Helen Evans Brown had cookbooks published in 1952 by Little, Brown. Their fan letters to each other set off their twelve-year correspondence. JB was beginning another book, *James Beard's New Fish Cookery,* and asked HEB's help with recipes for West Coast fish. In January 1953 he became a consultant to Edward Gottlieb Associates, promoters of French cognac and champagne. In April he made his first trip to California in thirteen years and visited the Browns. On the way back he attended the National Restaurant Show in Chicago. In late June he went to Nantucket for the summer to manage and cook for a restaurant called Chez Lucky Pierre. On September 22 he sailed for Europe, toured the Bordeaux wine country, spent time in Paris and London, and returned to New York in early November on the *Queen Elizabeth.* By early December, JB and HEB were planning to collaborate on a book of outdoor cookery.

36 West 12th Street
New York
May 23, 1952

My dear Helen —

There, you see, I have started. Thanks for your letter — and for the recipe for the Flapper Salad.[1] I showed it to someone who took it seriously. God, where can their sense of humor be?

I want to send you *Paris Cuisine* properly inscribed.[2] I think it is a pretty book. Little, Brown did very well by both of us this year. Monday night my very good friend Bill Palmer of the Café Continental is giving a dinner for the press and promotion people — about forty. Wish the two of you could be here. We are giving them chausson of lobster à l'Américaine, poularde Maxim's, rice pilaff, pineapple au kirsch and two of the cakes from the book. Champagne, a really wonderful Tavel '45 and liqueurs comprise the wine list.

Send me a couple of your favorite fish recipes, typically Western, for my fish book if you will. I'd love to have a few things from other people. Make it something you are really fond of.

All the best,
Jim

---

[1] A popular salad of the 1940s, in which half a canned pear or peach was decorated with shredded carrot, pimiento, and other items to create the face of a flapper. This was coated with aspic and served on lettuce with a sweet dressing.

[2] By James A. Beard and Alexander Watt, published in 1952.

[36 West 12th Street
New York]
August 4, 1952

My dear Helen —

In the middle of all this heat I am doing pictures of eggnog and all the holiday cheer. Then, come January, I will be doing mint julep. There is no rhyme nor reason to this life whatsoever.

I have never cooked abalone in my life and wonder if you would be good enough to send me two or three recipes which you can vouch for to use in the fish book. I don't want to take recipes from here and there, because I can't try them out.

If you are doing a book for Spice Islands I want you to include my (or rather Mary Meerson's) beefsteak Flamande. Mary really uncovered it when she and her husband [Lazare] were doing all the research and the designs for *Carnival in Flanders*.[1] It is nothing more than a lot of rosemary pressed into a thick steak with the heel of the hand and then grilled. But the flavor is something you wouldn't believe true. I like it better than any steak dish I know. I have also done it with a whole filet which was wrapped with fat. Stuck the rosemary under the fat and roasted the whole thing in a very fast oven.

Also try frying breakfast cereals in a little butter and garlic powder or celery powder, and add a few peanuts and almonds to it. Soupçon is doing that here and getting two dollars a quart for it.[2]

There is a movement afoot, with quite a little of the money already raised, to start a new food magazine. Know of anyone who might be a likely person to buy a share of it? — it is going in $5,000 hunks so far. And don't tell anyone who is close to *Gourmet* at this point, for several reasons. At any rate I think you should, when the thing gets going, apply for West Coast editor. I know it would be received kindly. So far we have Philippe of the Waldorf,[3] Peggy Wood's husband, Bill Walling,[4] Sam Field, the publisher, and my friend Bill Palmer, who has about ⅔ of the money in the world, it seems to me, and several others. I say "we" but I have nothing to do with it so far except they have called me in as a consultant about it. God knows, there is the need for a first-class food magazine.

I must stop this and get busy roasting about 15 pounds of beef so that it will look pretty for the damned picture tomorrow.

My best to you all,
Jim

---

[1] A 1935 French film about the seventeenth-century Spanish occupation of Flanders.

[2] A New York shop that offered specialty foods and accessories.

[3] Claudius Charles Philippe was general manager of the Waldorf Astoria Hotel.

[4] William A. Walling, a printing company executive and husband of the stage and television actress.

[36 West 12th Street
New York]
September 17, 1952

[Dear Helen —]

The abalone recipes, if I haven't already thanked you, were elegant. I could use a special one if you want to do it for me.

I am getting so fat that I can hardly move around. What I am going to do, God only knows. And right now is the time when everyone is giving parties and people are eating and drinking too much. And me, going to Europe in March unless TV prohibits. There is no help in us, as the prayer books used to say.

I have to fly to the bank and put in and take out. What a life — no one can save a bloody cent — I am always poor nowadays.

If you ever find another copy of *The Web-Foot Cook Book*,[1] let me know about it. I should love to have it for sentimental reasons.

All the best,
gastronomically,
Jim

---

[1] A rare nineteenth-century cookbook published by the San Grael Society of the First Presbyterian Church of Portland, Oregon.

Pasadena
[September 1952]

My dear Jim,

The second copy of *Web-Foot Cook Book* we find will be yours. The first, I selfishly admit, will be ours. We have tried to years to get one. . . .

I, too, am poor and fat. What a world!

H.E.B.

36 West 12th Street
⋅ New York
January 20, 1953

My dear Helen —

Last year I was nuts for the month before Christmas, with Sherry Wine & Spirits[1] calling on me all the time and having to do several articles and then doing three television jobs, including getting to the studio at 6:30 Christmas morn to roast a goddam goose.

My neck is being broken by the fish book. I have to ask you for some more help. It has been so long since I have been on the Coast that I forget some things. Salmon, smelts, halibut, sand dabs, porgies — most of them I remember vividly. But I am stumped by the rockfish — which is not what rockfish is here — striped bass, is it? And then the ling cod and the Alaska cod baffle me a bit, too. The Alaska cod I remember as being a very oily fish which bakes well and kippers well, and the ling cod I remember as a pretty good all-round fish. Do you get any whitefish from California waters? or red snapper? or fresh haddock? What kind of bass are there in the markets? And can you give me a couple of good recipes for the following:

Fresh tuna
Barracuda
Shark

Any unusual Chinese recipes — I have sweet and sour and fish with walnuts, etc. Anything else you might think of would be so appreciated I would practically crawl out on my hands and knees to thank you.

Fresh sardines — do you use them?

Herring?

I have taken on a job as consultant to the new cognac campaign they are putting on over here.[2] It is to run for a year and should be pleasant bread and butter for that time. I hope you have lots of things with cognac in them in print this year.

Tonight I have Alexis Lichine[3] and two others for dinner. I am giving them some charcuterie and a little bit of green to start with — then duck with turnips, mushroom sauté with parsley and garlic, cheese, and a chocolate soufflé, which is the recipe I use for chocolate roll and soufflé both — 6 eggs — beat the yolks with ¾ cup of sugar and beat in 6 ounces melted semisweet chocolate — then fold in the 6 beaten whites and bake. Simple and really good. I usually melt the chocolate with a little rum. We are sampling about four wines so I have more or less simple dishes to enhance them.

I hope you don't think I am imposing, asking you so many fish questions. I promise you your name in double caps in the new book.

Yours,

Jim

---

[1] Wine shop on Madison Avenue, in New York, run by Jack and Sam Aaron, for which JB was a consultant.

[2] JB was hired by Edward Gottlieb Associates, which handled public relations for the French cognac and champagne industries.

[3] Internationally known wine expert, wine producer, and author.

36 West 12th Street
New York
February 4, 1953

My dear Helen —

Thanks, thanks for your letter and all the help. I am writing on taste memory, as I remember the sablefish and the dabs and some of the other fish we had around Astoria and Gearhart. Your fish chart is a magnum opus.

Yes, Little, Brown are doing it, and it is going to be a rush job at the end, I can see that. Do you and Philip have that new book of La Monte's — *Marine Game Fishes of the World?* If not I shall send it to you at once — it's rather good. And have you all the books from the Department of the Interior, written by Rachel Carson,[1] on the fish of the Atlantic? If not, I shall ask Rose Kerr [of the Department of the Interior] to get me a set for you. They are worth adding to your collection for the information as well as the writing. And I'm afraid those days in Washington are gone when they have someone like Carson to do a job like that.

The soufflé, I find, cooks best at 375 rather than at the high temperature of the French recipes. I once discussed this with [Louis] Diat,[2] and we came to the conclusion that the hotel type of soufflé cooks quickly because the oven is always hot, but in the home unless your stove is perfectly insulated there is no chance that the soufflé will do the same job. Therefore 375 is really safer. It depends on the time — around 25 minutes, for wet, I find is right. You do my favorite soufflé, of course — a ginger one with gobs of preserved ginger in it?* And whipped cream with little bits of ginger? That is something.

Back to my fish.

Best,
Jim

---

[1] Marine biologist and author of *The Sea Around Us* (1951) and *Silent Spring* (1962).

[2] Chef at the Ritz Carlton in New York for many years who was credited with the invention of vichyssoise.

* Recipe.

36 West 12th Street
New York
February 26, 1953

My dear Helen —

Thanks a million for the recipes. I have incorporated them and have finished the first draft of the damn book except for the shark recipes you promised to send me.

They have just sent me the galleys of a rather charming book by Sophie Kerr and June Platt called *The Best I Ever Ate,* which is a series of reminiscences of gastronomic highlights in their lives, with recipes for the dishes they talk about. More and more I feel that the real future of the cookbook lies in that sort of book. Stories and recipes and gaiety — well, you did it to a great extent in *West Coast Cook Book* and it captivated everyone. If I were only a really good writer I would do something fabulous in that direction — but maybe I shall find someone to ghost it for me or do it with me.

My dear friends Kathi and Claude Sperling have an amusing place at Nantucket called Lucky Pierre. It is the first attempt on this coast to do a real West Coast hamburger and sandwich job — with fantastically wonderful decor and advertising, which has captured all New England. They can't be there during the summer so I am going up to be the manager — and if it goes the way we think it will, we shall take our lives in our hands and start the same thing here in New York. For the only thing of its kind we have, called Hamburg Heaven, with about six branches, is something you or I would spit on in passing — but it has made a fortune.

Tomorrow night Francis Guth, a tycoon in the textile business who cares only for cooking and eating and wining, is doing a dinner for fourteen in a friend's kitchen. We are getting a clear game consommé, a pâté of duck livers and grouse in artichoke bottoms, a cold roast sturgeon with his special sauce, a wild turkey flown from Yucatán, with another sauce, some sort of braised vegetable, cheese, and a dessert which slips my mind.

This, along with wines chosen by Lichine, should make a unique and wonderful dinner — many too many courses for me nowadays, but interesting anyway.

Thanks again for the recipes. You have a halo of truffles intertwined with old southern smilax and large goose livers.

Always the best,
Jim

36 West 12th Street
New York
May 18, [1953]

My dear Helen and Philip —

I haven't had time to catch my thoughts since I left International Airport almost a fortnight ago. The restaurant show in Chicago took all my time and energy, for that immense barn of a pier is one of the most fatiguing places in the world, and the walk to our booth[1] was almost a good mile, it seemed to me.

I have returned here with many ideas in my head. Firstly, I know that the Browns made me as happy as I have been for a long time. The wonderful times we all had during the days I was there in Pasadena are something I shan't forget. I am convinced that we should and will be a team — and if there is any chance of becoming tops in this field I think we can do it, with a few breaks. I felt yesterday that I would have given anything to have dropped into the Brown kitchen, run up some sort of an experiment and then chinned for a few hours.

As for my next step, either I keep on plugging along with all the things at hand or I find a new outlet. Perhaps the summer at Nantucket will help me make the decision. I am not so sure that the thing I want isn't a restaurant of my own — or with someone else — interested, Browns? I know that I never want to think of writing another cookbook or anything like it. Especially after getting the news that neither *Paris Cuisine* nor *West Coast Cook Book* has been publicized in Portland. In fact, several people asked me when my Paris book was to come out. Why do we waste time doing books when it gets us nothing?

The restaurant show showed more ways to imitate food than you can imagine. There were artificial onion soups, ice cream made from old rayon petticoats, barbecued sandwiches heated with a steam pipe in one second, cake mixes and pancake mixes by the ton, little doots to keep potatoes white, and so forth. All the equipment in the world and much that was fine. I may have a freezer as a result. But as for anything to make food better or more truly flavorful, there was nothing. A sad commentary on the future of food in this country. If restaurateurs are intent on cutting quality and giving artificially puffed-up food, there is no chance for any of us to do missionary work.

I dined at the famed Pump Room and had what I consider to be the end of all dinners for $13.00. I am going to give them a pumping when I write about it in *Apartment Life*. I was begged by the captain to try the — quote — "Sliced Beef Tenderloin cooked in Burgundy wine, Old French Market, buttered noodles (on Wagon)." Well, it was on wagon all right, but for the life of me there was no trace of the Old French Market. It included some rather large chunks of what may originally have been chuck but so cooked in something resembling red wine and thickened with cornstarch that I couldn't quite tell all the other things in it. This was served in a ring of noodles which had been heating away on the steam table for lo these many hours — and with no seasoning whatsoever. A half-bottle of Haut-Brion 1934 was served in a glass which you wouldn't think large enough for a liqueur. And for the first course two little pieces of king crab meat with mustard dressing — specialité de la maison — to the tune of $2.50. Of course there were the hot and cold running waiters in their hunting-pink jackets and their black satin knickerbockers and nylon hose. And there was all the usual pomp and glop to make it more chichi than ever. Thank God I can send the bill to the magazine.

I'm off now to do some errands and to learn how to make Crêpes Bretonne.

> All my love and kisses to
> the Browns,
> Jim

---

[1] JB was a consultant for National Premium Beer.

> [36 West 12th Street
> New York
> June 8, 1953]

[Dear Helen —]

My dinner at Dione Lucas's[1] was strange and wonderful. We started with the most indifferent bits of bread with smoked salmon, and cocktails. Then when we went to table she told me that she was ashamed of her hollandaise because the stove went wrong. She hadn't made it, but one of her assistants on the TV show had. It was sole poached in white wine with Mornay sauce and the Mornay topped with hollandaise and then truffles. With this, champagne. Then a chicken sauté which she made the point of calling "Stanley" — but Stanley is prepared by poaching and has a velouté with curry and other things added, and is served with rice. This was a sauté with bits of ham, truffle and mushroom, and a brown sauce. Truffles twice. Then asparagus hollandaise. Hollandaise twice. And potatoes and hot brioche. Then a huge salad and then a Dobosh Torte, which she said she had not made and which I could tell had come from a bake shop nearby. She ate nothing but watched every bite I took. And she questioned me later about leaving a small piece of fish on the plate. She fell asleep in the drawing room. She does all the shows I told you about and then goes away on weekends to cook for eighty people in some religious cult. It is her salvation she is working on. I am told she not only cooks for two days for these eighty people but that she buys all the food out of her own pocket as well.

Look at this month's *Town and Country* and read the recipes. The Lobster Américaine is all wrong. She is a great, great technician who doesn't know food.

Yesterday Ann Seranne[2] and I drove up to Philippe's and did lunch for fourteen. Smoked salmon and sturgeon with champagne, then a cold cream of pumpkin soup with nutmeg,* tiny baby lamb racks with a touch of garlic and Old Man on them (sample enclosed),[3] sirloin steaks, and a huge green salad with field salad, cress, romaine, endive and Boston lettuce. Then fruits with kirsch and ice cream (Waldorf) and a cake (Waldorf). It was a lot of fun and we think everyone had a whirl of a time.

Love and kisses to you both,

J

---

[1] British chef, cooking-school teacher, and restaurateur; author of *The Cordon Bleu Cook Book*.

[2] Executive editor of *Gourmet* and cookbook author.

[3] Southernwood (*Artemisia abrotanum*). HEB noted that it was also known as "Old Man's Love," "Lad's Love," and "Maiden's Rum." An ingredient in some European beers, it was an odd herb for JB to be using.

* Recipe.

[36 West 12th Street
New York
June 1953]

Helen —

I hope you have a copy of the letter you sent me. If not, I'll send it back. Here is what I think — rewrite it and let us tell bits of news and criticize whatever we wish but limit our letters to three questions each time so that they can be enlarged upon. Now I am doing a letter which answers your questions on brioche, on French names and on sugar peas. Then I am criticizing Dione's dinner, asking you about menu making, answering you on hams and smoking and discussing taste memory. I have spoken about a couple of books and may talk a little about a restaurant — the Waldorf, to be exact — and will bring in the Philippe lunch. We should make the letters — yours and mine together — about two thousand words.

Leave the holiday stuff for the second letter — I could write 3,000 words on why I hate cranberries alone. And we can fight over Christmas cookies and all that sort of thing. I can stand forth on my love of mince pie, and on how it is ruined by jellies and jams and by cooking. I think good mincemeat is cooked by cognac and not by heat.

Going to Cheryl Crawford's[1] for the weekend. We are entertaining about twenty on Saturday night and I am making carnitas and Poor Man's Butter and a salsa fria.*

About your roast with Adolph's [meat tenderizer]. It evidently didn't reach an interior temperature of more than about 130, which means that any Adolph's which was in there kept on tenderizing after cooking and made it mushy. It has to reach 150, internal temperature, before it stops working. I think the product needs the greatest care in the world. However, it does tenderize meat if applied properly. It is just like a hell of a lot of other things on the market which are not for us but which do the job they are intended to do.

Love and kisses,

J

---

[1] Theatrical producer and one of the founders of the Group Theatre. She and her companion Ruth Norman had a house in New Canaan, Connecticut.

* Recipes.

[Nantucket
July 1953]

Dear Helen —

I received your letter about the duck press and it brought a little ray of hope to me in the midst of all this madness. Although I can say maybe we should open a Lucky Pierre's before I lose the urge. I am having the time of my life and some grief thrown in. We are getting 95¢ for a cheeseburger, $2.00 for shish kebabs and $1.95 for four jumbo shrimps, deep-fried. I am thinking up all the gooey sundaes and making soup of fish bones and heads that sells for 60 cents a cup, hot or cold. I enclose the menu.

Yesterday I got here at 9:30 in the morning and finally fell asleep just as the clock in the church belfry was striking five. Then I was here at ten this morning. But the place is so damn gorgeous and the weather is so perfect that it makes up for it completely. Such an enchanting place I have never known anywhere. Last night was foggy and thick, and with this old whaling background, the architecture and the cobbled stones of Main Street, I felt I was starring in a Eugene O'Neill saga.

The natives resent the off-Islanders. We have had reports that we take dope and have sex orgies in the middle of Lucky Pierre's all the time. Then they come a-snooping and find out they like it.

Last night I had to write a book by long distance to be handed in to Schenley this morning. I hope to God it goes through. You and I should both be in the same place. We could cover all the food business in the country.

Love
[Jim]

[Nantucket
July 1953]

Dearest Browns —

I am writing a brief and wonderfully incoherent note probably. We have had fog and rain, and as a result have been so busy that we couldn't breathe. I have made about five or six chocolate rolls a day and all sorts of specialties, and have been taken off my feet by the doctor and strapped up, for overwork and being too much on the old pedals. So I only work twelve hours a day now instead of fourteen, as my assistant Mac sends me home about midnight with threats of death.

If the Browns want to be lambs to me, find some way to ship me a few nectarines and peaches now and again, as the fresh fruit on the Island is confined to bananas and overripe and moldy cherries from God knows where. Just the sight of six good nectarines would be a cheer.

I am importing an omelet expert [Rudolph Stanish] for two weeks, and I have steady streams of old ladies for onion tarts and quiche Lorraine every day. And we have invented another soup.

Had a drunk come in last night and order a hamburger and coffee at the counter and then walk out — only to return fifteen minutes later. When they gave him his hamburger and coffee — the first in a basket and the second in a mug — he ignored them and started eating relish and mustard out of the pots with the little plastic spoons, and then sugar out of the sugar bowl. He finally choked — not to death, unfortunately — on a lump of sugar and almost upswallowed but steadfastly refused to leave before he had finished all the mustard, relish, and sugar on the table. He never touched his coffee or hamburger. With that I leave you.

Love

J

[Nantucket
July 1953]

Dearest Helen —

Well, I feel like a new person. I have been so taut and nerve-racked that I couldn't sleep. But Joseph, the masseur, is here and has raked me over the rack of torture for two or three goes now, and I can sleep. He practically had to unscrew my head to loosen it, but with all the pain went a hell of a lot of worry.

I am sending you a recipe that is supposedly handed down from one generation to another here within a wealthy family. Try it and tell me how it works.

As for the madeleines — I haven't my recipe here but as I remember it, it is a half-pound each of sugar, flour and clarified butter, 4 eggs and either cognac or rum for flavoring. I mix the flour and sugar and then add the eggs and beat in the clarified butter. Then the flavoring. I am sure that is it. Try it anyway, and if it isn't right I will send you a pound of butter in the mail to make up for it.

We have been doing that Délice au Chocolat* from *Paris Cuisine* as well as the chocolate rolls, and it is so rich it walks out of the room.

My good friends the Palmers were here over the weekend. I took them to the Mad Hatter for dinner on Saturday night. It is the most glorified of tearoom food with a heavy Dione Lucas accent. We had Mrs. Martin's seafood bisque — it tasted like a great deal of cheddar cheese was melted in with the clams and scallops — a sour, strange taste with a smooth, creamy texture. I would guess she makes it in the Waring Blendor instead of straining it with rice, as I do when I make a bisque. Then we had the famous filet of beef, which she calls a "Gourmet Dish." She marinates the filet in olive oil, herbs — marjoram, thyme, bay and rosemary, is my guess — and a little vinegar and then roasts it very quickly. With this we had her patties of shredded potatoes, deep-fat-fried, young onions cooked in sugar syrup, which were unbelievably horrible, and spinach mixed with so much nutmeg that it was like a pudding. For dessert — her chocolate roll, which is the same as ours, only she gives one inch as against our three inches for the same money. This dinner cost $15 for three people without the drinks. She is making, need I add, a fortune.

We have had all the distinguished visitors — the [David] Sarnoffs, the [Alben] Barkleys, the [Leland] Haywards — and Mary Martin is supposed to come this week, and there has been a dribble of the lesser luminaries, whom my boys merely nod to as they wait on them.

We find that waitresses and maîtres d'hôtel are the best tippers. Send me a copy of the Angel's Kiss recipe.

Love and kisses,
JB

---

* Recipe.

Helen Dear —

I am worn out and can hardly put foot in front of foot. It is wonderful, though, for there are enough people who appreciate what we are doing to make up for it all. Last night we did a dinner party for eight, with the Portuguese sausage of the island, in puff paste, the lobster soufflé from the Plaza Athénée in Paris and then a St. Honoré gâteau — fun and games for a little hamburger joint. We have had Stanish doing omelets. That boy is wonderful. He turned out over two hundred last week in full view of the admiring audience, at $2 apiece, with salad and a roll. They clamor for him and pay $3.50 at night for a flaming soufflé omelet. Personally I have always felt that an omelet was the most overrated piece of food in the world. Stanish trained with Dione and at the Cordon Bleu in Paris. Thinks you and I know everything but makes three times the money we do. He came here merely to have the restaurant experience and works for little or nothing. He makes omelets for luncheon and dinner and all the chocolate rolls, which now amount to about twelve a day. We sell two a day to a smart restaurant that gives us a billing for them.

We have been getting the most delicious corn I have ever eaten, gathered in the morning and eaten within hours. It is wonderful cooked about two minutes. Or sometimes I scrape it off raw, mix it with whipped or sour cream and serve it as a cold first course. Did I ever tell you of the delicious corn ice cream I had in Yucatán — fresh corn and sugar added to the cream and frozen? It was one of the greatest food experiences I have ever had. Try it in your little freezer.

Send me your regular recipe for sourdough bread, and do you think we could do a starter here? The atmosphere is filled with wild yeasts. Maybe we could get a starter by air from California. If we could accomplish sourdough this summer it would be the end of all.

L & K,
[Jim]

[Nantucket
July 1953]

My dear Helen —

I agree with you thoroughly about our letters. We shouldn't sound like Jeanne Owen.[1] We have both been more than critical of those who carry around a pontifical store of knowledge and who cannot seem to get down below the mezzanine.

I am seriously considering giving up my apartment this fall or at least renting it for a year and getting settled in the next step. I'm ready to talk about running a resort restaurant with you. I have the cook, who will go anywhere with me. There is money to be made by the wheelbarrow load in a resort if you do the right thing and have a small amount of labor.

We are doing a wonderful business at Lucky Pierre's with snacks and certain specialties. During the two nor'easter days we were so busy that we couldn't stop. On top of that I had a party of the old dowagers — why do they all love me? — for Homard à l'Améri-caine. They raved. We ran out of everything that day and I crawled home at three in the morning for my sleeping pill and downy couch. And there is art to be put into a hamburger and into a bun. We have just started to bake our own hamburger buns. And I am making a pissaladière every day and sometimes a Swiss onion tart. They are all finding out that they can bring the children this year, that we are specializing in respectability and good food. We still have the drunks at night, but then, one must make a few weary dollars from them. I did order two drunken females out yesterday at the dinner hour and hear they are out after my hide today, but they fell off the stools and had to be taken to the john, and then topped it by insulting my food, and when they did that I just told them not to come back anymore.

Did I tell you about our chowder? We use a bit of green pepper with the salt pork and the onions, put some of the potato in the Waring Blendor with the clam juice, and use no milk but a dollop of sour cream in each bowl as we serve it. We get 60 cents a cup and the profit is very good.

The spareribs are a good seller. I do a Chinese marinade for them and parboil them as I often do at home, and then put them on the broiler for about 10 minutes and give them several bastings. The shish kebabs sell well, too. I never do the marinade the same twice, but they like it. We do a shrimp curry to order, with frozen shrimp, that is excellent, and we do a shrimp rémoulade. The hamburgers run from plain to those with a salsa fria and green peppers, with cheddar cheese and bacon, with my chili, and with herbs, which I think is awful. My God — how do you make a Catholic hamburger? I forget about Fridays.

We are serving chocolate roll for 40 cents a slice, which brings in a nice profit. And for the pissaladière we get 75 cents a cut and make $15 on a $2 investment. The menu is in broken and awful French, which Mac has a wonderful time doing up.

I think I may go to Europe for six weeks right after the season, on a business trip, and then out to the Browns to recuperate from it and decide whether or no we want to go into business and can see what the next step is. I think definitely we should tack ourselves together into some sort of professional marriage that will make money for the two of us and let us get ahead in the field, for together we can become a real power in the food business. I have Isabel [Callvert][2] in New York who can take care of everything for me and do it on an agent fee basis and who is good at fighting battles and getting things done.

I've got to discontinue this trolley of information, which I dare not read over, for it has poured out of my head like sweat off my brow onto the keyboard. I wish you could see me slopping together a gallon of rémoulade or trying to decide whether to make Eel Stifle or Blueberry Grunt* for dinner. How quaint are we New Englanders — and what money grabbers. Forty cents for a hot dog, come midnight. That's the kind of thieves we are, and $1.10 for a hamburger with melted cheese over it — but they pay it.

I ran out of catchup the other day and I had to guess what to make it from. I think I'll send the recipe to Jack Heinz.

Love and kisses,

J

We celebrated Bastille Day with pets de nonne on the house. I wish it were September.

---

[1] Executive secretary of the Wine and Food Society and cookbook author; a mentor of JB until a falling out.

[2] A Portland actress and scriptwriter who did radio work with JB in the 1930s. For many years she collaborated on his food writing. She was married to Ron Callvert, a vice president of AT&T.

* Recipe.

[Limoges
October 13, 1953]

Dearest Helen —

It's a rainy morning and all my stationery is in the car save this from the ship. It's been a most rewarding jaunt this time thru some country I know and some which is entirely new to me. The days in Bordeaux were wonderful, with the weather enchantingly beautiful and the harvest going along apace. We're skipping Burgundy. After a while another wine cellar becomes just another cellar. We went to the grotto at Lascaux yesterday, which is so magnificent. Had lunch at the Cro-Magnon Hotel — with stuffed goose neck.

I've got some wonderful new recipes to share with you. We had delicious peasant food in Bordeaux, for we ate mostly the food prepared for the pickers, with a few additions. The woman who cooked four meals a day for the seventy workers and the household (at $2.00 a day) is marvelous. I spent some time with her in the kitchen (100 litres of soup three times a day, and good!).

Yesterday as we drove from Bordeaux thru Bergerac to Lascaux we were stopped four times by a communist group, who had a one-day strike and demonstration. The roads were blocked and you were forced to take detours. One of them gave me a long speech about how much better the farmers fared in America and how I should remember as I drove thru the countryside that the French farmers were making nothing. They wished us a pleasant trip. Some were really nasty and others completely charming.

We stayed last night in a country inn in Uzerche, near Limoges — an enchanting town of fifteenth-century houses built up and down a tiny valley. The inn is delightful. Our dinner, which cost about $1.50 without wine (which was a little rosé of the country — 70¢) consisted of an excellent leek soup with pasta, a terrine maison (game and pork — and they bring the terrine to the table and let you cut your own), grilled pike with a sauce made with verjuice, a course of green beans in butter, grilled pork steaks with oceans of cèpes cooked in butter with garlic and parsley, then a cheese tray and fruit. There are cèpes by the millions now, from tiny ones to those as big as your head.

Remind me to send you the recipe for spinach gnocchi made by Bill Veach's[1] Italian houseboy. They are something pretty special. Also to send you a facsimile of the front-page editorial in *Figaro* the other day about cooking and menu terms in French. It's wonderful.

Save these letters, because I shall want to enlarge on some of the points when next we get going on our exchanges.

I thought yesterday I had seen enough chestnuts to supply the entire world with marrons glacés and polenta — or did you ever make polenta with ground chestnut meal? And I've found excellent canned whole chestnuts, which should be a boon to anyone who cooks.

We lunched the other day in Loué at an enchanting spot. The dessert was a superb soufflé with fresh raspberries soaked in Framboise dumped into the center of the soufflé, which was baked in a small silver-plated dish — with it, the famous tuiles, the thin rich cookies with shaved almonds which are molded around a roller while hot, except these were giant ones fully eight inches across — just three of them in a basket, one apiece, and startling they were to gaze upon.

And the other night at dinner in Poitiers they served our artichokes with the choke removed as cleanly as anyone could possibly do it — the outer leaves intact and the tender center leaves in one piece and inverted, so that the two shades of green showed.

I must stop. We are about to get underway. Try this — butter a casserole well, and add a layer of thinly sliced potatoes, a layer of thinly sliced carrots, parsley, potatoes, carrots, parsley, salt and pepper and butter.* Bake until tender and invert and unmold on a serving dish. Back to Paris on Saturday.

Love,
JB

---

[1] William Templeton Veach was an American expatriate who lived in Italy and France. He was a fine cook and host, and JB considered him a belated Edwardian. He wrote two cookbooks with HEB.
* Recipe.

36 West 12th Street
New York
[December 9, 1953]

Dearest Helen —

I have the colossal job of lining up all the show-ers for the Goddard Neighborhood House tasting this year.[1] It's in January, and this year's do is to be a buffet dinner with proper wines. We shall have a course of hors d'oeuvre with apéritif wines, then a fish course and hot and cold entrées, and then a selection of desserts, which is stupendous — after which, champagnes in the outer room with coffee and cognacs. And then dancing. All this for only $15 a person. You will be happy to know I am having some American choices as well as foreign, for all the food is to come from the great restaurants of New York and the great caterers. We are having enough fancy pâtés and hors d'oeuvre to satisfy a whole string of cocktail parties, and I shall be watching the average person wolfing them down before they attack the more serious business of the main courses. Cannot something be done to people who wolf down millions of doots and dinkles with their quaffing and then refuse your main dishes?

If you remember, when you were here we had our first course with drinks, which I consider a masterly stroke when one entertains in the vie de Bohème fashion in which I do. It is easy and people never have too much. The smoked fish were just enough to whet the appetite and fill one as precaution against the drinks. And then something as substantial as the Choucroute Garnie can be properly enjoyed. And wasn't it a good choucroute? It was even better two days later when it had cooked twice more. As you remember, we cooked it about five hours that day. And I don't think all the meat should be cooked with the choucroute, for that way everything tastes of the cabbage and wine. I also think you should cook the kraut with plenty of garlic and black pepper and wine. The chichi of putting a cold bottle of champagne in the center when you serve it so that you get a bubbly fountain of the blessed wine is wonderful. Wish we had tried it that night. And many people are surprised that I serve boiled beef with the cabbage rather than all pork. But to me the beef, pork, saucisson à l'ail, and frankfurters or knockwurst all make for a fine contrast of textures and flavors. What a dish it really is.

I served it again, you might be interested to know, for Helen McCully and the Pedlars.[2] We started that night with a new fish dish. Try it. I had two pounds of finnan haddie fillets. This I poached in a court bouillon of vermouth, water, tiny bits of bay, some of Spice Islands green onions and tarragon, a lot of parsley, and black pepper. The scent of the herbed bouillon was overpowering, and when mixed with the smoky wonder of the haddock it just tickled the olfactory senses. I cooled it well, chilled it and served it with a sauce most people might have called a rémoulade but which I called a bastard Sunday-night sauce. It had a good olive oil mayonnaise base, and I am still one who likes the flavor of the olive coming through. Into this went parsley, more Spice Islands onions, tarragon, pepper, lemon juice, a little red wine vinegar, mustard and plenty of coarse salt. I used tons of capers and blanketed the whole piece of fish with the sauce so that it could blend with the other flavors. Finally, before serving, I covered the fish with thin, thin rings of Spanish onion until the fish was completely hidden from view. It was sensationally good, and as far as cost goes, if we must talk of such things, it cost half what a piece of sturgeon or whitefish would and was every bit as good.

I made a Poire Maxim's[3] for dinner on Sunday night. I call it dinner because we sat at table. My mousse was as light and fluffy as a mousse can be, and the flavor of the Grand Marnier does something wonderful to the pears. I tried your fashion of cooking the pears and then skinning them, and I'm not sure which of the methods I like the best. Yours has much to recommend it.

I am doing something else which is against the founded principles of gastronomic procedures. I am now making my praline entirely with brown sugar, because it seems to carry a much better and more subtle flavor. And isn't there something rather thrilling about the sight of bubbling sugar as it reaches the melting stage? Always makes me think a little of the conception many people have of hell.

My days in the country were filled with dreaming up all the things for the Jerry Mason book [*Jim Beard's Complete Book of Barbecue and Rotisserie Cooking*].[4] I tried out the new Skotch Grill,[5] one of which I have begged the guy to send you. I did small steaks on it and hamburgers (and except for raw, I am organizing and heading an antihamburger society). It is a wonderful idea for the average small family, and if there is a fireplace handy it is wonderful for a New York apartment. But after I do this book and if we do one together, please never, never, never say outdoor cookery to me again.

Thanksgiving, you will be happy to know, was not a traditional one with me either. It was a couple of really fine juicy lamb chops in Kaysey's in New Haven — and with all the things which are supposed to be Thanksgiving. But why must they thrust a tired little glass of cider into your hand, to be gay, after you have had several cocktails and some rather spicy herring? The chops were wonderful, and for the life of me I could not see one person in all the restaurant eating turkey.

It breaks my heart that I can't visit you for the holidays, but I must stay and do all the things that are necessary to keep me going. Sherry's must have some time and others as well, and the goddam book does have to be finished.

Love,

J

P.S. [Louis] Vaudable[6] has arrived and the frozen food from Maxim's is really launched. It looks as if it might catch on. We lunched together yesterday — that madman and his representative here, who is sane, thank God. Then he couldn't decide whether to let Clem[entine Paddleford] interview him or Jane Nickerson.[7]

Sunday, Philippe's birthday party at the farm. I look forward to writing you what the great hotel genius serves for his birthday. I'll bet that I will work in the kitchen as much as I do anything else. But it is such a wonderful kitchen that I don't mind.

P.P.S. I think you are both the most wonderful people in the world.

P.P.P.S. I'm inviting about eighteen people the Sunday after Christmas for supper — this time it's going to be cassoulet and hors d'oeuvre, and, hold on to yourself, plum pudding with a foamy sauce and chausson of mincemeat. Well, the old fool is going traditional on us, isn't he?

JB

---

[1] An annual benefit dinner.

[2] Helen McCully, food editor of *McCall's;* Sylvia Pedlar, a designer of lingerie and her husband, William, a designer of hotel interiors.

[3] Poached pear halves arranged over a Grand Marnier mousse, with centers filled with vanilla ice cream and decorated with whipped cream.

[4] JB wrote several specialty paperback cookbooks for Maco Magazine Corporation. Jerry Mason was his editor.

[5] A portable pail-like grill that JB and HEB promoted while writing their outdoor cookbook.

[6] Director of Maxim's restaurant in Paris.

[7] Food editors of the *New York Herald Tribune* and the *New York Times.*

36 West 12th Street
New York
[December 13, 1953]

My dearest Helen —

I have thought of the title for our outdoor book — "Balls, Picnics and Other Outdoor Pursuits." I think that is a selling title. And then I have developed a real idea about our letters and feel that perhaps they should be sold as a book and be sort of a double biography and include more than we had originally planned — have a couple of chapters sold to *The Atlantic* or *Harper's* and then be thrust on the market for serious consideration as gastronomic literature. I tossed that idea at John Schaffner[1] yesterday when we lunched together and he bit on the bait. One more whirl of the floater and the fly and he will have it all and be swimming in the direction of Alfred and Blanche Knopf, who I think would fall for the idea at once.

I am filled with restlessness and nostalgia and cannot adjust myself to New York or find my place here. It is the most violent upheaval I have ever had about New York and I am not a little worried about the outcome. You might find me on the kitchen steps one day (what a big package the grocer sent) and again I might disappear into the mists of Mexico or France. Maybe I am just suffering from the return-of-traveler blues, but somehow it seems deeper than that.

I have had a rather amusing day at Philippe's in the country, the day having been his birthday. There were about thirty people for lunch and we all worked like slaves, with Philippe as the maître d'hôtel in his own home, as it were. Louis Vaudable (Maxim's) getting the caviar ready and toasting the bread, the head of Shell Oil company moving chairs and tables, Doris Lilly[2] being beautiful and useless, and everyone entering into the spirit of the game and really having fun. We had drinks and snacks — snacks, says he — a complete meal — a full 5-pound box of caviar, smoked salmon, smoked sturgeon, salami, raw vegetables, olives of all varieties, breads, crackers, pickles, et cetera. After a fully exhausting session of this and a short walk in the garden we started lunch — a six-rib roast of beef, two huge geese, steaks of venison, a huge casserole of beans à la Française, and magnums of red wine. Then to amuse the mouth while the dessert was being prepared by Ohrel, Philippe's first assistant, and me, there was cold ham, salad, and a beautifully laden tray of cheese, and more red wine in magnums. Then two baked Alaskas the size of a large tray and each one piled with three quarts of ice cream — and this, washed down with rehoboams of champagne, just so the gas bubbles would release some of the distress felt in most bellies by that time. Then just plain old plebeian coffee while the presents were being opened. It was Lucullan almost to the point of being vulgar. Confidentially, Brown, if you and I had had the kitchen, the raw materials and the time and all the rest of it, we could have produced a meal which would have been a milestone in American gastronomic history and would surely have brought the spirits of Carême and Montagné[3] buzzing around to make us Chevaliers of the Heavenly Host of Cook Book Writers, with double halos piped with phosphorescent duchesse potatoes. I think no one — and I haven't tasted yours — can cook a goose as well as I can. Period.

I did a program the other day with Irma Rombauer.[4] We talked of the readability of cookbooks and the difference between cookbook writing and gastronomic writing. She cited you as one of the persons of today she most enjoyed reading. And although we both do not like her book, I feel that is a compliment, for she is a person of rare charm and discernment.

I have a wonderful piece of hare in my kitchen which has been there since Friday. I bought a huge Canadian number costing $2.60 and brought it home and painted it well with my best French mustard and then stuck a bay leaf in its behind and sprinkled it with a little Spice Islands thyme seasoning powder and a touch of Spice Islands coarse pepper, and I turn it every twelve hours or so. Tomorrow night I shall roast it very quickly and serve it up with some chestnut purée and turnips. I shall send you a taste by typewriter. Then, from that heaven, I am obliged to go to the annual carol sing of the New York Newspaper Women's Club at Edith Barber's[5] — where everyone takes a 50-cent present and there is much carol singing and gaiety of the season.

Last night Alvin Kerr and Peter Carhartt[6] looked so tired that I bid them come to eat a plain dinner here. I bought the most wonderful capon I have seen in years. Fat as a eunuch and beautifully fleshed, this beast was covered with its own fat and sprinkled lightly with some Spice Islands tarragon, covered with foil and put in a 450 degree oven for an hour and a half. Then stripped of its covering and basted like mad, but this time at 350. It was really a gem and relished by all — such delicacy, such crispness — elegant. With it, mushrooms fluted by my fluter in scroll design and cooked on a bed of the stems and the flutings. And pineapple and tangerines laced with kumquats and spiked with bourbon for a most pleasing dessert. We drank a bottle of an extraordinary wine — Morey Clos de la Roche, absolute perfection in the Burgundy field.

Did I tell you that your Christmas may not get to you before February? It is coming to you direct from France. You need it and you'll like it. Boom.

I love you both dearly.

Best,

JB

---

[1] Literary agent, who then represented HEB.

[2] Publicist and author of *How to Meet a Millionaire.*

[3] Legendary chefs and authors of treatises on classic French cuisine.

[4] Author of *The Joy of Cooking.*

[5] Food editor of the *New York Sun.*

[6] Food writers and neighbors of JB.

[36 West 12th Street
New York
December 16, 1953]

Dearest Helen —

I went to Dione's to dinner last night and what do you think? She wants us to share a restaurant and cooking school! She has the idea that we are the two people here who stand for the same things and that we should have a small restaurant, tentatively an omelet bar, for luncheon, with fine hors d'oeuvre, excellent pastries and breads, and with a bar and a good wine list. Oh yes, and salads. We would gradually grow into food of a more serious nature. Then we would share the cooking school, with each of us doing our own specialities and one taking over when the other was not there. I am giving it thought and wondering what would happen. Of course the announcement of my name and Dione's together, in certain circles, would be like news of the Monitor and the Merrimac battle.

Dinner — well, it was simple and prepared by a French gal she has working there. Smoked salmon with capers and all the rest and buttered brown bread. Steak with French fries and cress. A magnificent purée of spinach, a tomato salad, and then a colossal mousse au chocolat with an acre of whipped cream. I think we should

settle down to a long discussion of mousses. That's almost a subject for a book.

Off to the wars, my dear.

L and K,

J

36 West 12th Street

New York

[December 28, 1953]

My dear Browns —

Well, the hurly is just about thrown and the burly is getting on
my nerves. I only wish I had fled to California, away from all of it.
The last days at Sherry [Wine & Spirits] were horrendous. But
then there was the pleasure of the couple of days of Christmas. You
will be amazed to learn I did not eat venison or goose. I ate a
traditional Christmas dinner, with turkey, stuffing made with Oregon filberts, creamed onions, yellow turnips, and pudding with
three kinds of sauce. All this I ate but passed the goddam cranberries by. Isabel cooked it, and it was really stupendous.

My party last night was fun. It was for John and Dorothy Conway,[1] who are at the University of Washington. We ended by being
twenty. The onions Belle Aurore were superb, and the finnan
haddie made an even greater hit than before. I also did a big bowl
of endive, cucumber and celery with ice — in a big new wheat-
pattern ironstone I got for Christmas. Then I had the cassoulet,
made with fine flageolets I found in the market. Saturday night I
had cooked a goose, and I used that, mutton, pork and garlic
sausage. Instead of sprinkling with crumbs I used sesame seeds. It
was really a dandy. I made it and served it in a copper braisière like
the one I am sending to you. For dessert I used the Soupçon
fruitcake and a beautiful pudding made for me in my kugelhopf
mold. I made a sauce with melted brown sugar, egg yolks, and
Benedictine, and it was quite good. I served a Corvo, the Sicilian
white wine, which is heavy and strangely bitter and excellent with
cassoulet. This particular wine is one of Frank Schoonmaker's[2]

importations and is one of the outstanding wines in Italy, here for the first time by a good bottler.

I have three more dinners to give and then finish. I have one next Sunday, and that becomes a progressive. Then Henri de Vilmorin and his countess and the Forme Becharats[3] on the Sunday following, when I think I shall have pheasant with sauerkraut,* because pheasant is so reasonable and is such a marvelous dish. On the other hand I am tempted by some of the tiny wonderful suckling pigs that are in the market this year from time to time. I love to stuff them with rice and liver and pistachio nuts, roast them, and serve them with baked plantains and thinly sliced apples sautéed in butter and a little sugar until they are browny-crisp at the edges. It is my idea of a noble but goddam rich dish, which requires champagne or rosé wine. Maybe the rosé champagne from California would be delicious — although I still think they should have another name for it.

Blanche and Alfred Knopf waxed enthusiastic over the idea of our book of letters. They see it as sort of memoirs and protest, with some recipes interspersed. I think we should both like a book from Knopf. They want to see some of it soon, so when I come out to the Coast I shall want to sit down quietly and get it thought out.

Did you get your Skotch Grill yet? I tried my town one out in the bathroom on Saturday. I bought a leg of mutton for the cassoulet and had two wonderful steaks cut from it. These I marinated in soy, grated garlic and ginger. I broiled them, and they were better than venison, except for the wonderful young venison one gets in Yucatán.

Talking to you was one of my great Christmas treats.

Jim

---

[1] John Conway, a professor of drama, had known JB since their theatre days in the 1930s; his wife, Dorothy, was a portrait photographer.

[2] Internationally recognized wine expert, importer, and writer on wine and food.

[3] Henri de Vilmorin was a wealthy French grain producer and member of the exclusive Club des Cent. Forme Becharat, unidentified.

* Recipe.

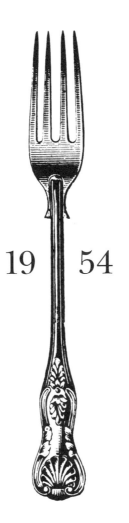

19 54

In January JB became a consultant to Skotch Grill and was given the first of his assignments for *Harper's Bazaar.* The following month he finished his paperback *How to Eat Better for Less Money* and came down with a case of shingles. In March JB and HEB signed a contract with Doubleday for their only book together, *The Complete Book of Outdoor Cookery,* and much of their correspondence during the year concerns food tests on various types of grills. JB met with the Browns in San Francisco in early April for a tour of the wine, cheese, and fishing industries, and they drove to Oregon, Washington, Idaho, Montana, Utah, and Nevada. JB returned to the West Coast in June for cognac demonstrations and touched down in Chicago and Cleveland as well. He started his long relationship with Restaurant Associates in July and also began as consultant to Chillingsworth Inn on Cape Cod. In November he made another tour for cognac and paid his third visit that year to the West Coast. On November 27 he sailed for Europe on the *Ile-de-France.* He visited Paris, Poitiers, Tours, Milan, Florence, and Rome before returning to Florence to spend New Year's Eve with his American friend William Templeton Veach.

Dearest Browns —

I am making fried beans and chili for dinner tonight for the Aarons. Only I am making the chili from turkey instead of beef. This is the Jack Aarons,[1] who have never been here for dinner before. Then with two more parties I shall be finished for the season. I am weary and gone. Last night I thought I would work but fatigue overcame me at 8:30 and I lay down, thinking an hour would help me. Finally I got up at one o'clock to take Cricket Crawford[2] for a walk and collapsed into bed again and slept until nine this morning, which is absolutely incredible for me.

I have been approached by Macmillan, who want a book on carving, and am seeing them on Wednesday. I shall do it in a hurry, with loads of pictures, which I think is what a carving book needs. And I am going to flaunt the experts in several ways. I like to carve a ham the French way and think it is easier for the layman and gives less waste. I also like to do a leg of lamb the French way instead of turning it over on the side and all that. But I'll show both ways, I guess, and let people fight it out for themselves. Have you or Philip any other ideas about it? I know that Uncle Philip is one of the great carvers of all time and should like his expert opinion. Has he ever been faced with having a sword handed to him when out in company and being asked to carve? It has happened to me twice with people who cannot forget the Civil War or the Spanish American War and must keep their memories green.

Why do people who give large cocktail parties put the food and liquor in separate rooms? You remember that Helen McCully did that at her party for you. And last Tuesday my landlord and lady gave a crush for about a hundred. The same thing happened. There was a table with turkeys cut into infinitesimal pieces, a fine Virginia ham hacked to pieces, a whole season's catch of shrimp, and vegetables galore, to say nothing of fruitcake and chocolate mints (ever try a chocolate mint with a really dry martini? — sensational). As a result people were falling on their faces and nobody ate any food. Then I went to another party the same evening and had food out of reach again, and I needed food badly. But you couldn't trek over twenty people to get to the table. Let us do something about that little evil — in fact, at this point let us do something about the cocktail party generally. Let us make it a champagne party or nothing.

New Year's Eve I had a very sane time and rather a fun one. I had been to Mac's for a reunion with some of the Nantucketers, of whom I grew very fond, then went to Aleks Bird[3] for a really delicious dinner — turtle soup, a chicken perfectly roasted with a farce of veal, pork liver and herbs. Peeled chestnuts roasted with the chicken for the last half hour. Wonderful homemade French loaves, crusty and delicious. With this, in honor of New Year's we drank champagne. For the rest, some excellent candies and coffee, and I had a kirsch.

On then to Lee and Paula Strasberg's, where the entire theatre and writing world happened to be. I continued with champagne there, and after the stroke of the day Paula had a buffet of Barney Greengrass[4] specialties that would have startled you. Enough smoked salmon and sturgeon and kippered salmon to cover the globe, with bagels and the other Jewish rolls that are soft and have a deep indentation like a navel in the center, with bits of sesame seed and onion in the dough — not the accepted onion rolls — I have to get the correct name. (What a wonderful story there is in bread.) We had tiny knishes, hot as hell, and all the wonderful Russian things that come with zakuska.

I had a fascinating talk there with Santha Rama Rau and her husband, Faubion Bowers.[5] They agree with me on the beginnings of French cookery being in China and we are going to have a full evening of their experiences in the far reaches of China and Tibet, and of Santha's times when her father was Indian Ambassador to Japan and China.

I got home at two in the morning, and sober — because of the champagne. I had the Conways here on New Year's day for breakfast at noon. Gave them champagne, hot spiced tomato juice, with cinnamon bark for stirring, Nova Scotia salmon, some of Mr. Bloomingdale's new imported prosciutto, some Holland ham, cream cheese, thinly sliced onion and fresh cucumber pickles. We drank a bottle of Sicilian wine with this and then ate some of my wonderful Roquefort and had tea. It was my favorite kind of a late breakfast — almost an hors d'oeuvre luncheon.

How I wish you were here to share the Roquefort with me. I made several jars of the spread* with cognac and butter the other day and took them around with a basket on my arm like Lady Bountiful. But it seems a shame to waste it that way.

I have been made consultant to the Skotch Grill for a year, and *Harper's Bazaar* called for an article. Happy New Year to me and to you and to us and to all.

> Love and kisses,
> and hope for my diet,
> JB

By the way, define hibachi for me. I am told by a reputable Japanese intellectual that you never cook on a hibachi but merely use it for heat. So?

---

[1] Jack Aaron, of Sherry Wine & Spirits, and his wife, Frieda.

[2] Cheryl Crawford's black cocker spaniel.

[3] A writer on food and wine.

[4] A restaurant on the Upper West Side of Manhattan.

[5] Santha Rama Rau, Indian-born novelist and playwright; Faubion Bowers, theatre critic and author of several books on the theatre.

* Recipe.

> 36 West 12th Street
> New York
> [January 5, 1954]

Dear —

Your wonderful cheery letter, with you in the doldrums, was the hope of my Monday morning. Your party sounds fabulous, and the food was what I believe party food should be. Even the turkey sandwiches sounded good. But for God's sake, how we beat our bodies to give a party, and other people give them with a box of potato chips, a can of deviled ham and ten cents' worth of sweet pickles.

My Mexican dinner on Sunday was a success. The mole was superb — as good a one as I ever made — and I did a new twist with the chilies rellenos. I stuffed them, put them in a buttered baking dish, poured the batter over them and baked them like a soufflé, then served them with a cold sauce.

This Sunday I am having anchovies with shallots and parsley, onions Belle Aurore, and mushrooms in a salad. Then a filet, potatoes cooked in goose fat, cheese, and chocolate mousse.

I have to do a cognac dinner the following Sunday — probably snails with cognac, Poulet Flambé with rice, and that old fool thing called a Tipsy Pudding — all decorated with angelica and crap like that. I mean a cross between trifle and Tipsy Parson* — pound cake and cognac, custard, whipped cream, raspberry jam, candied fruit and all the moola. Once in a while my soul just yearns for this.

Cheer up, dearie. Things will go tops before you know it and you will be sticking out your tongue at the editors who raise hell.

Love and kisses,
[Jim]

----

* Recipe.

Pasadena
January 8, 1954

Jim dear,

Your informant is wrong about the hibachi. It is true that they are used for "hand warming" and heating but they also make tea on them and many families cook on them. There is a larger charcoal cook stove called something like shichirin??? that is also used. I am doing research on the subject.

HEB

[36 West 12th Street
New York]
January 11, 1954

Dearest Helen —

I have decided to take the night off and spend it with myself. I am going to dine in style on the end of the filet I had last night, broiled au poivre in my Broil-Quik, some Idaho potato, which I sliced paper thin on the guitar with the skin on and which I shall sauté quickly in goose fat until just colored through, and cucumber salad. And perhaps I shall indulge in some chocolate mousse left over from last night, but probably not. Then I shall put myself into the downy early and sleep or at least relax. I haven't slept enough lately to count up.

The snow changed my whole party last night. The Forme Becharats were snowbound on Long Island, and so I called Cecily [Brownstone][1] and said come over, and Wendell Palmer[2] was here in New York, and I roped him in. The onions Belle Aurore were elegant, and the anchovies came off perfectly. The cucumber salad was yours,* in mayonnaise, and I surrounded it with thin slices of the first good tomatoes I have had in ages. We drank the Italian wine [Corvo] with that. My filet looked beautiful with tiny carrots, peas, beans and fluted mushrooms around it. Then cheese and Pommard, and I had made two chocolate mousse or mousses or whatever the hell it is, and Helen had brought me a fruitcake with a thick goo of almond paste on top, which my Scotch blood warms to. We had a bottle of champagne with that and coffee and liqueurs. We sat late and were very gay, and when everyone left I said to myself, I'll just sit and rest a minute. I awakened at six this morning fully clothed, with the lights on and the door open for all to see. Then that horrible thing of getting undressed and making up the bed and sleeping another hour or so. I had a radio program this morning[3] — it was a network show, too, and I don't think I told you to listen in.

I lunched with my editor at Little, Brown [Alex Williams] and then went to look at a house, which was not at all what I thought it might be. It belongs to the Fountains — she is Leatrice and Jack Gilbert's daughter and looks enough like your correspondent's old friend, the late lamented star, to shock anyone who had known him as well as I did from the age of something up.

Philippe called me the other day with a problem. What did they eat for great formal dinners two hundred years ago in New York?

Love and kisses,

JB

---

[1] Food editor of Associated Press and one of JB's most cherished colleagues.

[2] JB's former editor at Little, Brown.

[3] "Make Up Your Mind," on CBS.

* Recipe.

Pasadena
January 14, 1954

Jim dear,

What wine do you like with ham? I think it makes a lot of difference if the ham is a Virginia one or a tendered horror. Also don't you think that the way it is cooked has a lot to do with it? . . . I came across a recipe the other day — printed in a "cook" book, called "Just Dump." Isn't that frightening? And, I fear, true?

HEB

[36 West 12th Street
New York
January 18, 1954]

Dearest Gourmette —

I have just had a long talk with John Schaffner. Evidently Clara Claasen[1] wants our outdoor book in a hurry. Well, we can put it together when I am on the Coast. We have all the material at hand. What do you say to your making an outline and sending it on to me? I think we should include portable cookery, picnics, off-shore cookery, and hibachi and smoke cookery. There should be luncheons for a day's outing on train, boat or plane, where there is no cookery to be done. We can afford to be a little chichi in this book and give them something new. And shouldn't we call it "At Home Off the Range," or would you prefer "doing it outdoors," in small letters, as if it were by e. e. cummings; or would you like "Helen Evans Brown and James A. Beard Cook Alfresco"?

I am cooking sauerkraut with garlic, beer and pig's feet for Ann Seranne and me to eat for dinner. Smells divine. Also making a dessert with some stale macaroons in cognac with a topping of praline and canned pineapple (the second case I have had sent to me), cooked down to thickness and topped with whipped cream flavored with vanilla. I shall tell you what it was like if we live through it.

Saturday night we settled down for a photographic session, with ducks in the rotisseries and chickens and steak on the Skotch Grill, when out went the fuse. The landlord and lady were out for the evening, so we pranced up to 55th Street, with all the equipment in two taxis, and continued there. I did the duck with curry, honey and lemon,* and it was beautiful. A new drink: vodka with pineapple juice. I am becoming a vodka addict and like it straight on the rocks now.

Ham, I think, takes one of two wines — champagne or rosé. With a fine Virginia or Kentucky ham champagne is the ideal wine. With a tenderized job or a canned one — well, a rosé is wonderful. And I like to cook it in rosé or in red wine, with a topping of crumbs and mustard or a rubbing of dry and wet mustard and sometimes a little mace or nutmeg. I also like hams baked in crust as well as any. And the old stuffed ones from Maryland are superb. I once stuffed one with nuts, raisins and spices. When it was served cold the slices were like marble. It was naturally a hell of a lot of trouble, but it was worth it to see the pinkness of the flesh marbled with the motley bits of fruit and nut paste. Your ham pâté sounds right. Try a few truffles with it and see if that doesn't make it extra special.

We do work too hard and everyone expects us to be fresh and wonderful all the time. Today the goddam telephone has gone one hundred and twenty-five times. I am going to be so relieved when the Goddard tasting is over. I have long sessions with people every day about this and that, not my own work. Well, it is for charity, I suppose.

Try marinating a chicken with black olives, garlic, olive oil and just a bit of rosemary for a day and then spitting it with the garlic and olives inside* — and serve it with sautéed potatoes and water-cress, along with red wine and herbed bread, and add some rosemary to the bread.

Your [1770 New York dinner] menu[2] was sensational. I am passing it on to Philippe.

I must now write out some recipes for bridal punches and he-man recipes using cognac, then settle down to restaurants for Mrs. Snow.[3]

Let us feast.

Love and kisses, heartily,
Jim

---

[1] JB's and HEB's editor at Doubleday.

[2] The 1770 menu: "Turbot / Remove for two ducklings / Crayfish in Jelly / Pigeons Stewed / Chickens / A Ragout of French Beans / Potted Lobster / Green Pease Soup / Melon in Flummery / Creams and Jellies / Dish of Snow / Green Pease Soup (Again?) / Haunch of Venison / Potted Liveret / Forced Cucumbers / Tongue or a very small Ham / Lamb Stones Fricaseed / Veal in Jelly/ A Dessert."

[3] Carmel Snow, editor of *Harper's Bazaar.*

* Recipe.

36 West 12th Street
New York
[January 23, 1954]

Helen, dear —

Well, the Goddard tasting is over and what a night. The two prima donne kept me on the jump and the food was there in such profusion that I couldn't look at it. I ended at Longchamps at midnight with a large platter of steak tartare — and very good it was, too. I'm sending you Clementine's bit on it, but the thing itself was really distinguished, and such clothes I haven't seen since the war. We grossed about thirteen thousand and will clear about ten — not bad for a one-night stand. Dione made a hundred and fifty omelets, Madame le Douzen[1] did crêpes till they were practically rolling on the floor, and there was food and wine enough for legions. In fact we are selling some of the wine off now. But what a hell of a lot of work. And now to start planning next year's, on Monday.

Tried a new restaurant yesterday — Romeo Salta — Italian, naturally, and simply enchanting. We ate magnificent scampi with a warm sauce of egg, olive oil, tomato, basil, oregano and parsley, with an overtone of shallot, thick and very sharp. Then [semolina] gnocchi — the pasty kind made with pâte à choux almost. These, with tiny roulades of veal sautéed quickly, each about 1½ inches wide, with chopped ham and shallot and herbs for stuffing. They cook everything to order and in Revere Ware, and serve it in the pans in which they cook. Excellent service and nice surroundings. Restaurants are such a bore, however, when you are there perpetually. There is such a sameness about it all, and I get tired of being fawned over.

Love and kisses,
[Jim]

---

[1] Philomene le Douzen, owner of Paris Brest, and later of Crêpes Suzette, restaurants in New York's theatre district.

[36 West 12th Street
New York
January 29, 1954]

Helen, dear —

I did a dry-run party for the Skotch Grill yesterday, and it worked beautifully. We did shrimp, which had marinated in garlicked oil and lemon for 24 hours, right in the house on a really hot fire. The steaks we did out on the terrace — sliced them thin on bread, with onion sauce. I think we used about 10 pounds of steak and God knows how many shrimp for this groaning mass of hungry executives, and they wanted more.

By the way, the chef at the Plaza said that he couldn't possibly equal the sauces that come over here with the frozen Maxim food, and he's right. The sauce for the veal is fabulous, and the one for the sole incredibly good. If they would only put up the sauces alone, what a break it would be. Maybe that's for us — to freeze the mother sauces for the market.

Tuesday, believe it or not, we are going to Lynbrook [Long Island] to shoot pictures outdoors at night with a new unit that the boys at *Argosy* have designed.[1] I am going to do shrimp, mutton steaks, herbed bread, and a huge salad with beefsteak tomatoes, red onions and greens. We shall be sitting and cooking at the same time — something new and different, I am told. I hope they take stroboscopic pictures so they can record the shivers, for it will probably be about six above zero. I suppose I should wear a kilt. Maybe we should follow the old French habit of carrying a hot baked potato in each pocket for additional warmth.

Love and kisses,

JB

---

[1] JB wrote "he-man" food and wine articles for *Argosy*.

[36 West 12th Street
New York
February 1, 1954]

Helen, dear —

Last night's party was a whirling success — except that B——
had had no lunch, drank three double martinis and almost
crawled out of the place, leaving her small Dior hat here. Clementine was in fine fettle and called this morning to say it was as
nice as any party she had been to in years. We munched some
nuts with a beautiful Moselle for a cocktail — except for B——.
Then we sat down to a Terrine de Body.[1] The veal from Tingaud[2]
was perfection, and I used Canadian bacon sliced paper thin,
plenty of shallots, and cognac instead of white wine. I served it
with the little French dill pickles and the last of my pickled
onions. Then the filet with all the vegetables, and I used attelets
with scalloped mushrooms. And Teleme and pears with chocolate and praline — and my candied violets and some beautiful
marzipan. And good wines. We sat at table till almost midnight,
and I was sorry to see everyone go home. I do love to entertain.

I was invited to dinner last night by a friend — say, rather, an
acquaintance — whose love for good food is known. Well, he was
fried when I got there and became more so. When we finally sat
down to table it was not to a badly planned dinner but to one
which had long since lost its savor. A magnificent veal cutlet,
cooked to perfection once, with golden onion rings atop and
sour cream, had rested about twenty minutes too long. The same
sad story with broccoli. And a mess of endive. When you have
endive in all its beauty why ruin it by cutting it into hash? Leave it
whole or cut it into quarters, and let people have a knife with
their salad. Are we such slaves to Emily Post that we cannot adapt
the French and English habits of cutting our salad greens? It was
one of the most frustrating dinners I have had in ages and made
me think that somehow we must get in a few digs at people who
leave things too long in the goddam casserole. But seriously, if
people want to drink forever (and the host collapsed into bed
during dinner), they should serve food that is heavily on the hors
d'oeuvre side, but substantial. I would rather have sat down to

some good sardines, strips of endive and tomato slices and the beautiful cheese they had.

And now I must to market to buy my summer dinner that we are to photograph tonight. I'm hoping I can get my A&P butcher to cut lamb steaks so that I don't have to go downtown this morning. I know I can get shrimp here and everything else I need.

Just got a $10 check from *McCall's* for a recipe. Well, it buys a few things, I suppose, and I should be grateful for it. But is this what we work for — a series of small checks?

Love and kisses, please, everyone,

JB

---

[1] A terrine made with veal scallops, bacon, onions, white wine, and seasonings.

[2] Tingaud was the classiest of the New York butchers.

36 West 12th Street
New York
[February 4, 1954]

Helen, dear —

I have just had a most elegant low-calorie luncheon, made in the broiler — sauerkraut, mustard and two thin pieces of Canadian bacon. Crisp on top and beautifully krauty — and filling.

My midwinter pictures at the barbecue were good, I trust. I was ankle deep in mud at the end of the period of shooting but hot in the middle because I was practically straddling the damned cooker. You have no idea how ridiculous you feel in summer clothes grilling lamb steaks and shrimp over charcoal in the middle of winter after dark.

L & K
JB

36 West 12th Street
New York
[February 9, 1954]

Helen, dear —

I had fun teaching Ruth[1] and Cheryl to make omelets in the fast
fashion while I was in the country. You can do them in half a
minute if things are favorable for you. I used their old iron pan,
which has been used for everything and thus substantiated a
theory I have always had — that this special-pan stuff is a lot of you
know what. I bought a French iron one yesterday and am going to
keep it exclusively for omelets and then try it against others.

I'm going to make some of that wonderful red caviar "cheese"
[taramasalata] that the Greeks make to take to a friend's
tonight — red caviar, soaked bread, onion, lemon juice, olive oil
and slow, even beating. I do mine in the electric beater and
sometimes add parsley and a little garlic to it.

Tomorrow night I'm making a pot-au-feu — I'm longing for
it — and shall do it with a nice piece of beef, a small chicken,
cabbage, celery and turnips. With sour pickles and horseradish. I
can taste it now. Let's go in the pickle business. Where can you buy
good gherkins in the French manner, put up in wine vinegar with
garlic and tarragon and a few shallots added?

Got to go and dress and meet Frances Smith of the Fisheries
Council, who will write everyone on the Coast that we are coming.
We have a date to sit for photographs in Seattle, for Dorothy
Conway, who is considered the finest portrait photographer in the
country now.[2] They come from Europe to have their pictures
done. She is anxious to do us. So look your prettiest.

You can now buy your lox and cream cheese mixed together and
called Cheezlox. Grr-r-r-r!

Love and all that,
JB

---

[1] Ruth Norman, a food consultant and co-author of *Cook Until Done*,
became manager of the James Beard Cooking School. She was a companion
of Cheryl Crawford.

[2] Photographs from the session appear on the jacket of this book.

[36 West 12th Street
New York
February 15, 1954]

Helen Dear —

Well, it's my turn now. I have a lovely case of shingles — frayed nerve ends — but then I am not surprised for it continues to be a race for existence. I have so much to finish up this week, besides three luncheons, four theatres and a dinner, that I am crazy. I am looking forward to our little trip with great enthusiasm.

We are invited to a mandarin dinner the night of April 11th in San Francisco by Ken Zwerin, who was here this week. He is a lawyer who is very interested in wine and food and has never been admitted to the holy of holies of the Wine and Food Society because he is Jewish. However, they all cater to him, and he is invited to everything and gives wonderful parties. He wants to order a special dinner for us, so he is planning it for the night you arrive. He is one of the most intelligent persons I have ever met — studied for the rabbinate and turned to law after that.

I had him here for dinner on Saturday, for an onion tart and a choucroute — and a 1952 Alsatian, which was like drinking young gold it was so fruity and fresh and delicious. You can have all the old wines you want. I am finding more and more that I belong to the school of the youthful wines with no pretensions. Of course a big wine of stature is delightful once in a while when there is a great dish to prepare and eat.

I think you are worrying too much. You are one of the few people in this country to have what it takes to make gastronomic history of what we are living through. We all have to take shit from people sometimes. The important thing is to know your power and your strength and above all that you are one of the instruments through which the knowledge flows. You are not a trained homemaker nor a home economist but a true prophet in a world where prophets are needed. So just gird your apron a little tighter, wield your skillet and spatula with an added flourish, and toss the crêpes a little higher in the air.

Love and kisses,

JB

36 West 12th Street
New York
[February 21, 1954]

Honeys —

The party for the Skotch Grill went beautifully. I have had the most wonderful letters from it and am getting pictures in any number of magazines. The party was rough and ready and different. The atmosphere of Peter's Backyard[1] is so different from all the uptown jobs, and with the big grill at the back it was perfection. We had Skotch Grills around with shrimps on them so that the minute guests arrived they got a noseful of the odor of charcoal cookery. They had all they wanted to drink and then wandered up to the big grill for steak sandwiches. We grilled millions of pounds of thick sirloins, sliced them thin on the bias, put them on split extra long loaves of French bread, which had been garlic-buttered, and then cut them in healthy hunks. They even asked for sandwiches to take home to sick mothers and whatnot. Then there was a huge table of beautiful pastry and coffee. Everyone sat where they wanted and gossiped with whom they pleased. Helen McCully sent me a real mash note about it.

I'm having John and Perdita [Schaffner] down the night I have Hildegarde Popper[2] for dinner. Going to give them lobster à l'Américaine, now that I find out, years later as it were, that all I have to do is ask for lobsters and I get them free.

We did a big conch dinner the other night, but the best of all was the raw conch, which I mixed with chives, parsley, and mayonnaise, for an appetizer.

Had lunch on Friday with Marjorie Deen of General Foods and among other things told her about your chocolate [and sourcream] icing. She waxed interested and may write to you about it. If they use it they will probably pay you for it and give credit. We had some last night — Aleks Bird made a chiffon cake and brought it down here, complete with your wonderful icing.

I shall be in San Francisco a few days before you arrive, so I can see anyone you think I should. Do we want to go to Petaluma to see the Brie and the Camembert? What about Idaho and the potato country if we go across to Salt Lake? I'm in your hands. A great big smacker on both cheeks to you.

Upward and onward with gastronomy,

JB

---

1 A steak house in Greenwich Village.
2 Editor at *House and Garden.*

[36 West 12th Street
New York
February 24, 1954]

Dearest dieters —

I have a large pot of octopus stewing on the fire — for the television show tonight ["I Have a Secret"]. Braised it in olive oil and garlic and then added basil, red wine and parsley, and it is simmering. Smells divine. Did I tell you to watch me on this show?

Made one of those last-minute decisions last night for dinner which gave me a brand-new dish. I was going to make a quiche of crab, and when I arrived chez fishmonger there was not a hair or shell of crabmeat. So I bought a pound of bay scallops and sautéed them lightly in butter with shallot and parsley, dumped them into the pastry shell, covered them with the custard and baked.* Everyone raved, and I felt it was good. Then came the filet, with a sauce like a Marchand de Vin, and strawberries, pineapple and raspberries with Grand Marnier. We drank a really sensational Johannisberger Riesling from the Rheingau, which Sam [Aaron][1] brought down the other day for me to try.

I must get myself together for the evening's show.

Love and kisses to you both —
JB

---

1 President of Sherry Wine & Spirits and co-author, with JB, of *How to Eat Better for Less Money.*
* Recipe.

[36 West 12th Street
New York
March 1954]

My dear Helen —

This business of reducing is terrible. I must lose some more before we start out. Mary Hamblet[1] writes me from Portland that Dr. Ed Harvey, who is the head of the Oregon Fisheries, is planning a day of activity in Astoria for whatever we want — smoking, canning, fishing, and all the other bits and pieces. Also there is a nut place near Portland owned by one of the Dittenhofers, who wants us to see what they are doing. The Conways have started things in Seattle, and so it would seem we are on the way.

Does anything taste better in your life than the first few messes of asparagus you have in the spring? We are getting fairly good stuff now, and it does make you believe in the wonders of the season.

Try to get to a television set and see the new program "Home," which I hear is pretty awful. Poppy Cannon[2] is the food person, and she did a vichyssoise with frozen mashed potatoes, one leek sautéed in butter and a cream of chicken soup from Campbell's.

[JB]

---

[1] A friend of JB's from childhood, both in Portland and at the beach in Gearhart.

[2] Food editor of *House Beautiful* and author of several cookbooks, including *The Can-Opener Cookbook.*

[36 West 12th Street
New York
March 8, 1954]

Dearest Browns —

I'm so happy you like the fish boiler, and you know that the second piece is still to arrive — your braisière. I find it is my most useful piece of household equipment, and I love to serve in it. I also have the omelet pan and the crêpe pan and shall bring them along. Then we can omelet and crêpe to our heart's content when we get back to Pasadena. I think we can even do crêpes in our outdoor food book. We used to do the most wonderful griddle cakes on the beach when I was a kid, so why not crêpes with trout rolled in them or whatnot?

Tonight I broiled some flank steak and had a broiled tomato and a raw endive, mushroom and green onion salad, with my diet dressing of mustard, capers and lemon juice. I felt so goddam virtuous about it all. Today at lunch I bought four ounces of corned beef and a Temple orange and went back through the streets to jury duty munching my bit of food. Gourmet is as gourmet does.

Going to have Ruth and Cheryl here for a quick bite on Wednesday, and then we go to see the premiere of *Threepenny Opera* down here. Marc Blitzstein has done a new book and lyrics for it, one of my old friends [Scott Merrill] is playing the lead, and Lotte Lenya is singing her old part, so it should be a wonderful thing. I guess it'll be steak and salad and cheese, for it has to be hurry or nothing — or maybe I will do little squab on the rotisserie.

Love and a bit,
JB

[36 West 12th Street
New York
March 12, 1954]

Dearest Browns —

Well, we are co-authors, with Doubleday. That is settled and on the way. We shall have plenty of time to get it all together and on paper. We have a lot of it already. This combination should go far. Maybe we shall do three or four. I still have my eye on Knopf for our mutual memoirs.

Love and kisses, co-author,
JB

P.S. I have just paid my tax and the first installment on next year's estimate, and a few other bills. But I have my California mad money in my stocking.

[36 West 12th Street
New York
March 24, 1954]

Dear Helen —

Yesterday I made a new recipe for brioche mousseline* I found in a little French book. It is fantastic and as good as the one the little French gals charge a dollar a loaf for. Bake it in a tall round can or mold. I used a charlotte mold. Dissolve a package of yeast in about ½ cup of warm water. Add 1 cup of flour and make a paste of it. Put it in a warm place. While it is rising a little, combine 4 cups of flour, ½ pound of butter, ⅔ teaspoon of salt or a little more, and 1 tablespoon of sugar. Gradually add 6 whole eggs, one at a time, and work until you have a smooth lovely paste. Now combine with the yeast-flour mixture, and work well. Cover and let rise till double its bulk. Work in about ⅓ cup of warm milk and turn into buttered and floured molds. Let rise again and bake at 375 until browned and cooked through. Next time I am going to substitute cognac for the milk and see what happens. The grain is perfect and the flavor unbeatable.

We had a recipe given to us by a Turkish woman which is a new variation on the shish-kebab theme. She alternates sweetbreads with marinated lamb and bits of tomato and onion. She also gave us eggs boiled in half coffee and half oil for four to five hours. The flavor comes through in a strange and wonderful way, and the color is sensational.

The Reynolds Grill is the one the aluminum-foil people have put out this year and which is portable. They have a diagram for cooking on it, using a small amount of charcoal and foil. It is not as good as the Skotch Grill. And it is more trouble. But we probably should include it.

I'll send the capers next week and anything else new and fabulous I can find.

Love and all that,
your confused and busy
JB

---

* Recipe.

36 West 12th Street
New York
[March 28, 1954]

Dear Browns —

This is the last gasp. I am pooped, bitched, bushed, buggered and completely at sea. But off we go. I have to take six people to luncheon today at the new Chinese place I found, then back to work for another hour or two, and off to Paul Bernard,[1] who is having a party for me, the nice guy. Then a week of hell to face, including a dinner I am doing, which I trust ends the entertaining season. It's going to be simple — asparagus with grated cheese as a hot hors d'oeuvre, Jambon à la Crème,* polenta with spinach, and a Turinois — one hour's work.

After my long session on Friday with RKO Pathé, I am convinced that if we think up a short idea — 8–13 minutes — we can put it over. It is up to our three wobbling medullas.

I leave Saturday. If you want to get any messages to me I shall be at the Palace [in San Francisco] after Monday.

Love and a bittock,
JB

---

[1] A publicist and friend of JB. They shared birthdays in early May and sometimes celebrated together.
* Recipe.

36 West 12th Street
New York
[July 8, 1954]

Dearest Browns —

My *Harper's Bazaar* restaurant article ["Eating Out in New York"] seems to have made quite a furor, and Mrs. Snow is hot on my trail to do more. She had two letters waiting for me when I got home, and all the restaurants in town have invited me to eat.

A television offer again — this one really quite a good one with good money. I shall let them know in the next week or so.

At Ruth and Cheryl's over the weekend, they wanted a Chinese meal and so I did it. There were eight for dinner on Sunday. We had planned to do it outdoors, but it poured rain all day, so we had it indoors. I did chicken in paper, and as we all sat down I had a thought about the pieces still to be cooked. Instead of deep-frying them, I put them in a 400 oven for about five minutes, and they were divine. I had no Chinese parsley, so I used Old Man in the dish. You must get a plant of it. We had Chinese peas from the garden. Also did spareribs and fried rice and made a huge egg foo yong in a great iron skillet, finishing it under the broiler.

The next day I took the leftover chicken out of the paper, chopped it coarsely and mixed it with almonds and mayonnaise. We took it over to Rose Franken's[1] for cocktails, and everybody loved it. Made the best sourdough over the weekend I have ever made. I started about noon on Saturday and by Sunday morning it was working. On Monday morning we had wonderful pancakes. I have left it for this week to see what comes of it all. We picked wild huckleberries and blueberries in the back part of the garden, and they were heaven.

Love and kisses
JB

---

[1] Novelist and playwright, author of *Claudia.*

36 West 12th Street
New York
[July 13, 1954]

Helen dear —

The Cape was beautiful. But I worked my tail off at Chillingsworth.[1] There were forty people for dinner on Saturday night, and they were special parties, so I finished off dinners for most of them. I did forty portions of Poulet Flambé — did béarnaise as well as the flambé sauce — cooked three batches of rice pilaff, did string beans amandine for forty people, and did a soup that was the invention of the moment but delicious.* I chopped up about 4 pounds of ripe tomatoes and brought them to a boil with salt and pepper and a little thyme. Then I put them through the blender. I took a number 5 can of Snow's minced clams and put them through the blender until they were creamy, and combined them with the tomatoes, a touch of broth and a little more thyme and butter. It was absolute heaven and thick as a bisque and pink as hell. They loved it. I was hanging over the stove from 5:30 till 8:30, dished up everything as well and even cut some of the chocolate rolls. Finally we went down the road and had a club sandwich at ten o'clock, and I was dead. However, it is wonderful to see how the place has caught on and how well people like what they get. Dinner is $4.50 or $5.00 and lunch is $2.00 — no liquor, although people may bring their own.

We had a nice party at Peggy Lesser's[2] last night — with two HEB recipes — the onion salad with tomatoes, oregano and parsley and the spinach with mushrooms and sour cream. Also a beautiful roast of beef. This was all for good-bye to Kiki, who goes to school on the morrow. She has become a real personality this summer and may or may not make it in the theatre.

I am starting to work as a consultant on a full-time basis for the organization known as Restaurant Associates. The first thing is to develop rum drinks, then inexpensive dishes with wine, and so on. They are a wonderful group of people and I am only hoping they know what they want as clearly as they seem to know it. I shall take you to their top place at Newark Airport [The Newarker] when you are here.

Love and kisses,

J

---

[1] Chillingsworth Inn, near Brewster, Massachusetts, for which JB styled the menus.

[2] A children's book editor at Doubleday. She was married to Norman Foster, a sculptor, and Kiki was their daughter and JB's goddaughter.

* Recipe.

[36 West 12th Street
New York
July 27, 1954]

Dearest Browns —

This is plain hell week and last week was heller. I am late with Jerry Mason's book [*Jim Beard's Complete Book of Barbecue and Rotisserie Cooking*] — very late, and more to be done on it. Then I spent four days photographing for the big carving article in the November *McCall's*. We did color pictures on the hottest days in summer with no air-conditioning. I worked under lights about eight hours a day and nearly collapsed. We had so much beautiful Tingaud meat that we were covered with it.

Then in the midst of it all I had ten for dinner on Saturday. It was one of those things that had to be. We had prosciutto and melon and pears with drinks. Then I did a Vitello Tonnato in aspic (Tingaud's best white veal at a huge price), a Salade Niçoise, and thin polenta crescents with cheese and butter. Made herbed bread and had a magnificent white wine of Lichine's — a Riesling from Alsace. Had an Italian rosé with the melon. Then a raspberry soufflé made with white of egg only and some marvelous German kirsch.

Worked all day Sunday with two typists who were lousy — I could do the work in half the time but you wouldn't be able to read it. Tore through Monday and went up to New Canaan to see Cheryl's new show [*The Thirteen Clocks*] in Westport last night and back to the harness this morning.

Thursday I have the Lynn Farnols[1] and Ann Seranne for dinner — a quiche of crab, a chicken chaudfroid, Salade Russe, herbed bread, and fruits with kirsch.

I have my new shower in and am getting the entire bathroom [=kitchen] done with white metal cabinets with lights at the work level, new electric lines, a portable dishwasher, and a new refrigerator eventually — and a room divider in the bathroom so that you can pee without falling into the salad dressing. It's going to be sweet heaven on earth, and soon.

By the way, if it interests you, the rolled veal I did for the cold dish the other night was cooked at 325 until it reached a temperature of

160. It was removed from the oven, after which it arrived at 170, which is the perfect temperature for it. It was just juicy and not pink and not dry. For the *McCall's* pictures we removed all the beef at 120 and let it rest. It was perfect when carved 30 minutes later. The lamb we did at 140 and when carved was barely pink. The turkeys we removed at 160, and they were just slightly overdone in the breast when we carved.

The Chinese whose restaurant [Nom Wah] was in my *Harper's* article did us a dinner the other night that was superb. We had bird's-nest soup, stuffed shrimp with a kumquat sauce, then butterfly lobster — his idea, with rounds of lobster, slices of water chestnut, and bacon dipped in a batter, deep fried. Then slivered duck with Chinese peas and a huge mound of lightly sautéed long rice, with bits of ginger and pork in the sauce — sensational — it's called Snowflake Duckling. Then beef with vegetables and oyster sauce, followed by kumquats and fresh lichees, and to cleanse our palates, chrysanthemum-blossom tea. They are going to teach me to make Chinese dumplings. I can go down and spend as many mornings as I want in the kitchen and see the whole process. Come on along, and we'll do it together and start a restaurant.

Through Alexis Lichine I was offered Bemelmans' restaurant in Paris — he is evidently bored with it. Fifteen thousand dollars with a 100-year lease. But I'm afraid I have too much to do already.

I can tell you, I miss the peace and quiet of my little Pasadena house and garden. I am dead from the neck up and down at this point and no letup in sight for months. I'll never get to Europe unless I go for Christmas to Morocco, where I have always wanted to do a Christmas — nothing traditional but beautiful desert and spots around Marrakech.[2]

Love and kisses,

J

---

[1] Lynn Farnol handled public relations for a number of clients in the food industry.

[2] JB did not get to Morocco, but spent Christmas in Florence.

36 West 12th Street
New York
[August 10, 1954]

Dearest Helen —

I did turkey steaks on Thursday last [in New Canaan]. They were about 2 inches thick, from a 12-pound hen. They took exactly one hour and were good but not sensational. I still think turkey is best when it is roasted.

Friday night we did mutton steaks — real Canadian mutton, which was absolute heaven. They were about 1 ½ inches thick. Ron Callvert likes his well done, and I did that one for 30 minutes. Isabel and I like ours rare, and they were on for 20 minutes, browned to a turn, lusciously pink and juicy inside. We had the rice and chilies and sour-cream dish with it,* using mozzarella. I find that 15 minutes at 400 is better than 30 at 350. Also that it needed more sour cream.

Had the Jerry Masons Saturday night for supper and gave them a turkey chili with the rice again, done in double quantity, and they raved. Also a huge platter of Bibb lettuce, beefsteak tomatoes, Italian onions, and sliced pickled beets from the garden. And a new appetizer* — a can of crabmeat and a can of clams, drained of their juice, grated onion, chopped pickle, tarragon, mayon-naise, chopped parsley and a huge slug of rum. Let it stand for an hour, drain in a fine sieve and turn out on greens for a wonderful spread. I served it with Melba toast. Did a huckleberry soufflé for dessert — or rather two of them, with no flour, and they almost carried the oven away.

We were invited to dinner last night where they cooked two 3-inch steaks until they were pot roasts, over a fire much too hot. And they had had them specially hung and treated with great care — and they liked them that way.

Love and kisses,
JB

---

* Recipe.

[36 West 12th Street
New York
August 13, 1954]

Helen, Dear —

I had dinner at Cecily Brownstone's last night and cooked a 7½-pound 3-inch steak on the Reynolds Grill. I think it is fabulous in some ways and not too hot in others. The steak took almost 35 minutes. Separating the pieces of charcoal does help at the beginning, but when the fat had collected in the foil it caught fire once and caused a major conflagration. There was a hell of a lot of smoke, and very greasy-smelling smoke, during the whole procedure. However, the steak itself was superb.

Cecily borrowed her sister's apartment, with the garden. We had shrimp with a dill and tarragon sauce, the steak with a garlic and ginger butter sauce, which is delicious (grated garlic, butter, and grated fresh ginger), then onion rings,* dipped in a batter that you may or may not have had — 1 egg, beaten, 1 cup buttermilk, 1 cup flour sifted with ½ teaspoon soda and ½ teaspoon salt. Soak the onions in ice water, batter them and fry at 375. Cecily put them into the oven after frying. They were wonderfully crisp and better than any I have had for ages. We might call them Cecily's Onions and suggest using them for drinks also. Then she had hot pears in a crust with a form of praline — delicious.

My kitchen is just about finished, and while I am away next week Agnes White[1] will put in the sliding panels in front of the john and basin. I have to get a marble top for the cupboards, and then the walls will be painted white with a black ceiling and green trim. In the various panels between the lower and upper sections we are using the jacket of *Paris Cuisine* for decoration. It is really going to be pretty smart.

To the country for ten days.

Love and kisses,
JB

---

[1] Agnes Crowther White, an interior designer from Portland, decorated JB's two apartments on 12th Street and his 10th Street house.

* Recipe.

[New Canaan
August, 1954]

Helen dear —

The limes came, for which I am grateful, and I shall return in kind in the way of capers, on my next trip into town. I have been here all week, with one trip into town, which was a rush, and that on the muggiest day in summer. It has been delicious here with nights cool enough for blankets and days brilliant and brittle.

I have finished Jerry's book and am starting another for him at once and then one more for next spring. He thinks I will eventually do three a year. It is a glorified magazine job, that's what it is and what it should have been right along. I think we should think of something really stupendous for our next collaboration. It might be our respective menus for all occasions.

Did two 5-pound chickens on the spit the other night with low heat, and they took exactly one and one half hours and could have stood ten minutes more without being overdone. They were not rare, the joints moved freely, and they were basted but once during the cooking. It was dinner for Jane and Alex[1] and the Jerry Masons. Had herbed sourdough French bread with drinks. Used acres of green onions, basil, parsley, chives, with a slight overtone of mint and garlic, and it was wonderful — crisp on the outside so that it sounded like rock crushing. Then the chickens and a barley and mushroom casserole,* corn, gathered ten minutes before it was cooked, red onion salad with greens from the garden, and a clafouti of pears — Bartletts, with the butter-milk-flour dough dripping into the fruit like dumplings. We drank two sensational wines — a 1953 Niersteiner and a 1952 Montrachet from Monnot, the greatest single white wine in the world. There are only about 25 cases available in a year.

The following night I did a 2½-inch sirloin on the coals, and it was done in 35 minutes over low heat — charcoaly without being charred or black, tender and delicious, with little shrinkage.

The puppies have finally opened their eyes and are attempting to walk. Cricket grows more bored by the minute and will be completely fed up in a short time.

The garden is wonderful — peppers, tomatoes, corn, and a few beans. The McIntosh apples are just right. We are doing a pie tonight. Also making some more sourdough bread and trying out a brioche mousseline, which, if it is good, I will forward to you.

Love and kisses in three languages from Cricket and her three and me.

JB

_____

[1] Jane Nickerson and her husband, Alex Steinberg.
* Recipe.

[36 West 12th Street
New York
August, 1954]

Helen, dear —

Your package was delayed somewhere en route. It didn't reach here till eleven o'clock last night, and it was postmarked the day before. So I gather someone sat on it for a long time to defy the possibility of delivering. Alas, the tamales were sour, but the fish and the pastrami were in fine condition. I don't know when I have eaten better pastrami. The fish has a marvelous flavor but it is different from any smoked or kippered fish I have ever known. I guess the smoke was rather hot on it, wasn't it? It has a more salmony taste than most — in fact, the salmon flavor overshadows the other flavors. I looked longingly at the tamales. Why don't you send me the recipe and I shall try them myself.

I did a chicken casserole last night that you must try. It is a whole chicken steamed over julienne of vegetables. But the stuffing is something for the world. Chop 60 ripe olives, combine with a pound of ground veal, 1 large chopped onion, 3 chopped cloves of garlic, 2 tablespoons flour, 1 egg, salt, pepper, nutmeg and thyme or rosemary. Stuff the bird, place on the vegetables, and steam in a slow oven for two hours. I think you will like it — especially cold.

I am leaving for New Canaan and am doing a whole baron of

young lamb on the General[1] tomorrow night. I shall let you know at once about it. I have to go and pick it up. Hope your capers arrived in good condition.

JB

---

[1] Also known as the Bartron — the best barbecue equipment on the market, designed by retired Air Force General Harold Bartron.

[New Canaan
August, 1954]

Helen —

I can now tell you more about your package. The salmon were both interesting. I prefer the one that was dry-cured and that had quite a salty flavor. It seemed to have had the most oil left and the greater delicacy, despite the salt. It was not smoked salmon, as is the Nova Scotia, but it had a great distinction. The kippered was very good, but it was just well-kippered salmon, delicious but not really unusual.

I am inclined to agree about the clove in the pastrami, though I feel it is as excellent a pastrami as I remember. I would like a little more coarse pepper on it, but that is a purely personal taste. I learned a little secret the other day from Mort Clark,[1] who did the finest hams in Virgina I ever ate. Mort says the secret of good ham in Virginia is that people use borax in the curing — straight 20-Mule-Team borax. Maybe a little with the pastrami might be a good idea. I'll ask if Mort ever did pastrami. But we can have his ham and bacon and sausage recipes as well as his recipes for rillettes and for pork-liver pâté with truffles.

Helen, I did the baron of lamb on the General Saturday night. It weighed 14 pounds. I spitted it more or less diagonally through one side of the saddle and the fleshy side of one leg. I tied the two little legs together and had perfect balance. Stuffed a piece of Old Man up the ass and crushed some rosemary on the skin. Inserted slivers of garlic in the flesh here and there. He spitted for exactly 2½ hours to an internal temperature of 160, which meant there were certain well-done spots and some that were pink — none you would call rare. He looked so beautiful on the platter, with the lovely brown crust, tiny tail standing up and well-rounded bottom aloft. Sliced perfectly, and eight persons gobbled a lot of him, with plenty left. Had him with rice, corn from the garden and a ratatouille. Good cheese and a silly apple pie from the trees in the garden completed our dinner, along with a couple of bottles of Cos d'Estournel 1943. You may want to add the baron to the book. Cost ten dollars and was U.S. Prime.

I am so tempted to take one of the puppies. They are so darling. But I know better.

Love and a great hug, dear,
JB

---

[1] Morton Gill Clark, scriptwriter, novelist, and author of several cookbooks, including *The Wide, Wide World of Texas Cooking.*

[Pasadena
August, 1954]

Dear Jim —

No wonder [the pastrami] tasted like too much cloves. The recipe called for ginger. But I thought the second batch better than the first and so my third will have half ginger, half cloves. I also agree with you & increased the pepper.

HEB

[36 West 12th Street
New York
September 1, 1954]

Helen, Dear —

Just a hurried note. I do the sourdough starter just about the same way as you do — 2 cups flour, 2 cups water, 1 tablespoon sugar, 1 teaspoon salt. I take a cupful when I use it and replenish with a cup of flour and water and a little more sugar and salt.

I did French bread again last week and split it and herbed it. Used a cup of starter and a yeast cake, 4 cups flour, 1 teaspoon soda and a little more water (optional). I let it rise quickly in the warming oven. Shaped the loaves and let them rise again for only about 15 minutes. Brushed them with beaten egg and baked them at 400. It is wonderfully chewy and well-grained that way.

Also did loaves using a yeast cake, soda, 3 cups flour and 1 cup cornmeal. Made the most delicious bread for slicing and the most superb toast I have eaten in ages.

Try this for an outdoor dessert.* Cream ½ pound butter with 1 cup sugar. Add 1 egg yolk, 3 or slightly more cups flour and 1 teaspoon cinnamon. Spread out in a sheet pan or cookie sheet and brush with the egg white, beaten. Sprinkle with chopped almonds or filberts and bake at 350 until lightly browned and crisped. Cut in squares or what you wish. It is simple and so good. I used to sell it like mad on Nantucket. The recipe is Viennese, and I found it one day in *Larousse Gastronomique*.

When my kitchen is to be finished is in the laps of the gods of the kitchen.

Love and kisses,
JB

_____

* Recipe.

36 West 12th Street
New York
[September 1954]

Dear Helen —

Isn't it wise for us to be thinking what we should do for our next book? I should like it to be something out of this world exciting and something no one has ever done before. Maybe we should do a book of historic menus and the story around them, and give certain recipes from those menus. Or maybe we should do a book of our favorite dishes collected over the years, with memoirs of where and when we first ate them. Or maybe we should do an alphabet of foods and our favorite recipes for each food.

The food editors' conference is going full tilt and we hear the results are horrifying. Soon, we are told, there will be no fresh foods on the market — just canned or frozen (this came from the lips of the Secretary of Agriculture).

I did a sauce duxelles the other day, for the Bloomingdale's tasting, that was so simple and good. The butterfish in foil with ham, tomato purée and whatnot was delicious, as was the fillet with mustard and mushrooms. And the pompano with the duxelles,* etc. was sheer delight. Alice Hutton, the publicity dame there, spooned out the sauce from the papillotes to make sure she got it all. It is the ideal modern way for fish. I had about one hundred there on Monday, which they consider very good.

Love and kisses,
JB

---

* Recipe.

36 West 12th Street
New York
[September 19, 1954]

Helen dear and Philip —

I have just finished reading our manuscript for the second time. I am convinced that it is a magnificent tome and that we have something no one else has ever started to accomplish.

I also feel, after John and I saw Clara, that she will not accept the book as is. I have instructed John, and he is firmly in accord, that if she says anything at all he is to offer her the advance and we will take it back — and we can have it sold in two days. It would be given better treatment by Knopf, Viking, World or Little, Brown. I am certain she is going to say it is too fancy and not as good as the *Sunset* barbecue book. Please don't worry, it will come out all right. Anyone will be happy to take a book by the two of us, don't forget it.

One thing in the manuscript I am changing. If we are going to have the Virginia-style ham in it, we are going to have an authentic one. Morton Clark is giving us his directions, which they used when they were in business and their hams were considered the best in the country except for Smithfield. Also, his rule for Virginia bacon is going to be there, unless you have any objections.

Helen, there is so much work to be done I am thinking very seriously that we should form a combination. I still think we should have a small snack bar or something like that. Ruth is so anxious to get into the business. My old cook from Nantucket is dying to come here and work for me. The boys at Quo Vadis[1] want to help out on anything I'd do. Give it a lot of thought. We should be on the bandwagon, with Philip doing something along with us. Even a school part-time and a snack bar would give us enough to be able to close for two months a year and go abroad or wherever we wanted to go for the summer.

Last night I made a wonderful turkey casserole. We have a new turkey-in-parts division in my chicken place. Small ones cut up. I took a half breast, cut in two, two legs and two wings. Dipped them in flour, batter and sesame seeds, browned them in butter, placed them in a casserole with cognac, tarragon and a little Madeira, and baked them, uncovered, for 1½ hours at 300. Added ½ pint of heavy cream and baked another 15 minutes or so. Served it with baked potatoes with green onions and sour cream. It was delicious and simple as could be. I did use a good deal of pepper, too.

I made a soufflé with a cake mix that was sensational. Maybe we can sell it to General Foods.

Also, made a mistake with your chocolate icing and put in twice as much sour cream as you call for.[2] It was something incredible on an angel food cake. Made in a fish mold.

Au revoir,

J

---

[1] The owners of Quo Vadis, one of New York's best restaurants at the time, Gino Robusti and Bruno Caravaggi.

[2] HEB's original recipe called for ½ cup of sour cream and a pinch of salt stirred into 5 ounces of melted semisweet chocolate.

[36 West 12th Street
New York
October 16, 1954]

Honey, this is Saturday and I have been trying to find time to finish what I started earlier in the week. I have had a time running around like a fool. Yesterday I did the carving party for Helen McCully, including both a right and a left leg of lamb. We had about forty there, and there was luncheon — a beautiful party, really. She can do things with a terrific flair, that girl, when she wants to.

Then a pineapple party. Then a Swedish woman came and did a long interview with me and took one of the pictures of the two of us together, for a Stockholm paper. She is a fascinating person and is buying *West Coast Cook Book* and *Virginia City Cook Book* to take back with her.

The final bits of work on our book were so minor it is silly to even think of them as being changes. Helen has the manuscript now, and *Woman's Home Companion* gets it next. I think perhaps Mrs. Snow might get it, too. I had a note from her yesterday saying only,

"I can't begin to tell you how much I enjoyed your article on the markets." I was touched.

Madame Tannenberg gave me the idea for two things. One is a pancake made with heavy cream or sour cream — 5 egg yolks, 3 tablespoons flour, heavy cream or sour cream and then the egg whites, beaten stiff and folded in — dropped by spoonfuls on a hot griddle and cooked only on one side, then piled with fruit or served with sauce or honey and butter.

Also, crêpes cooked large and spread with coarsely chopped shrimp mixed with either hollandaise or béarnaise and rolled. This is something.

My friend Orsini who has the coffeehouse [on West 56th Street] has started serving one hot dish a day. Yesterday he had zucchini, split, cooked slightly and stuffed with tuna fish, garlic, and tomato sauce and browned under the broiler. Absolutely delicious. It could be served cold as well, cooked with olive oil, herbs, and a little tomato purée.

You asked about the pot roast. I had a rump roast, rolled and barded. Studded it with garlic, then seasoned it with rosemary, salt and freshly ground pepper, and put it in the oven at 450 for 30–40 minutes. Added 6 carrots, bay, 1 onion stuck with 2 cloves, and ½ cup red wine (for an 8-pound roast). Covered it and put it back in a 300 oven. It had body, texture and individuality — and was not a brown stewed piece of meat.

Would you be interested in being in the jelly business? And pickles and food specialties, under our own label?

Love and kisses,
JB

Helen, the pancake recipe is ½ litre of heavy or sour cream with the 5 eggs.

[Pasadena
October, 1954]

Jim dearest,

The fish book came. Jim, I am crazy about it. Read every word before I fell asleep. It is, without doubt, the best book that has ever been done on American fish and I am inclined to think the best book you've ever done.

H

[S.S. *Ile-de-France*
December 2, 1954]

Helen, dear —

I intended to do a lot of work on the trip, but I have done nothing but relax and be lazy — and that was a job in itself. When you and Philip go, this should be the boat, and cabin class, with first-class privileges. In cabin, we have Professor Toynbee,[1] a cabinet minister, one of the top French political reporters, Gerald Sykes[2] and his wife, Buffy Johnson, and a host of others. I have eaten magnificently but simply.

Today I had the fun of spending an hour with the chief baker and the others, watching them make bread from beginning to end, for the bread on the ship is fabulous. They use two parts hard wheat to one of American flour. The first fermentation takes about an hour. Then they cut it up by hand for the small rolls — the long ones — and knead the pieces into balls. Each man does two at once. They slap and beat and fold. These are covered with flannel and allowed to rise for fifteen minutes, after which they are rolled into toothpicks and placed on grooved pans and allowed to rise only a few minutes. Then they are slashed and put into a 450 oven with steam and baked for about 15 minutes. The flutes of bread are kneaded only once and shaped and put to rise on a board covered with a piece of flannel, and each one is nested in between folds of the material. They rise about 20 minutes and are then baked in the same way. No fat in the bread at all. Merely yeast, flour, salt and water. We weighed some of them, and despite the fact they were done by eye, they weighed, almost to a fraction, the same.

Some of the good food — well, for hors d'oeuvre, fennel poached in oil, vinegar and water, with herbs, served cold with strips of pimiento and anchovies. Also a wonderful potato, egg, tuna fish and parsley salad, with oil and a little vinegar. A lovely partridge was mine the other night. Also scallops with a white wine sauce, mushrooms, shallots, parsley and fresh tarragon, served in shells with a little Parmesan over it. Crêpes folded with pastry cream sprinkled with praline, flamed with kirsch and covered with kirsch-flavored hot heavy cream for a sauce. Sugar in the sauce and a little praline. The best bouillabaisse I ever ate. Last night for the gala dinner we had filets, sautéed very quickly, flamed with cognac, and topped with a tiny bit of chopped fresh tomato, béarnaise, and mushrooms; little fingers of duchesse potatoes rolled in shaved almonds and deep-fried for just a minute; braised endive.

I had dinner with Peggy Lesser the night before I sailed. Took Bill Kaduson[3] down. They came to the boat, which was quite a send-off. Sam Aaron sent six bottles of champagne, and Bill brought six, so I still have some. There were about fourteen at the boat, and others were too late because they overslept. It was rather fun to get high on champagne at ten in the morning.

Love to you both,

J

---

[1] Arnold J. Toynbee, English historian and author of *A Study of History.*
[2] British wine and food authority.
[3] A vice president of the cognac and champagne promoters Edward Gottlieb Associates.

[Paris
December 6, 1954]

Helen, dear —

Saturday night André Quaintenne[1] took me to a new place,
which is in what used to be the kitchen of a sixteenth-century
convent. The huge fireplace is used to prepare food — part charcoal cooking, with two gas burners to keep things hot and such.
We had a head cheese made of wild boar, a terrine of boar, and
a hot hors d'oeuvre of pork, which you will want to try. The pork
is coarsely chopped and quite lean. Mixed with a little salt,
crumbled bay leaf and a good deal of pepper, it is formed into
cakes about 3 inches across and 2 inches thick. These are
wrapped in parchment and broiled over charcoal until the parchment is practically burned, then served in the parchment with
the top cut off. We ate them with a good Bordeaux, followed with
more wild boar. This was from the ham and roasted hanging in
front of the coals, served with a purée of chestnuts. Cheese and
coffee. Superb but expensive. Fifteen dollars for two. The place is
very chic at the moment, and one sits around the fire and
watches the food being prepared. They have a set of knives with
stag handles made by an old-time artisan here. I have ordered
some of them. I have never seen anything to compare with them
for their efficiency or their beauty.

Last night we dined at Le Table du Roy. All show but very good
show. I shall send you the menu. The dessert was worth trying.
Done in an orange cleanly scooped out. Half filled with soft ice
cream mixed with grated orange rind, orange juice and Grand
Marnier. (You should really make a frozen custard with those
ingredients and use that instead.) Then a little port wine poured
over, covered to the top with sour cream, and capped with orange
and a little stem of angelica.

A man — larger than I and a camp of the first water — makes a
sauce for quenelles at table. In a copper sauté pan over alcohol
(and I've found the proper alcohol stoves) he puts about ½ pound
of butter, then sliced mushrooms, baby shrimp, and fines herbes,
then blazes with enough cognac to drown in. To this he adds a
sauce béchamel, lobster bisque — very thick — and a sabayon

made with white wine but no sugar. This simmers, and he adds vermouth and, at the last, whisky, and pours it over the quenelles. We didn't have it, but he brought me a little of the sauce to taste — it was fabulously good. Instead we had Truite au Bleu with a white wine sauce, brought to the table in its copper cooker over alcohol. A little of the carrot and onion from the bouillon was brought out and put on the plate. Then we had a young chicken roasted on the spit in front of us, with a tarragon butter. Not as good as your or my tarragon butter but very good.

I love you both.

[JB]

---

[1] A publicist for Renault.

Hôtel de France et Choiseul
Paris
[December 11, 1954]

Honey lambs —

I have been in Cognac for three days and returned to have dinner with Simon Arbellot, the president of the Société des Gastronomes, and the editor of *La Gastronomie,* which I am sending you as part of your Xmas. Cognac was a lot of fun. We had dinner the first night with the Hines,[1] folk of whom I have been fond for a long time. We had poached fresh eel with a sauce poulette, with tiny bits of sour pickle sliced into the sauce. Then grilled veal steaks, boiled potatoes, petits pois from the garden, cheese, and, for dessert, a savarin drenched in Hine with Hined pears in the center and heavy cream. Elegant. Then the next day we lunched with M. Renaud, the head of Remy Martin and the richest man in Cognac. He is a darling of 72 who loves pinching girls' bottoms and breasts and who lives magnificently well as far as food and drink are concerned. It was a beautiful luncheon — a Friday meal. First a huge colin poached in a very delicate court bouillon, with a magnificent mayonnaise made with olive oil and stiff enough to cut in cubes. With this, boiled potatoes. Then cèpes, the loveliest mushrooms in the world, sautéed in butter with acres of parsley and sliced garlic in great quantities, and the garlic was served as part of the dish. Then a salad with walnut oil and petits pois cooked à la Français. Then a selection of cheeses. Then a tart of the district — two meringues with chopped filberts, cooked brown and chewy, with a cognac-flavored cream between them. Three different wines and then cognac — natch. And much good talk. Renaud is a man of the world and a man with a wonderful sense of humor.

That night we were at the Hennessys' — Patrick's[2] — in a magnificent rebuilt old farmhouse with the most marvelous collection of Vallauris in the shapes of everything — the kind of stuff for which I am a sucker. A simple dinner — Channel sole meunière with lemon, a gigot with rissole potatoes and fresh spinach, cheese, salad, and a cabinet pudding and fruitcake soaked in you know what.

On the way down we ate in Cazalis's [Henri IV] in Chartres, one of the good restaurants on the road. We had a dish M. Cazalis invented last year, and what flavor it has. A veal kidney per person with all fat cut off. Rolled in a paper-thin escalope of veal, with loads of veal suet, Italian parsley, and a little shallot — and, for me, it would be better with a little tarragon. This is buttered and grilled until the veal is cooked through and the kidney is pink in the center. Served with fried parsley.

The night before we left, I had dinner with Genevieve Seznec[3] at Lasserre. A first course of fresh foie gras, sautéed with butter and goose fat, with white grapes and dots of fresh truffle. Unbelievable and so rich you could hardly dare to think of the calories. After that we had a simple chateaubriand for two, with a little béarnaise and watercress — and out of respect to Alexis a bottle of Lascombes.

Henry McNulty, the Gottlieb Associates boy over here,[4] is taking me to Alice Toklas. I love her book [*The Alice B. Toklas Cook Book*]. We may go there for lunch one day this week. I leave on Thursday for Florence for the Christmas holidays.

I am learning a great deal, which is the important thing, after all.

Love to you both. I miss you.

JB

---

[1] Of the cognac-shipping family.
[2] Also a cognac shipper.
[3] With the Paris office of Edward Gottlieb Associates.
[4] Head of Gottlieb's Paris office.

Hôtel de France et Choiseul
Paris
[December 14, 1954]

Dear —

Macmillan's, who want the carving book, want to pay only ten percent of the wholesale price. What with the money the photographer, Anton Breuhl, would get and the money for the meat and the time consumed in writing and photographing, it would amount to absolutely nothing in the world for me. I am through with books. At least for a year. I shall do the one with you and one book of gastronomic memoirs, and I think that is all.

Tonight I dine with Louis Vaudable, chez Maxim's. Louis always has so much to talk about, I shall be in stitches before I leave there. And very fashionable — nine-thirty for dinner.

Sent you a few little luxuries for your Christmas table yesterday. I told you where I would be. I shall dine in regal splendor with Bill Veach, overlooking the Arno — and, I am sure, with elegance and a bit of old home week. He is from Sacramento. So it will be cosy. Probably with three princesses and two duchesses.

Last night we ate at the Gare de l'Est. See *Paris Cuisine*. The chef is the first chef of France and practically no one in Paris knows the place. He was so nice. Offered us foie gras he had made himself the day before, as a token. Then we had sole split down the center, stuffed with hollandaise made with fines herbes, and grilled in white wine and fish broth heavily reduced. Served beautifully browned with its own sauce and three thin slices of fresh truffle.

Then tiny mignons of lamb grilled very rare, with a white wine tarragon butter — mostly butter sauce — with a little truffle. A heart of artichoke filled with mushrooms cut very fine and cooked in cream with salt and pepper. And a thin little pastry shell filled with small — but small — potato balls sautéed in butter. A bit of cheese and good coffee. With it we had a half-bottle of a wonderful Pouilly-Fuissé and a bottle of Château Léoville-Las-Cases 1950. A really elegant and perfect dinner. Oh yes, little cookies and tuiles and tiny palmiers with the coffee. We dined for almost three hours in quiet and peace. It was a beautiful experience.

Sunday night I dined with Sandy [Alexander Watt] on a wonderful pot-au-feu and cheese. The baby there is something. Seven months old and it ate almost six ounces of steak and three potatoes and carrots and cereal for its dinner. And slept for twelve to fourteen hours after that.

I'll finish this in the morning and tell you what we had chez Maxim's.

Eggs poached in cream with a topping of hollandaise in an oval shell of puff paste, first. Then a loin of venison with all fat removed and roasted so that it was perfectly browned on the outside and red rare but not raw on the inside — and heavy, wonderful venison as tender as butter. With this, two little tartines of duxelles and prunes stuffed with foie gras, and hot. Then a cake which Philip would love. Génoise with a fruit and cream filling, edged with praline and topped with a thick layer of blackcurrant purée.

At any rate I got a job out of it. The frozen Maxim's sauces are coming into being. I am to do the editing of all the recipes and get them into shape. I'm going to dinner tonight to taste the various ones. It will be more or less of an adventure.

Next word, from Italy.

[JB]

[Florence]
December 26, [1954]

Darling Browns —

I loved my little gift, which I unwrapped just before lunch yesterday as we were having our tree and presents.

This apartment is so beautiful and filled with such treasures that it is like a dream world. Bill has spent his life surrounding himself with beauty and elegance. I am hoping you are going to start a little correspondence with him, and please send him your *Patio Cook Book* and *Chafing Dish Cook Book*. His collection is to be left to the University of California.

The drawing room and the dining room look out over the Arno and up the hills to the great palazzi and beautiful villas. Both rooms are filled with priceless furniture and things which have been collected from Sacramento to Florence.

We were five for lunch yesterday. While Bill has a wonderful cook and servant, we both did most of the cooking. We decided upon a pumpkin pie. It turned out that we didn't have quite enough pumpkin, so I created. I used half pumpkin and half puréed chestnuts with the usual spices and cream, eggs, and sugar — and, dear, it is so much better. The chestnuts seem to give it an entirely different texture and quality.

Then we stuffed the turkey with a collection of things. We had fresh truffles, which we slipped under the skin, and made a stuffing with parsley, onion, puréed chestnuts, bread crumbs, some rice pilaff left from the day before, mushroom stems, plenty of fresh truffle slices, and a little Madeira. The turkey was about 10 pounds, the largest we could get in the oven. We started with some beautiful foie gras Bill had brought down from France. Then the turkey and puréed potatoes, a salad of endive and beets, the pumpkin pie, and cognac and coffee.

It was a dreamy day, the sun beat in on us and we were very gay and happy, all five of us. Last night after a cocktail party in one of the palazzi we came back to early bed and settled down with plates of cold turkey bits, and I had a red onion sandwich and read till late.

I have learned to make a fonduta, that wonderful mixture of

Fontina cheese, eggs and milk, covered with paper-thin slices of fresh white truffles. It is an exotic that cannot be duplicated. I shall send you a couple of tins of the white truffles and see if you can get the same effect. If you can't get Fontina — and I think you can — you could use Jack or even Teleme or a very mild cheddar.

Love, love, love,
Thanks, thanks, thanks,
J

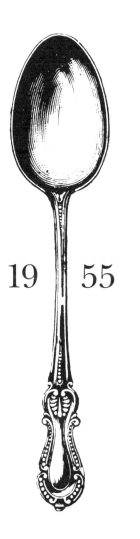

19 55

Continuing his European visit, JB went to Torino, as consultant for Cora vermouth, and on to Paris, where he met Alice B. Toklas, and then toured the Bordeaux and Champagne districts. On January 28 he sailed for New York on the *Liberté*. He was promptly sent to Doctors Hospital for tests and an operation on his right leg. In March he was approached by Dell Books to write a basic cookbook for paperback publication (*The James Beard Cookbook*). That same month and the next he traveled to a number of cities, including Detroit, Kansas City, and Houston, to do promotion demonstrations for cognac. In April, also, *The Complete Book of Outdoor Cookery*, written with HEB, was published. In May JB spent a week in Mexico and took a second, longer, trip there in July.

The Browns paid a visit to JB in September. In November he started performing on an NBC radio program, "The Weekday Show." On December 10 he sailed for Italy on the *Independence* and again spent Christmas in Florence.

Dearest Helen —

The New Year's celebrations have gone along with no trace of fatigue on my part. I came back from Rome on Friday to find Bill quite wrapped up in cold. We had been invited to a party in the Terristori Palace and decided at eleven-thirty that we would get dressed and go, but fate stepped in. Bill put on his shirt and a large diamond from one of his evening studs dropped out, and we spent the next hour on the floor looking for it. I finally found it. It was then too late to go partying. We consumed a bottle of bourbon between us, ate cold beef sandwiches and went to bed about one.

Rome was simply beautiful the three days I was there. Ate so much baby lamb I almost feel I shall produce a wool crop this year. It is the season for them, and roasted, with or without garlic, they are delicious, with a flavor that is unlike any other type of lamb. I had it with finocchio, steamed and served with olive oil and lemon, and with rosemary fried potatoes.

Did I tell you of the chicken Romana? It is sautéed and covered with strips of roasted sweet red peppers and a tiny bit of tomato purée. Delicious. And artichokes in the Roman fashion. Cut with long stems, which are carefully peeled, and the bulb as well. Then all the spines are cut off, and they are steamed that way. Served upside down with the stems sticking high in the air, and eaten with oil and lemon for an hors d'oeuvre — two to a person.

Ate a lovely fritto misto — brains, mussels, scampi, artichoke sections, potatoes, chicken croquettes — very tiny — each thing dipped in egg and flour and fried.

This Italian habit of having a whole plate of pasta every meal is something I cannot follow. I see people eat a steaming plate of noodles or spaghetti that would serve for a full course anytime and then follow with meat, potatoes, vegetables, salad, cheese and dessert.

Next time you make a curry try Bill's eggs. Hard-boil them — one to a person — prick them well with a fork, and let them stand in curry powder for an hour or so. Then sauté them whole in butter and serve them with a curry dish. Each person mashes the egg into the mass. It is elegant.

Yesterday we had luncheon at Doney's, one of the best restaurants here, and had their special chicken — pounded breasts, sautéed at table over an alcohol flame, blazed with you-know-what, with paprika and mushrooms added and then cream and a little brown sauce, cooked down and served very hot.

I leave here day after tomorrow and go to Milan and then to Torino, where I get the material for the new job Bill Kaduson got for me, for Cora vermouth. I am also going to the place where they make the most beautiful copper utensils in the world — true works of art.

Love and kisses,
JB

Found a cheese which is almost exactly like Teleme, although done in round cakes about two inches thick and eight inches in diameter. Called Pecorino Toscano (see your cheese book), it is absolutely delicious and creamy and has that slight acid taste that is Teleme. The waiter in the little restaurant where we go often suggested I try a little freshly ground pepper on it, and the difference is simply wonderful.

Pasadena
January 5, [1955]

Jim dear,

The Entertaining book [*Jim Beard's Complete Cookbook for Entertaining*] is out and to be perfectly honest I am a bit cross with you. You have included stuff that is in our book and that I have been studiously avoiding using until it was published. I know that you won't resent it when I tell you, dear, that I really think you have repeated yourself too much in your last few books. That is why I think you ought to rest on your laurels for a while.

H

[Hôtel de France et Choiseul
Paris]
January 13, [1955]

Helen, dear —

Well, I'm back in Paris, with your last letter having just arrived. I think that is pretty good — it is postmarked January 10, 9 p.m. I shall be here for another two weeks, with a trip to Champagne on Monday for three days and then to Bordeaux for three or four days.

After my wonderful stay with Bill I went to Torino by way of Milan. Torino is the home of vermouth, and I did a two-and-a-half-day inspection of Cora (which is, by the way, the finest of all dry vermouths) prior to doing a booklet for Schiefflin on how to eat and drink with vermouth. The Italians, who are the largest vermouth drinkers in the world, never use it in cookery. I'll send you the complete list of herbs they use if it interests you. And what is our term for abseentium?[1]

My opinion of Italian cookery is not too high. And getting my first piece of French bread on the train yesterday made me realize again what masters the French are at that art. It seemed to me that even the food on the wagon-lit restaurant car was better than all the food in Italy, save at Bill's and at the fabulous Giannino's in Milan. And last night, late, Henry McNulty and I went to the Régence for dinner, and just my simple meal of marrow on toast, a grilled kidney and some cheese tasted like ambrosia.

Today Henry and I lunched with Art Buchwald at dear Madame Pannetrat's little restaurant [Aux Bonnes Choses] — on a truffle omelet, confit d'oie, done with white beans, and a bottle of wine.

Art is doing a crazy column on me which may be very funny. He is a
sweet guy and has done wonderfully well.

You are so right about the Entertaining book. Those recipes
were included by mistake, for when the ms was typed, other
sheets got mixed up in it. I thought I had caught most of them
until I saw the galleys. I don't want to do any more cookbooks for
a while. I still think the fish book is the best thing I have ever
done and after that, *Paris Cuisine* and *Hors d'Oeuvre and Canapés*. I
have a lot of new recipes and wonder if "The Best of Beard and
Brown" isn't a good idea. I'm sure that if Doubleday won't take
it, or Little, Brown, that Donald Friede[2] will, for he once said
he'd like to do an omnibus of mine. And I like what he did with
the M. F. K. Fisher[3] omnibus [*The Art of Eating*]. Thanks for giving
me the goosing.

Scampi are what I have always said they were — like a lan-
goustine. They are a cross between a shrimp and a langouste,
and pinky and white-shelled. They come in various sizes up to
the size of a small lobster. These last ones broiled are excellent.
Bill did a pilaff of scampi one night with a curry sauce that
was tremendously good. In Milano I had some medium-sized
ones deep-fried, with a sauce mayonnaise. They have a sweet
taste, not at all fishy or shellfishy, and are not as firm as
shrimp.

One thing in Italy which is beyond belief wonderful is
the prosciutto, both cooked and uncooked. We had some from
Vittorio Lambretti the other day, which is supposed to be the
finest in the world. Our Virginia ham is the closest thing
to it.

I shall have to diet like a fiend when I get back.

Love, dear,

J

P.S. Spent the morning with Alice Toklas. She loves your *West Coast
Cook Book*, which evidently someone sent her. I thought it would
cheer you to know you are on her "favorites" shelf. She was
delighted to know we are doing a book together.

I am to do a party for Skotch Grill on the 17th, so that means I sail on the 28th and arrive the 2nd or 3rd of February on the *Liberté*.

---

[1] Artemisia Absinthium; HEB responded correctly, "I suppose wormwood is the answer."

[2] Of the publishing firm Covici-Friede.

[3] America's most highly regarded food writer, also author of many volumes of fiction, essays, and travel pieces.

Pasadena
January 19, 1955

Jim dear,

You're a sweet lamb not to be mad at me for bawling you out. I did it only because I love you so much I didn't want you to make an awful mistake. Also maybe because I was a little jealous at your being smart enough to make so much money. . . . Lord, I wish we were with you. It all sounds heavenly.

Helen

[Hôtel de France et Choiseul
Paris
January 23, 1955]

My dear Helen —

Back from another trek — this one into the horribly flooded district around Bordeaux.

Yesterday M. and Mme Cruse, the shippers, and owners of Château Pontet-Canet and La Dame Blanche, gave me a luncheon in the château. They entertain in the most enchanting way possible. It was she who did the luncheon with the thirty-six solitaires on the table and the great Strasbourg goose. Yesterday she planned a typical Gascon luncheon of dishes which have been in her family for generations, and with the exception of the first course everything was grown on their farm or made in their kitchen.

We started with a novelty — caviar from the Gironde River near Bordeaux. Not as large as the Russian but less salt and delicious. With that, the Dame Blanche 1950. Then slices of goose liver which had been steamed in white wine and covered with a sauce similar to a hollandaise but without the lemon and just a touch of vinegar in it. This, garnished with homemade sausages and eggs fried in goose fat. Then the confit, which, as Madame Cruse said, may have been the same goose who gave the great liver (one liver served eleven persons admirably). The confit was cooked in its own juice and served with cabbage leaves cooked till just soft enough to fold and form into tight rolls about two inches long. Tiny new potatoes cooked in goose fat till brown and crisp went with them. The confit was perfectly carved in rather thickish slices and small joints, and the cabbage leaves served as a garnish all around the platter. With this a Pontet-Canet 1928 — and a fabulous one. Cheese — a plain cheese from the farm, rather like a cheddar, and then one from Gascony. The dessert Mme Cruse had prepared for me especially — a réduit Taillan. The cook arose at five and put a great quantity of milk on to cook with some sugar, and that is what it is — six hours' reduction of milk and sugar until it is like a firm custard, with a rich flavor unlike anything in the field you have ever tasted. It is crusty on top and rather caramelly on the bottom — like crème caramel but it has no eggs. It must be done either on top of the stove or in the oven at a low, low temperature.

I know of no home in France where luncheon or dinner is so beautifully done. Such a difference from the rather bad meals one eats in Champagne.

Had an interesting dinner at Alexis Lichine's place on Thursday night. An excellent cheese soufflé for the first course. Then a thick rump steak of beef roasted rare, with cèpes, which they had canned themselves, cooked with oil, garlic and parsley, and quantities of braised endive — a perfect combination of flavors, along with red wine. Cheese for the end of the meal. The beef was what many French consider the best. They take oxen which have worked in the fields for years and retire them for one year to pasturage, where they relax and eat like fools. They are then slaughtered and aged and have plenty of fat and flavor. It is completely different from the beef to which we are accustomed.

I have just returned from lunch and a long walk along the river. There are millions of people out to see what is probably the highest recorded water level of the Seine in the history of Paris. It is rather frightening to see trees simply inundated.

For lunch, in a Belgian restaurant, I had green eels and water-zooï. The eels were excellent and jellied with all their herbal delights, but the waterzooï could have been better. The broth was not chickeny enough. I think they cooked the death out of the bird and then added more water after they had decanted the real broth. This is one of the happiest days I have had, for I had no engagements and could wander around as I pleased and eat where I pleased.

Thursday I have to invite several people here for drinks. I shall have champagne, of which I have plenty, and vodka martinis and cognac. I can get the most delicious salted almonds here, and from Rumpelmayer's, enchanting little sandwiches, and I'll have some cheese sticks. I shall be able to pay back old debts in a pleasant way.

Would you like to do a collection of our recipes called "Recipes and Recollections"? About two hundred recipes from each of us with a little story about each one and the appropriate accompaniments. And we could tell in each case why we included it in the list of the greatest eating we have known. Think about that. And I think that our outdoor book should be done in French as well, for they are just beginning to do the outdoor thing.

Love and kisses,

J

Hôtel de France et Choiseul
Paris
[January 26, 1955]

Helen, dear —

I am going on a permanent diet — really and truly, without fail. I have gained so much that it is pitiful. But there is always the comfort of knowing I have learned new things.

This is the last letter from here for the time being. How I'm going to get everything off the boat I don't know. Cognac arrived, and Robert de Vogüé[1] has sent champagne to the ship — well, I can always drink that with someone.

Last night I was invited by Simon Arbellot to dinner with him and four gastronomic writers to taste cassoulet at Grand Vefour. As if that were not enough for one day, I had to lunch with the Hennessy group, and we went to the Table du Roy again, and had a fabulous mussel dish for a first course. You could do it with clams, too, I think. It was done at table in a large copper brasier on a double alcohol flame. We were five. First, almost a half-pound of butter, then about ⅔ cup shallots, the same of parsley, 2 bay leaves, fish broth — about 2 cups — and 1½ cups brown sauce, and this with a little fines herbes in addition to the parsley. A good slug of vermouth and of cognac, and the whole thing was allowed to come to a boil, then a dash of salt and pepper and celery salt. The chef added the cleaned mussels in their shells, grabbed the covered brasier by the handles, shook it vigorously like a cocktail for a minute, returned it to the flame and let it simmer just until the shells opened. Then a great glob of heavy cream, so thick it stood like whipped cream, and another smack of butter were stirred in. A touch of tomato somewhere. When it was dished out, we had the tender mussels and we had the sauce as a soup. It was rich beyond belief and magnificent. But this was followed with kidneys and mushrooms with a mustard sauce, which was just as rich as the first course. Then cheese and fruits. I was laid out.

I went to the de Vogüés for cocktails and to a party for me given by the Williamses,[2] and then to this test dinner, wishing I never had to think of food again. We had a good whisky at the bar. Then we sat down to the first cassoulet — Castelnaudary — with luscious tender little lamb chops cooked in the bean mixture just long enough to flavor them and still remain rare. Also mutton cooked with beans and garlic and parsley, and a delicate and wonderful dish it was. After this came the Toulouse cassoulet, made with goose, pork, mutton, country sausages, and Toulouse sausage of pork, with fresh truffle slices and pistachio nuts in it, and slices of salt pork. Elegant and to my taste it was the first which had something divinely subtle about it.

We drank a light Morgon from the Beaujolais district with this and then followed with a Bordeaux with the cheese, a fabulous piece of Brie. By the time I had had coffee and a cognac I could hardly walk. Three miles later I had a beer, then on to a quart of Perrier and six charcoal tablets. I finally felt I could get into bed without a gas explosion rocking the hotel and slept like a baby, only to awaken to a feeling of being weighed down with food. Thank God, I'm lunching today with friends who like to eat lightly, and we shall lunch on eggs and a grillade. Then McNulty and I have twenty coming for champagne and drinks, but that doesn't mean I have to eat, although I'm going to have a farewell dinner with Sandy and Grete [Watt] and McNulty.

I went to the Ritz Grill for lunch the other day, always one of my favorite places. Had eggs baked in a rich bouillon for a first course and then one of their great specialties, sheep's trotters poulette. They cook the dainty little feet to perfection, bone them and serve them smothered with a magnificent sauce poulette, sharp with lemon. And for the first time since I have been here I had a piece of pastry for dessert, for they make a Gâteau Pithiviers — which is my favorite — like no one else. The puff paste is buttery and crisp and the cream of almonds freshly made.

This concludes the chapter entitled Voyage 1954–1955.

Love to you both,

J

---

[1] The Comte de Vogüé, principal owner of the Chambolle-Musigny vineyards.

[2] Of Williams & Humbert, sherry producers famous for Dry Sack.

36 West 12th Street
New York
[February 11, 1955]

Dearest Helen —

Just a note, because I shan't be able to use the typewriter again for a week or so. The doctor is putting me in the hospital to make some tests and whatnot, and I shall be bedded down for about five days. I have been bothered for the last few weeks with something, and we are going to trace it down at this point. I shall be in Doctors Hospital. At least I'll be away from the telephone.

Love and kisses,

J

[Doctors Hospital
East End Avenue
New York
February 19, 1955]

My dear Helen —

I'm trying typing in bed to see how it comes out.

I came in last week on [Dr.] Jack Sullivan's orders, for rest and tests. I guess I had been overdoing and was terribly overweight and had a bad thumping. However, the tests came through perfectly. Then Jack decided it was time to take out the varicose veins. So that was done on Thursday. I'm to be here for a few more days and am on a 1000-calorie diet and getting plenty of rest. I'm inundated with flowers, books and champagne and have a beautiful view of the river, the mayor's house, and all the garbage barges going up and down. The dietician makes the trays attractive and you wouldn't really know you were getting as little as you do. Sam Aaron keeps a running service of champagne splits going — not for me as much as for the personnel and visitors.

Of course, I have the goddam Skotch Grill party on Friday and have been giving out from the bedside with ideas and advice.

Just had lunch. Shrimps with lemon, a beautiful lamb chop, tomatoes and cucumbers, and a pear preserved in water. It is the first real meal I have eaten in two days, except for last night when I ate a bit of cold sliced chicken and some Melba toast.

Now I have the problem of getting all my work done and plenty of rest as well. I am going to slow down on a number of things and just aim for the biggest. I go with Bill Kaduson to Boston, Philadelphia and Washington next month and then in April or early May to Detroit, Kansas City and Houston. At that time I hope I can sneak out to you for a few days or a couple of weeks — if I have any money left after this is all done.

Lots of love,

J

[Doctors Hospital
East End Avenue
New York
February 21, 1955]

Dearest Helen —

I feel a lot better and am confident that I shall be a better boy from now on. Everyone has been so wonderful to me — Philippe, Alexis, all the importers — I could have a fully stocked bar here if I wanted it. I never knew so many people liked me, really.

My right leg is so heavily bound that it makes walking somewhat difficult. I realize that I was overly ambitious to think I would be able to get out this week and do the party. But I do want to get home and finish some things which are pressing and which can be done at the typewriter and desk without overdoing anything at all.

Helen McCully has asked me to do a diet piece, and I think I have struck a new idea. It has occurred to me that since being here in the hospital and dieting I have been renewing my acquaintance with the honest and true flavors of foods. The difference is wonderful. Why everyone diets with ersatz things is something I don't understand. For lunch yesterday I had a little filet. I ate it slowly and realized that here in America we have the finest beef in the world. It was well aged and had flavor and texture. Never have I eaten such a piece of beef anywhere in Europe. And with it, were broiled mushrooms, tasting of the earth, and a little asparagus. Again last night, with celery and shrimp, I felt the same thing. It can be a glorious fresh tasting experience, this dieting.

Love and hugs,

J

[36 West 12th Street
New York
March 8, 1955]

My dear Helen —

I rehearsed all morning for the Home Show and put in a plug for using you, which they were glad to have. Then I had an endless chain of things to do that kept me uptown all through dinner, and I was exhausted when I got home. I'm still oozing in the groin, but the penicillin poisoning is going away, and I hope by the weekend when I leave for Boston that things will be much better.

Had a beautiful dinner last night with the Surmains.[1] They are offering a fabulous trip to the great restaurants of France this summer, for twelve people for $3,000 apiece. We had a double chicken consommé — André uses an old recipe of his mother's; makes a rich broth with one chicken, removes the chicken, adds another one and cooks till the broth is richer. Then tournedos Dijonais, cooked with a slice of smoked ham on top and served with a red wine sauce made from the pan juices. Artichokes with butter. Crisp stuffed potatoes. Then a salad of endive and cress. And a heavenly mousseline of apples. Seven pounds of apples were reduced to a pulp — the apples peeled, started with a little butter, then mixed with sugar and eggs and baked to a golden brown on the bottom. It was a sensational dessert. I adore to see young people like Nancy and André take such pains with their food and such delight in cooking and serving. We were eight, and they did it all, with a maid to do the cleaning up and odd jobs.

Philippe just called me to see if I would like to be the assistant at the Newport Casino this year. I shall have to see what is wanted and whether or not it is my dish. Anyway, it is one of the things on the fire.

Bill and I leave at nine on Sunday morning to drive to Boston. I have never driven with him, so don't know what is in store for me, but I imagine he should be a fairly good driver. But you know me—

I'm scared of drivers unless I have the utmost confidence in them. Give me a plane pilot a hundred times over.

Love,

J

---

[1] André and Nancy Surmain. André, a young Frenchman, was an airlines caterer when JB first met him, and the Surmains' house on 50th Street (where he later started the restaurant Lutèce) was the setting for the first session of the James Beard Cooking School.

Easy Living Co.[1]
677 Madison Avenue
New York
[March 19, 1955]

Helen, Dear —

I drove up to Boston with Bill on Sunday and enjoyed it, for it was crisp and beautiful, and we drove half the way with the top down. Monday night saw Cheryl's show [*The Honeys* by Roald Dahl], which needs a lot of work but which is funny. Food — one woman killing her husband with oysters, the other with a leg of lamb, and then at the end they are eating the evidence with the police, who are looking for the weapon.

Tuesday, the TV show, which went very well this time. I had a lot of people there viewing me in that capacity for the first time, so I was on the qui vive — and I felt like hell.

Drove back on Wednesday, stopping in Newport, where they have asked me to do the Casino this year, and it tempts me more than anything else — delightful spot and the potential seems tremendous. I suppose you wouldn't like to join me for the summer, would you?

Thursday was the party for Buchwald, and it turned out to be a dilly. We had it at Lynn and Nell Farnol's, and we had all New York. The Kreindlers and Bernses from "21," the Bennet Cerfs, the Schusters, Richard Rodgers, and on and on and on. I did a terrine of liver and pork, a terrine of veal and ham, a duck pâté, and a chicken liver pâté, and Vaudable sent me a partridge terrine they had made. I also made about three hundred onion sandwiches,* and Lynn had bought a Virginia ham and beautiful cheese. For the first time in my life I saw people flocking around the buffet table, digging in like crazy. Renaud Dolfi, of the liqueur family of the same name, said that he had never in all his trips here eaten food which tasted so authentically French, which of course made me swell with pride.

Monday I go to *Reader's Digest* for lunch, after several delays. Keep your fingers crossed, will you? Tuesday Dell Book's manager [Frank Taylor] has asked me to dinner to discuss a project, and there are two commercial things on the way. So I guess the next few months are taken care of all right, but I need the money, for last year while being a good one financially was a catastrophic one in some ways. My kitchen cost me a hell of a lot more than I figured, and it is still costing, for I really must have a new stove and refrigerator to make it complete.

I'm doing dinner for Camille Timberlake[2] on the 30th, before she sails for Europe. Going to do a quiche of crab, baron of baby lamb, potatoes with rosemary, asparagus with lemon butter or heart of palm sauté, and a very simple fruit dessert — with coffee and some of the mirabelle I brought back with me this time. A German wine — a light and wonderful one — with the quiche and a lovely young Fleurie with the baby lamb.

Had lunch at the Pavillon yesterday and it was not good. I had a little smoked eel, which *was* good, then their great specialty of Friday — striped bass with an oyster and mushroom sauce. They had more than overcooked the fish — and at $3.75 an order as well. Then, because it was the Pavillon, I indulged in a morsel of their Pithiviers, and lo and behold the puff paste had been made with the saltiest butter on record, all of which seemed to have oozed out through the crisp leaves. What Vaudable must have paid for the luncheon for five with wine and drinks, I cannot imagine. I will take "21" anytime. And I had a delicious dinner in Boston at Locke-Ober's, with a perfect grilled mutton chop. They astonished me by saying they are serving no more oysters this season because they are not up to their standards. Rather than serve something they didn't like they were removing them from the menu completely.

Toujours,
JB

---

[1] A short-lived mail-order business offering wine accessories, run by Sam and Jack Aaron and JB.
[2] A San Francisco socialite of the Guittard Chocolate family.
* Recipe.

[Pasadena
March 1955]

[Dear Jim,]

I am writing an article called "I lost five pounds in twenty years," a diet story. . . . Dear god, man, you have energy! All that work for your party — those terrines & onion dos (they are still my favorite appetizer).

[HEB]

[36 West 12th Street
New York
March 28, 1955]

Helen Dear —

It looks as though the *Digest* was serious about a series of things if I can satisfy them with the first one.

The wife of the editor, Paul Palmer, is a Bulgarian, and she did a delicious lunch for us. Mussels rémoulade, tiny cheese strudels about the size of a test tube, homemade bread, a Bulgarian version of meat loaf, with lamb and pork and seasonings, molded around eggs and baked with mushrooms and broth, rice with shredded carrot and onion cooked in it and much paprika. Cheese and fruit and two wines. A really stupendous luncheon.

Tuesday night, dinner at Chambord with the editor of Dell, who wants me to do a basic cookbook for him. A wonderful guy and a wonderful dinner. (I told him to do your *Holiday Cook Book* in paper.) We had lobster cooked in cream and blazed with Pernod — in the shell, as it is with Américaine — and cut into small bits. Also a soufflé, which I didn't eat but tasted, made with candied and brandied fruits. The dinner for four of us was so astronomical in price [$110.00] I guess I have to do two books to make up for it.

Wednesday I went up to Pound Ridge for two days to do pictures with Lizza [Josephine] van Miklos on casserole stuff for Jerry Mason. We started at eleven in the morning and by six in the evening had done eleven complete dishes and shot thirty-six rolls of film both in black and white and in color — and had done process shots, of me cutting up a chicken and a duck, chopping parsley, slicing onions and such like, all with strobe lights so that we didn't have to stop. Took a lobster dish, a chicken casserole with white wine and a pot roast done in the oven over to Jerry Mason's for dinner. Up at seven in the morning and did soufflés in color and black and white till I had to get a train back to New York in time for lunch and a lot of other things. I could hardly wait to get home and get my clothes off, for I had had to get my leg dressed that afternoon, among other things. It was brutal.

Saturday, took Ken Zwerin and Paul Bernard to Quo Vadis to lunch. Had the Italian version of pot-au-feu, bollito misto, which they do to perfection — beef, veal, chicken, salt pork, and great thick sausage, all poached and served with vegetables, potatoes and mustard fruits. It was as good as the best place in Milan.

On Friday I went to Marion Brown's pickle party for her new book [*Pickles and Preserves*]. She had brought up about a trunkful of pickles, and they served them along with cocktails. Well, I might add that spiced pears, sweet tomato slices and pickled peaches are not my dream of what to have with a martini, but the pickles alone were handsome. I liked her bread-and-butters as well as any I have eaten, and you know how queer I am for pickles anyway.

Sunday, had twelve for breakfast, which was a mistake, but it was fun. Smoked whitefish, carp and salmon, and four types of German sausage, with scrambled eggs. Peggy [Lesser] did a batch of her superlative ones with parsley, and I did a batch with dill weed. The usual B. Marys and Golden Screws beforehand. Coffee, coffee cake, wonderful marmalade (and I suddenly remembered how Mrs. Fiske[1] used to eat great bowls of Scotch marmalade with heavy cream) and cream cheese. They stayed on forever, till I was frantic, for Isabel and I had a hell of a lot of work to catch up on.

Did you read Poppy on how everything in cookery originated in Ancient Greece?

Love and kisses,

J

---

[1] The American actress Minnie Maddern Fiske.

Pasadena
April 1, 1955

Jim darling,

What is this *Digest* deal? You haven't told me. And the casserole book? I thought you were through with that kind of book. My god, man, you will kill yourself. Don't, we love you.

H

[36 West 12th Street
New York
April 3, 1955]

Helen Dear —

The dinner for Camille Timberlake was elegant. Agnes worked all day here, practically. My antique cupids arrived from Italy. I have the big copper lavabo up again, and I had about six dozen or more daffodils in it with the spotlight from above. The new café curtains are of gold cloth with little clips. The cupids are gold — Agnes says we are in the gilded era. I had pâté; the shad roe was succulent and really the treat of the year; and the baby lamb was so cute it was difficult not to put it under glass. I had a beautiful Moselle and a Fleurie, and a La Tâche '42 with the cheese, and some of my precious mirabelle with coffee. We sat until almost one in the morning.

Helen, the way to do the [dried] morels is to soak them in water, then cook them lightly, water and all, with butter and very finely chopped parsley, and add heavy cream. Serve them with a sautéed or roast chicken. They have a rich flavor which is different from any other mushroom.

Try making thin crêpes with no sugar. Put a lightly poached egg in the center of each one and fold toward the center. Cover with sauce béarnaise — the most unbelievable experience.

The *Reader's Digest* deal is a plan Paul Palmer has in mind, which involves about six or eight articles on the general theme of food in America. They pay $1,500, to begin with. If the thing goes over, his idea is that I would be their official food person. But it has to get past Mr. Wallace as yet, and he is strictly a bourbon and chocolate-sauce boy.

Did you see Art Buchwald's crack aimed at Little, Brown in his column? One of the unpleasant things about America, says he, is the publishing business. Publishers scramble for your books and then keep the fact that they have been put on the market a dead secret.

The casserole book [*Jim Beard's Casserole Cookbook*] I did over the year, and Jerry Mason is publishing it in the fall. He is doing more commercial tie-ins, so he feels I can have a steady income from him for the next ten years. I am trying so hard to sell him on a book for you.

I had dinner at a rather nice restaurant [Pablo's], where I had heard the food was something special. It is run by a man who has had a place in Provincetown and in Key West. There is a more or less steady menu, including satés, various international specialties, and a wonderful version of the Argentine and Brazilian steak, sometimes called churrasco — grilled over coals and served with a sauce of onions, vinegar, peppers, parsley, celery seed and other seasonings, but mostly onion and some hotness. They even do a whole rack of beef that way. At any rate, they had the best gazpacho (we were there on Spanish night) I have ever had, but it was more like the Russian soup okrochka than gazpacho. Made with veal broth, it had bits of smoked ham in it and crisp garlicked croutons, as well as the crisp vegetables. So much better than the water one. Try it.

Love,

J

Pasadena
April 6, 1955

James dearest,

Was the churrasco the ribs? Cut two to a steak? I don't know okrochka. Tell me all. . . . Your house sounds too too elegant! You won't want to stay in our shabby old dump after such grandeur. I do hope the *Reader's Digest* thing goes through. It will. You're tops.

Love,
Helen

[36 West 12th Street
New York
April, 1955]

Dearest Helen —

I think our book looks elegant and so does everyone else who has seen it. I did two shows for it in Cleveland and shall do two for it in Washington next week.

Then I have been asked to address some fashion group in Philadelphia the 2nd of May on the subject of casual fashions in food — this, in relation to the book. I shall be doing shows in Detroit that week and then in Texas the weeks following. I do a Bloomingdale's do for it. I'm also on the Ted Mack Show and the Make Up Your Mind Show — so if the goddam thing doesn't sell I cannot tell what will.

The show in Cleveland was rather fun, because people were eager to know more about the use of cognac and what glamorizing meant. Then we were introduced to the most revolting buffet I have ever seen, with great joints of well-done beef, turkeys which had been steam-roasted till they burst their skins, and platters of commercially canned pickled fruits with all their artificial colorings.

I must say, though, on the plane coming home that night very late they served the best chicken sandwiches I have ever had on dry land. I always have said that on shipboard the sandwiches they sneak into your cabin are best in the world.

Wednesday I had another dinner party — Helen McCully, Alexis Lichine, the Jack Aarons and Sylvia Pedlar. I served them some really interesting pâtés that Henri de Vilmorin had sent me, mushrooms stuffed with snails and snail butter, with a fine Erdener Prälat; then tiny squab chickens roasted with butter, vermouth and tarragon on a slice of sautéed polenta; your asparagus,* which was the sensation of the eve; cheese; and I made the crêpes with bananas and pastry cream that you and I did for the show last spring. Served a fine Meursault–Les Perrières with the chicken, and with the cheese, a Vigne de l'Enfant Jésus and a La Tâche. Six people finished off six bottles with great aplomb.

Have you had the Eskimo Cook Book? It comes from Alaska Crippled Children's Association, and if you order, have Philip order for me too, will you?

Agnes and I have had a long conversation with Bill White[1] re taking a small shop around the corner from me and doing a sort of Soupçon and small-sized Balzer.[2] We would have handsome specially done accessories for the kitchen and dining room, a few food specialties, good kitchen and table things, fine antiques for the culinary offices, and books (we would be happy to have things of Philip's on consignment — rare food books and that sort of thing). In no way should this interfere with whatever else we are doing. We shall decide this week.

Had a small ham from the Amana Colony in Iowa. They sent me ham, bacon, cervelat, smoked sausage, etc. — real good honest smoking, and the bacon cut from the rind, and the rind sent along for cooking. They also make the great walk-in freezers, strangely enough.

The Newport thing is off. I'm just as happy, for it would have killed me off by the end of the summer.

Love and kisses,

J

---

[1] William Alfred White, a real estate agent and Agnes White's husband.
[2] Balzer's was a fancy-food store in Los Angeles.
* Recipe.

Pasadena
[April 1955]

Jim darling,

I read part of your letter about one of your dinners on the air the other day. They loved it. I will do the same on the "Cavalcade of Books" on Sunday. . . . How's the weight? Mine is the same. I just can't keep below 135 without killing myself. I think that's what god means me to weigh.

H

[36 West 12th Street
New York
April 26, 1955]

Dearest Helen and Philip —

I'm so torn about this small shop thing. But I feel it is so necessary to start something which is going to be a bit of security for the old age. We are talking again about a cookery school. Maybe that is the answer, with a branch out there. You and I could loan our names and be the heads, respectively, of the Los Angeles and New York branches, with perhaps an omelet bar and a shop to sell the necessities. Then visiting teachers each year. If Dione, why not us? I am going with Ruth Norman on Thursday to discuss this thing further with the Surmains.

I ate Crab Imperial in Washington and think it could be

improved with Dungeness crabs. Try making a fine béarnaise and combining it with crab and a little onion in the shells, add buttered crumbs and parsley to the top, and gratiné. Tell me if I am not right. I can't get the flavor I want with this crab, but I'm perfectly sure I can with the other. I shall hang on your words.

Love and kisses to the Browns from the Beard, who dined off broiled kidneys, asparagus, and an onion-and-tomato salad with mineral oil dressing. I hope it works.

J

Pasedena
[May 1955]

Darling Birthday Boy,

I have started speaking of you on the air as *the* foremost authority on cookery in the country. What the hell, you are, aren't you? . . . I think you are right that we should have something to fall back on in our old age but Philip thinks your ideas sound like too damned much work. I still think that a column by the two of us could sell, specially if this book goes over.

Much love,
Helen

[36 West 12th Street
New York
May 7, 1955]

Helen Dear —

Isabel gave me a steak-tasting last night as a birthday party and an experiment. She did one in the rotisserie, Alvin did one in the oven broiler, I did one with a red hot pan and a little salt, and John Ferrone did a steak pizzaiola — sautéed in olive oil with a sauce of tomato, garlic and oregano. Of all of them the one done in a hot pan tasted the most like a charcoal-broiled one — everyone voted for it. Next in line came the pizzaiola. John had used one tin of plum tomatoes, three cloves of garlic and a good seasoning of salt, pepper and oregano. This cooked down in olive oil and was poured over the steak on a platter.

We did knockwurst with sour cream and pepper for a with-drinks do and some canned pasteles from Puerto Rico. Isabel had a salad bar with dinner. Peaches with bourbon and two birthday cakes followed.

There was a party for Jack Aaron the day before. I think I told you he was being honored by the importers, the French Government, and the champagne producers, and received the Chevalier de Mérite Commercial. The room of Carlton House was done with Toulouse-Lautrec pictures and millions of "Can Cans"[1] (the reason for the decoration) and Can Cans with magnums in them. It was my pleasant duty to introduce M. Beaujard,[2] who gave him the order, and then Dick Blum,[3] who gave him the scroll of the champagne producers — quite dramatic. Then he received a birthday cake which Ann Seranne had made in the shape and size of a Can Can, with the decor in butter cream and little black paper legs coming out here and there. I also got a birthday cake — a bottle of Beard Brut 1903 with a garland of flowers. I can't imagine having had a more delightful party for my birthday.

Have you read *The Tenth Muse* by Sir Harry Lukes? I am enjoying his potty Britishness.

I don't think there is a better restaurant in this country than the one Lester Gruber runs in Detroit [The London Chop House]. I went there at his invitation. The first night we had Dom Pérignon 1943 and Coronation Cuvée 1943 for pre-dinner drinks, to contrast the two great cuvées from one house (both Moët). Then on to a strained onion soup enriched with Madeira. After that filets of lake perch, amandine, with a Bâtard-Montrachet 1949. Then the most delicious chateaubriand I have eaten in years, with some of the fat left on — with this, a Château Latour '28 and a Château Ausone '28. After this, watercress salad, pineapple with kirsch, and cognacs and framboise and every other thing until about two in the morning.

The next day for lunch we were invited for tiny grass-frogs' legs and the special hamburger of the house, which is a noble dish — fourteen ounces of fine meat grilled perfectly and served with a sauce maison. The chef, who is a Latin American, started talking about dishes we both loved in Latin America, so he planned the menu for that night. Lester had asked several newspaper people and a few of Detroit's food-conscious to a dinner for me. We started with champagne again, had a strained marmite and then escabeche of whitefish — and with it, magnums of Meursault Les Perrières (Alexis's wine). A fine bit of arroz con pollo with the chef's own personal touch followed, and pineapple with port this time. Lester has asked me to come twice a year or more and stay as guest host for several weeks at a good fee, with a chance to innovate and perhaps have a class. I am sorely tempted to do it.

Tomorrow, thirty for cocktails. I told you of the two dips I am going to do.

Running off to start dinner — saddle of lamb and eggplant and tiny potatoes.

Love and kisses by the score,

J

---

1 Ten-gallon tin wine coolers decorated with Toulouse-Lautrec poster art and offered by Sherry Wine & Spirits as part of a promotional campaign.

2 Representative of the champagne producers of France.

3 Richard L. Blum, Jr., president of the importing firm Julius Wile Sons & Co.

Pasadena
May 10, 1955

Jim dearest,

My god, what fine meals you have. But how in hell can you keep from gaining tons? . . . I am keeping all your letters. I think they will be valuable to you in reminding you of the wonderful food you've had.

Much love,
H

Sherry Wine & Spirits Co.
Stamford, Conn.
[May 11, 1955]

Helen dear —

Doing my weekly stint in the new store with not much to do
except get out a few letters and do some phoning. Stayed last night
in New Canaan. Ruth and I had a nice dieting dinner of a baked
stuffed pike, asparagus, salad and melon. We had a long discussion about a cooking school and what it can do.

Been trying to think of our next book. I would like to do one on
shortcuts to entertaining. There is room for a book on snacks,
hors d'oeuvre, buffet dishes, dishes that wait, and breakfast and
luncheon dishes that are easy to do. "The Snickersnack Book of
Gnoshing" or something like that — a cookbook of light bites.

My various dips on Sunday came out all right. I must confess that
in the chili dip I created I used peanut butter, and it gave the most
superb texture you can imagine. I grated onion into olive oil and
let it just melt, then added garlic, beef gravy, chili powder, coriander, oregano and the p butter. It was much admired and went
magnificently with carnitas, chilled celery and Swiss cheese fingers. I made some marinated banana fingers to dip into curry, but
folks started dipping them into the salsa fria, and it turned out to
be the discovery of the age.

I used the remainder of the salsa fria to make an arroz con pollo
for a photograph yesterday, and it was elegant, with the addition of
a little saffron and a bit more pepper. I also had to do a pot roast
and some pears in red wine. Gave Agnes the pot roast and gave
John Ferrone the chicken dish. God, when you have to do anything like that the food certainly backs up on you.

Love and kisses,

J

West 12th Street
New York
May 14, 1955]

Helen, dear —

Well, I'm all set for my little Mexican foray. I have a list of
restaurants that I am to try out next week. I'm hoping that my
friends the Guths will have some time to take me to their favorite
spots. And I shall try to get some more morels, for they sent me a
magnificent necklace of them last year. If there is anything else
you want shopped for in Mexico City let me know at once.

This is my duck weekend. Mabel [Stegner][1] sent me three. John
Ferrone is coming tonight, and I am spitting one and serving it
with a version of béarnaise — the first time I have ever done that
to a duck. With it I am doing some turnips, naturally, and mushrooms. And for dessert, strawberries which have soaked in fresh
pineapple juice and are blessed with rum at the last minute.
Tomorrow I shall do duck with sauerkraut, garlic and pepper, and
serve it with steamed onions.

We went to the Rodgers' to dinner on Thursday night in Scars-
dale. It was at Gladys Rodgers' in Portland where I held my classes
in cookery lo these twenty years ago. A crown of lamb filled with
mashed potatoes, green peas, a salad of avocado, tomato and
lettuce with a sweet "French" dressing, homemade strawberry ice
cream and homemade coconut layer cake. Also homemade cinnamon bread with the dinner. No wine. The bread was of such an
elegant texture and flavor that it should have been the main
course. I should have loved it with sweet butter and perhaps some
cheese and practically nothing else.

Contrast that with luncheon yesterday at Baroque — just gou-
jonettes of sole, with fried parsley, a little Chablis and a
macaroon — delicious.

Love and kisses,
[JB]

---

[1] A home economist and food consultant.

36 West 12th Street
New York
[May 15, 1955]

Helen Dear —

The duck béarnaise was superb — the duck crisp and delicious and the béarnaise a fabulous accompaniment. But the béarnaise was so different. I had a bottle of sherry wine vinegar with tarragon — one of the deals with the leaves in the bottle. So I used that for my reduction. The sherry flavor stayed rather than the vinegary one, so it gave the sauce a nutty, rather delicious flavor. It almost overpowered the tarragon, and I had put a lot of extra tarragon in it. Had a barley casserole with it and asparagus with capers and mustard sauce. The strawberries with pineapple and rum were sensationally good. I let them infuse in the pineapple for two hours in the refrigerator and added the rum about fifteen minutes before serving. There is no reason why you couldn't use the canned chunks. And you do the same thing I do, putting frozen raspberries over canned pineapple chunks and letting them thaw. And pineapple with crème de menthe also. And of course I think a pineapple Hélène, with ice cream and chocolate sauce, is heaven, and a pineapple Melba is too.[1]

Has anyone ever made a finnan haddie bisque? I have some milk left from poaching a piece. If I had my Waring here, I would blend the rest of the haddock and the milk, add butter and have a superb soup.

Love and kisses on a bright and glorious Sunday — the kind of day that makes you aware that New York can be beautiful.

J

---

[1] HEB was working on a pineapple article.

Pasadena
May 17, 1955

Jim darling,

The béarnaise sounds wonderful. I will try with sherry and also with sherry vinegar. However, I do wonder why it wasn't too rich with duck. I have done a finnan haddie chowder. Very good and of course a meal in itself. Thanks for the pineapple ideas . . . What's a goujonette?

Kissily,
H

[Pasadena
May 1955]

Dear Jim,

Was the gazpacho that you had — the one like okrochka — put in the blender? . . .

I heard you on the air on Friday — "Make Up Your Mind." Your voice is really magnificent. I think, however, you made a mistake taking that crack at women cooks. Remember *they* buy most of your books.

Love,
H

[36 West 12th Street
New York
May 28, 1955]

Dearest Helen —

I don't know where to start with the seven-day stay [in Mexico]. It was a gastronomic tour of the country, for Francis Guth knows his food and just where to get it. Some days we were tasting all day long, it seems to me, and I learned a great deal about dishes we do not usually have. For instance, the best food in Mexico City, from a native point of view, is a Yucatecan place. There are two women on a little balcony making fresh tortillas, and their tacitos are famous — with an escabeche of chicken, with a mole sauce, with cracklings and grated pork, with chicken and bean sauce, and on and on. You can hardly stop eating them. Then there is another dish with large tortillas wound around turkey and chicken and a sauce of pumpkin seeds and a very delicate chili; and still another of layers of toasted tortillas with shark, which has been poached in a court bouillon, chilies and a tomato and chili sauce, similar to a salsa fria but hot. But to me their crowning achievement is a corn cake made with 10 eggs — these, not separated and beaten into the batter one at a time. First cream 1 cup of butter with a cup of sugar, add the eggs, 3 cups flour and 2 ears of corn kernels blended with 1 quart of milk. They bake it in a deep pan, about 16 x 20. Incredibly good and sticky, like a fine pound cake, but much more coarsely grained.

The majority of the salsas fria we had were made of the green tomatoes [tomatillas] entirely, and the variety of guacamole is endless. We went to the best place for maguey worms, and in one wonderful bar (for men only) they serve a shrimp broth at the bar made from dried shrimp, potatoes, onion, and a bit of chili — this, served in small cups along with your drinks. And another place serves — with drinks or for an appetizer — tiny cups of broth set in a deep saucer filled with boiling water. The broth is made from pressing raw beef, heating the juices, pressing again and seasoning with salt and pepper and a little chili. Rich as hell.

We went to Puebla one day for the mole at the Royalty Hotel and their tortilla Española, which is a pancake omelet with potatoes and onions. The mole is fabled all over the country. Also the seviche there is famous, with olives, green chilies, lots of oil and onion, and a little broth.

Okrochka, such as the one I have in *Paris Cuisine,* is more common in Paris than the one made with kvass, which is gassy and does not have the flavor of champagne, there being a Madeiraish taste to it. There is also a non-meat okrochka, with a mixture of shellfish, cucumbers, tarragon, chervil, sour cream and kvass or white wine and soda or champagne.

The gazpacho I spoke of is not blended in the blender. However, the escamadura gazpacho is done in the mortar until it has the consistency of mayonnaise. Then the cucumbers, seeded, salted and squeezed, the seeded and chopped tomatoes, and the pepper are added, with chervil, tarragon, and a little vinegar. Bread crumbs instead of croutons are added to this — these, previously soaked and squeezed, but I like the crisp croutons better.

We were asked to a dinner party at the home of a Colombian woman one night for 8:30. They served cocktails steadily till 11:30, when out came the most beautiful buffet you have ever seen, with two enormous turkeys, sliced and the skin back in place so that they looked completely uncarved. A real honest-to-goodness aspic with vegetables, not a gelatine salad. A chestnut and almond stuffing, with oregano in it, for the turkey. After this and wine, cognacs, coffee and such, people danced, and at 3 in the morning they served a second complete buffet! Entirely different things. It turns out the woman pays her cook at the rate of a first-class hotel chef. The Colombian Embassy pays all her bills, and her ex-husband lets her spend as much as she wants. But she can never have a cent of cash. Cute, huh?

I'd love some bow ties. They should be 38 inches long to be perfect.

> Lovily and kissily,
> [J]

[36 West 12th Street
New York
June 3, 1955]

Dearest Helen —

I had dinner for the Gottliebs, the Sam Aarons and Jeanne Stahl of *Life* magazine last night. Bill Veach had brought me a large selection of a wonderful pâté de foie. I had one can of that with drinks, then mushrooms with snails, which everyone adores more than the snails in the shell. My lobster à l'Américaine was about the best one I ever made. I used three lobsters for six people. They weighed exactly thirteen pounds (just what I weighed when I was born). They were as tender as they could possibly be, and Petrosino gave them to me for fifty-five cents a pound, just about half what other lobsters are. I did rice with chicken broth and a shade of saffron, a cucumber salad, and toasted protein bread. Then I made chocolate crêpes,* with half Mexican chocolate and half semi-sweet, piling one upon the other, for fifteen pancakes. Put them in the oven for two minutes and served them in wedges with whipped cream flavored with cognac and vanilla. We drank a Pouilly-Vinzelles and a Corton-Charlemagne, and a bottle of champagne with dessert. And Sam had brought some of the first marc de champagne ever imported into this country. Everyone rolled out at midnight.

I was sick over the weekend in the country. When I got up Sunday I couldn't walk and I was in agony. I called Jack Sullivan, and he said I had been doing too much and to stay off my feet and get them up in the air. Cheryl and Ruth made me be quiet, and I obeyed. I did a bit of supervising. We had a beautiful time. Marilyn Monroe even enchanted Bill Veach, and that is saying something. Eli Wallach brought her up. She was so quiet and unassuming and little girl that I couldn't believe it. Judith Anderson popped in in the middle of the afternoon and was herself, and on the way to France for the festival. Still talking about the caviar omelet we gave her at Eleanor Peters'.[1]

Came back on Tuesday midday, and Bill decided he should come down to take care of me on Tuesday night. Made finnan haddie with a half-pound of butter and almost a half-pint of heavy cream. Made mashed potatoes for the two of us and used over a pound of butter in them. Made asparagus with almost a half-pound of butter, and a coeur à la crème with a pound of cream cheese and heavy cream. I took three tablespoons of mineral oil after it was over. The potatoes were the most elegant I have ever tasted. But it was rugged to get through it all. Besides, Bill ate a half-loaf of bread with almost a quarter-pound of butter.

Next Tuesday is the day of the big party for Bill — I think there will be fourteen. Whole foie gras in aspic, terrine of veal, cucumber salad. Then a huge mushroom pie with puff paste, Virginia ham, and the casserole with gizzards. Toasted buttered protein bread again. And the strawberries Martiniquaise. I can't be bothered with the elaborate menu I planned before. But still it will be a hell of a lot of work.

I'm having dinner alone tonight. Broiling chicken with chopped garlic, chopped parsley, a little basil and chili powder. Some asparagus, a romaine and tomato salad, and a mango. Not too awful and not fattening, God knows.

Ta ta,

J

---

[1] A former Portlander living in Los Angeles who was a patron of the arts and a good friend of both JB and the Browns.
* Recipe.

[36 West 12th Street
New York
June 6, 1955]

Helen, dear —

I have been thinking that perhaps the next book should be classic recipes and their variations. We could give 100 or 200 recipes in their original state, as far as we are able, and then give the various things which have happened to them. This would be a fascinating book for reference as well as a fascinating book to use. I thought about it the other day when I was using the new Dione Lucas book with Ann Robbins as co-author [*The Dione Lucas Meat and Poultry Cook Book*]. It is so full of wrong attacks on the standard things that it made me feel something should be done to make this a better world for honest cookery.

Then I began to wonder where beef à la Stroganoff came from, for there are so many different recipes for it (Jeanne Owen's in *Wine Lovers Cookbook* is by far the best). It is not in any of the great authoritative French cookbooks, not even in *Larousse* [*Gastronomique*], which makes me think it was created by someone during the Russian restaurant craze. The closest thing to it that I can find anywhere is bitok, which is chopped beef with sour cream, and there are several recipes for Stroganoff calling for chopped beef. At any rate, wouldn't such a book be fun and enlightening?

Love,
JB

Pasedana
June 7, 1955

Jim dearest,

What's happened to your diet? All that butter. Shame on Bill Veach . . . And *stop* overdoing . . . I forgot to say that the bread we are going to have with our party is corn (fresh), cornmeal, green chilis and cheese. Sublime. Sort of a cross between spoon bread and corn bread.

[H]

[36 West 12th Street
New York
June 13, 1955]

Dearest Helen —

I have just had a letter from Francis Guth and shall surely be going to Mexico on the 13th of July. Hope to God you all are still planning on driving down. I recommend the Maria Christina if you want a hotel. It is oldish and delightful and not overly expensive.

In the meantime I am going ahead with a floor-through [at 36 West 12th Street] and the shop with Agnes, and, I hope, with a cooking school in a small way this year. I am thinking of Philip as a possibility for running the shop, because of his knowledge of books and food, his ability to do so much, and his approach and personality. That would make you free to do things here in New York and to work with me in the school and in other projects where we could combine. But maybe you don't want to tear up stakes and come here. It is merely something tossed in the air to be washed and ironed.

My trip to the Cape was interesting, and the restaurant [Chillingsworth] and shops are going to be startlingly beautiful and, I think, a success. For this year I am going to plan five specialties for dinner for them — lobster à l'Américaine with green rice; flounder of the Cape, sauté meunière, with bananas; cold striped bass with aspic and green mayonnaise; filet of beef in crust with young vegetables; and probably Poulet Flambé with rice. For desserts, chocolate roll and a crème brûlée, and they already have a wonderful apple crisp. For brunch and lunch I am doing other fish things, curried seafood and scallops Provençale. I have vegetables planned for them and a few hors d'oeuvre, but this will be the backbone. The Poulet Flambé is superb now that I have changed the recipe to sour cream and egg yolks instead of sweet cream. No one serves a good lobster à l'Américaine, and it is so good and uses the large lobsters, which are cheaper in price.

Helen, would you send me the recipe for the potato chocolate cake we had at that potato party last year?* I though I had saved it, but I didn't and would love to have it.

I did another Bloomingdale's stint this morning — a Poulet Flambé and the green rice from our book, with fresh basil, parsley, chives and watercress in it. Then we did the homemade ice cream from the book, and I did the flaming strawberries with concentrated orange juice — instead of the one we did last year — and it works wonderfully. We served the berries over the ice cream.

We had a fine crowd — about seventy, I think. There are about twenty regulars. One woman brings her cook each time to get new ideas for their repertoire at home.

Off to roast a chicken on the spit and cook some peas. Not very thrilling but just what I want for dinner somehow. I have nice romaine and some really good tomatoes also. So I shan't starve. Yesterday I made sandwiches for eating on the way home, with wonderful oatmeal bread — some with rare lamb and chutney, some with chicken and chopped watermelon pickle and mustard, and some with tomato and cottage cheese with quantities of black pepper. They tasted awfully good with a bottle of California Chablis, and we all were so much happier than if we had stopped in a traveler's rest somewhere and been fed horrors.

I made a lobster curry on Saturday night with a lot of cooked eggplant in the sauce and a little tomato. I thought of you when I ate it.

Love and kisses by the millions to all the Browns from the Beard.

J

---

* Recipe.

[36 West 12th Street
New York
June 16, 1955]

Helen, dear —

We have a place for the school, and I feel it is just the beginning of what will come later. The shop is going to get going in a month or two and then open about November 1st. Agnes and I have, between us, a lot of stock, and with other things we can order from France and Mexico, and with what can be made to order, I feel confident we shall have a tremendous business for the holidays. We are getting excited about it and feel you must be one of the faculty of the school in one way or another.

My supper last night for the Chillingsworth Inn people to taste all the things for the restaurant was an eating festival for them. We had four hors d'oeuvre, as I told you. The sole with bananas came out beautifully, the scallops Provençale were good, the lobster à l'Américaine was really elegant, the Filet en Croûte with a blanket of chopped mushrooms under the crust was sensational, and my chocolate roll came out as none has for a long time. How they got through it all, I don't know, but they seemed to have the time of their lives. I gave them very small helpings of everything.

You asked about the mushroom pie. I did it with sautéed caps topped with the chopped stems cooked down with butter, flour, cream and a little garlic — just a hint. Then I added a little cream, chilled it, and covered it with puff paste. I used the big casserole, like the one I gave you, the oval one. And did I tell you that with the barley and gizzard casserole I included pine nuts and chicken hearts, the latter sautéed in butter before being added? Also a bit of tarragon.

Will you please give me explicit directions for your new corn bread with cheese and chilies and all in it?* I am going to do a supper for Dargent,[1] the champagne man, at the end of the month, and I would like to give an all-American meal. That should be a fabulous dish with the baked ham with mustard sauce I am planning to serve. I thought I would have vegetables and a home-made terrine of some kind and maybe an escabeche,* which is American in its way. Then the ham and corn bread and a cole slaw with tomatoes and cucumbers, and for dessert, a superb straw-berry shortcake with heavy cream.

My mouth is set for the pig — hooray — for I've wanted one for ages.[2]

Try this — cream together a quarter-pound of butter and the same weight of sugar, gradually add 5 egg yolks and 3 fresh rolls which have been soaked in a little milk, pressed dry and crumbed. Finally fold in the 5 egg whites beaten stiff and arrange the mix-ture in a buttered tart mold or flan mold, and top with pitted Bing cherries. Bake at 350–375 for about 45 minutes and serve warm or cold, sprinkled with powdered sugar. It is charmingly different and delicious.*

Love,

J

---

[1] Joseph Dargent, head of public relations for the Comité Interprofession-nel du Vin de Champagne.

[2] The Browns were planning to roast a thirty-pound pig when JB visited.

* Recipe.

36 West 12th Street
New York
[June 27, 1955]

Helen, dear —

I leave today for the Cape and shall spend the next three or four days in the kitchen with the cook trying to get the entire menu set. I may have to make one more trip before I go to Mexico.

John Schaffner was here for dinner on Saturday night. I gave him some spareribs done with soy, ginger and sherry* and poured off the liquid as they cooked so that they came through with a wonderful glaze and almost dry. Also sautéed string beans with bits of my Virginia ham. And we had capelletti — fresh ones we get now that are delicious, with fresh basil, fresh parsley and Romano cheese. Then just fresh raspberries for dessert with sugar and Grand Marnier. We had a long discussion of what there was to do and of what you and I were to do together.

Now that we are practically in the clear for Doubleday I have a hunch that Clara is going to want us to get busy again, but I think we must have a very thorough and finished plan for her. I am convinced that if the book is priced at less than four dollars it will sell better than a more expensive one. For in this great Republican era people have no money to spend for food and allied arts because they spend it all on installment-buying and cars — and refrigerators — and then have no food to put in them. Only tuna fish and potato chips and Campbell's soup seem to sell, if you can believe the recipes.

Love and kisses,

J

---

* Recipe.

36 West 12th Street
New York
[July 2? 1955]

Dearest Helen —

I'm just back from the Cape, where I did a full week working with a woman who has done tearoom food all her life and now at sixty is changing over to Continental food. We tried out all the possibilities for the menu this week, and I go back this weekend for testing with the cook. Dinner will include Filet de Boeuf Wellington, lobster à l'Américaine (and I have concocted a salad from the cold lobster and a cold soup from the sauce and shells so there will be no waste), filet of flounder or haddock sauté meunière (the cold fish goes into an escabeche for a first course), bay scallops Provençale, and Poulet Flambé, with a new sauce which I shall show you (and the cold chicken goes into a wonderful hash with the sauce, almonds, peppers, and grated Romano cheese). Only these entrées this year for dinner, with soup or hors d'oeuvre, homemade rolls or bread, fresh vegetables, and a choice of chocolate roll, chocolate mousse, ice cream with a fabulous cake or your lemon tarts, apple crumble, etc.

The clam hash for luncheon is good, as is the chicken hash, the cognac beans, Elena's[1] rice casserole, Finnan Haddie Delmonico, curried fish and seafood, and any number of other things. I am having a different hot bread each day for brunch — such things as brioche, brioche mousseline, croissants, cheese popovers, oatmeal bread, scones, corn bread, corn spoon bread, etc. Brunch will be $3 and dinners will vary from $4.50 to $6, and no liquor — too close to a church. But if you bring your own wine you may drink it there from Baccarat crystal, and you eat on bone china with fine silver. The waitresses are in eighteenth-century costumes, with little caps which tie under the chin.

It is like an oven here today. I had to come back from the Cape to get some work done so that I can get away to Mexico. It is at least fifty degrees hotter here than there, and I am sitting with no clothes on, dripping with perspiration.

I shall try and do the notes on the beef article and surely will get them done on the plane. I have a wonderful French recipe for beef with a spoon. Also, I think we should do pot-au-feu and the beef salad after it. Pot-au-feu is the favorite recipe for beef in the French manner in the U.S. and the most eaten beef dish outside of steak and roast beef.

Love and kisses,
JB

---

[1] Elena Zelayeta, a West Coast cook and cookbook author who specialized in Mexican and Spanish food. She was blind.

[36 West 12th Street
New York
July 4, 1955]

Helen, dear —

I forgot to tell you that I tried a recipe, not yours, for the chili bread.* I had neglected to take it with me to the Cape and so tried to rely on my memory for it. I used 2 cups each of flour and cornmeal, 1½ cups cream-style corn, ½ pound grated cheese, 1 cup finely cut pimientos (no chilies), 2 cups sour cream (no butter), 3 eggs, salt and pepper, 2 teaspoons cream of tartar, and 1 teaspoon soda. It was wonderful, notwithstanding. The second day it was better, and the third day I sautéed slices of it as a base for a chicken curry, instead of the eternal rice. Cornmeal and curry are really made for each other.

The curry was a different one, too. I sautéed a tremendous chicken, cut up. When it was beautifully browned in butter, I added curry sauce made from onion, puréed summer squash, in lieu of eggplant, a bit of tomato paste, fresh ginger, curry powder, mustard, hot water, and a good shot of Worcestershire sauce, and let it steam in the sauce. It was served on the sautéed chili bread with cognacked raisins, cucumber relish, mustard pickle (sweet), marinated banana slices, chutney, and almonds. It was Ceylonese without the eggplant. I like curry that is not loose. I went out to dinner last night and had too much to drink but have been plugging along all day trying to go through the pile that is my desk. Isabel and Ron [Callvert] are coming down and we shall no doubt go to Chinatown for dinner, to BoBo. It is a bitch of a day, about 90 in the shade and muggy. Ruth and Cheryl wanted me out there, but I couldn't face another trip on top of the one yesterday. Anyway, it is divine here in the quiet of a holiday weekend. Absolutely no one around and nothing stirring.

Love and hugs all round,

J

---

* Recipe.

[36 West 12th Street
New York
July 7, 1955]

Helen Dear —

I was supposed to go to Ruth's tonight, but a commission from *Life* to plan two picnic menus by tomorrow — for an article for next year — came up and I couldn't go. Then I have to do a story for *Gentry* this week, and Mrs. Snow gave me two things to do for *Harper's Bazaar*. It is a mad whirl, but I love it.

Had Clara, John [Schaffner], and Ann last night for dinner, and it was as hot as the lower regions of the intensely hot parts of Hades. So I changed my mind and didn't have choucroute for Ann's and my benefit. I gave them little toasts with some pâté on it for a bite with their drinks, followed by prosciutto and figs. Then a beautiful lobster salad, with a tomato, watercress, and egg garnish and a dish of cucumber salad. I passed paper-thin rye bread and butter sandwiches. After that, fresh raspberries with Grand Marnier and whipped cream. We drank a Pouilly and after dinner had some Chinese rosé wine and cognac. Clara stayed long after the others and told me the story of her life, practically. She is now of the opinion that we are the greatest thing that ever happened to her, so let us go along with it. My opinion is that we are.

I leave on Wednesday morning for Mexico and shall come to you about the end of the month. I am sending you a ham from Candlewood so you can taste one again and we can have a party with it when we are all together

Had a quiet dinner for myself tonight. Grilled a piece of flank, had a little potato and some of last night's cucumber salad, and fresh raspberries — you know my weakness for them — I only wish they were in season twelve months of the year — I would turn away from every other fruit.

Love and embraces,

J

[36 West 12th Street
New York
July 13, 1955]

Helen and Philip —

We signed a lease at 68 Fifth Avenue yesterday for the Boutique Gastronomique. If you are interested in tearing up roots, would Philip like to be in charge of it? It would be a different sort of approach, with books, articles for the kitchen and dining room, new and old, and some foodstuffs. I feel, and so does everyone else, that it will pay off in its way.

This would give you a chance to work the New York field. Also to sell to the shop certain food specialties you might want to put into production. It would give you a chance to teach in the school when it comes along, and it would allow you to pull yourself out of the California climate, which you have said you want to do. Think it over and send me a note to Callejón del Santísimo, 10, San Angel Inn, Mexico D.F.

The plane is delayed so I can write a little more.

The space we have taken is on the first floor — European style — up ten steps. We have about 25 feet of frontage on Fifth Avenue, all windows. There is a good-sized showroom on two levels, behind that a room for demonstration and teaching. Then an office room, a bathroom, and a small terrace. We have enough stock to see us through six months. It is going to be smart, smart, smart. Although Agnes [White] does not know Philip — and God knows, he may not be interested — she feels from what I have said that he has the quality to make such a thing go. We would hope to open in time for the Christmas trade this year.

There should be some food things. For instance, at Christmas time I would like to make a specialty of wonderful stollen — like yours — Helen Brown's Own Recipe for Stollen. I am trying out an old Southern fruitcake with lots of chocolate and almonds and pecans to see if it is worth selling. Also a white cake — a pound cake, really — with 2 pounds of sliced citron and 2 pounds of sliced almonds in it. I want your ideas.

I'm still waiting to hear about the plane. There is nothing worse

than being ready to go somewhere and then having to wait around
and stew in your juice.

Love and kisses,

J

Pasadena
[July 1955]

Jim dear,

As for your shop. How about various dinner packages? One for
curry with powder, chutney, cognac raisins, etc. with recipe. One
for Japanese food, one for Chinese, one for Mexican, etc.?

Love and kisses,
H

Callejón del Santísimo 10
San Angel Inn
Mexico, D.F.
[July 1955]

Dearest Helen —

I'm disappointed and so is Agnes, to whom I spoke on the
phone last night after reading your letter. We had hoped you could
see your way clear to New York. But maybe the West Coast branch
will take shape and then we can all work together on it.

As for the book, of course I want to do it and I shall give you
some definite ideas of what I think we should do. There is such a
need, my darling Helen, for a book which tells people the whys
and wherefores of entertaining and which gives recipes that are
simple and good and different. And much as I hate to say it, I am
coming to the point of saying that we have to follow some of the
trends and give quick-and-easies, and perhaps time each recipe
and show shortcuts for most of them. Even here they are supermarket mad and frozen-food mad. I'll hate us for taking the easy
way out, but I know damned well we'll make money if we can make
the easy things taste better than the others can, and I think that is

probably our mission in life. The more I think of "How We Entertain," by Helen Evans Brown and James A. Beard, the better I like it.

I have been loaned, and Francis Guth is translating for me, a precious manuscript cookbook from the grandmother of a friend of mine who is part of one of the most distinguished families in Mexico. These are family recipes from before the Empire. We shall see what we can do with some of them. Now they are in huge amounts — 50 eggs in a recipe is absolutely nothing.

We trekked to Puebla the other day. We ate two different moles, both wonderful in their way, and a dessert of chilies rellenos, with a sweet sauce made of pounded fresh walnuts, milk, sugar, and Chinese parsley, and sprinkled with fresh pomegranate seeds. The chilies were whole and stuffed with meat and cheese and cooked the usual way. Also had beautiful fresh corn tortillas made with whole kernels and, I think, cornstarch and eggs, cooked in lots and lots of butter. And a lovely Enchilada Suiza at my favorite bar, the Mirador.

I think the curry powder idea is a natural. We should do two, with hot and medium strength. And let us give them some little difference. What else would you like to package?

I leave here next Thursday or Friday. I hate to say I won't be going California-wise, but you must understand this time. I shall break my neck to go to the Hilton opening if possible.

Loads of love,
[J]

36 West 12th Street
New York
[July 30, 1955]

Dearest Helen —

I just got home last night and have a house full of things to do. But I want to tell you that I shall arrive on Sunday next on the TWA special plane and I only have to go to three parties the whole week. We can spend the rest of the time planning the book if you are able and willing.

I shall tell you all about the Mexico trip when I see you. I am glad you didn't do the drive down, for there were so many washouts on roads that many of the Guths' friends were held up for as much as two days at some of the little towns. Last weekend in Acapulco the road from the airport to the city had boulders as big as your living room on it here and there.

I did a hell of a lot of cooking that weekend, including dinner for sixteen on Sunday night. We had an avocado soup* and a beautiful roast leg of pork, which I cooked long and slow. With roast potatoes, sautéed apples and pineapple, some native cheeses and native wines, and fresh peaches with bourbon. Monday night I made a curry with blended frijoles as the thickener. Ate the best tamales there I have eaten anywhere, including the big and wonderful ones you made, but excepting the fresh corn ones. Went to a breakfast on Monday morning where the pièce was scrambled eggs with frijoles, chocolate, toasted tortillas and rolls, tons of melon, and orange juice, with which they passed wheat germ.

By the way, Francis Guth's restaurant is the Passy. San Angel Inn is a residential section where he lives. The reason Eleanor [Peters] couldn't get the number is that, as is true with all telephones in Mexico, it had to be bought from someone and that means he is probably listed under a factory or something like that.

I'm going to Helen McCully's for a bite of dinner with her and Eleanor Noderer[1] tonight, carrying my own corn over.

> Love and kisses,
> [J]

---

[1] An associate food editor at *McCall's.*

* Recipe.

[36 West 12th Street
New York
August 20, 1955]

Dear Helen —

Things just begin to pop. Now that the restaurant [Maxfield's] is beginning to take shape and I have done the menu, another restaurant comes along and wants the same thing. And now the spot on the Cape needs a chef again because the old gal who was doing it wants to quit. So I guess I shall have to train another person for that job. Wish I could find someone absolutely right for it.

Monday night Restaurant Associates have a date with me to go to one of their restaurants, in Newark Airport [The Newarker], and then to discuss the possibility of going on their payroll as consultant. Ann says that she and her partner, Eileen Gaden, are getting into public relations so fast they don't know where to turn. They now beg me to go into the firm with them. But I don't think that is the right thing for me to do either.

I, too, am dieting seriously. Tomorrow Isabel and Ron are coming here. I have a small leg of lamb and a huge plate of antipasto, and that is it. I did some of your best beans the other day, and they are ready, and I'll have the usual fresh things and a lovely salami. Then peaches with bourbon.

Monday we do the two picnic shots for *Life* — finally settled on ham en croûte for one and squab for the other. Pâté for one and soup for the other. Melon for one and cheese and fruits for the other. Watercress and romaine with no dressing for one and assorted vegetables with a dunk for the other. I think they will look rather wonderful — they have beautiful props.

Here is an Entrecôte Infernal, which I thought you might like to try. Chop a medium onion and a large clove of garlic, and brown them quickly with 2 peppers cut in julienne. Add 2 large seeded and chopped tomatoes, and add salt and cayenne — to substantiate the "Infernal" epithet. Let it cook down a bit and serve over a grilled entrecôte with a garnish of French-fried onions.

My cupboard is full of weevils. They probably came in the

cornmeal or something and spread like mad. I threw away about twenty-five dollars' worth of food today.

Love and kisses,

J

Saturday, the 20th. I was on Buontempi's program this morning. One hour of Italian cooking with enough commercials to throttle you.

[36 West 12th Street
New York
August 26, 1955]

Helen, dear —

Helen McCully and I have chosen October 4 as a date for your cocktail party at her house. I would like to have you to dinner on the 7th if that is agreeable. Then we can lunch at "21" on the Saturday after that and perhaps do something on the weekend.

For your dinner here I may make it buffet, since I promised you lobster à l'Américaine, and have about twelve. I'll start with snails and mushrooms, a few bay scallops done specially, some of the real imported prosciutto with pear slices, and greens of some kind, and then do the lobster, removed from the shells so it is easier to eat buffet, and rice. Then I shall probably do the chocolate crêpes in a couple of huge piles. Would that satisfy you? And for the night you arrive a huge tin of pâté awaits us, and we shall probably have one of Mr. Albert's best legs of Canadian mutton done to a fine turn, some turnips and mushrooms, and something else to surprise you.

If you are at the Van Rensselaer you can always come over here for your tea and papers in the morning. Philip can have his hamburger, and there will be everything here to do with.

The Morning Show yesterday on CBS had me and the book. I did a steak flambé on the electric skillet at seven-thirty in the morning, and they ate it with great relish. Why not? It was a very nice spot and goes network.

J

[36 West 12th Street
New York
August 31, 1955]

Dear —

Helen and I are sending out invitations for the 4th. Stanish is going to do the party, and I think we shall have about sixty. I am inviting twelve for the Friday buffet, and put down in your book that Isabel is giving you a brunch on Sunday the 9th. Bill Kaduson is planning something for you, and I think Peggy Lesser wants to give you a party.

The *Life* steak article is awful. They took a bit from everyone, put it all together and called it steak. The picture of Mr. Quincey Jones[1] broiling steaks over hot flames is enough to make you woops.

Did a leg of baby lamb on the spit at Cheryl's on Saturday. Very young lamb bought from the Greek butcher on Ninth Avenue. It got to 150. I brought up the coals and let it burn and flame for about 3 minutes till it was crusty and brown. Then it coasted for 20 minutes. Well done on the outside and just pink on the inside. We had it that night and had some cold for lunch the next day, and it was juicy and delicious. Marilyn Monroe was there again.

Last night Bill Palmer came to dinner. We had a bottle of Orvieto, a tin of foie gras and some toast, a piece of cheese, and coffee and a little rum. A perfect dinner, which sent him home raving. I love to do a simple thing like that and have people happy. He has offered me a job. I'm being offered jobs all over the place, it seems. But I don't mind, for then I can pick and choose which is to carry me through my old age.

Love to you both,

J

---

[1] A Southern California architect.

36 West 12th Street
New York
[September 9, 1955]

Helen, dear —

You asked about the shop. When we found Philip was not in the running, Agnes and I decided the time was not right. We gave up the lease, and we are selling some of the stuff through her own shop. The idea is by no means dead. We may start a small mail-order thing this year to build up to it.

I have your reservations made at the Van Rensselaer. You and Philip have a bedroom, sitting room and bath, and it is seven dollars a day. You can come here, as I said, for breakfasts and have the run of the place.

I guess the *House and Garden* wine column ["Corkscrew"] is settled, at least for six months, and I am to do a few food pieces for them too. The wine column is good for me from a prestige angle, and Gottlieb and the others I work for are delighted to have me in that kind of a position.

Tonight Isabel and Ron are coming down. I am doing a new veal recipe. A piece of rolled shoulder browned in butter. Then ½ pound of pork skin and 1 glass of wine. Let the wine cook away. Add a bouquet garni, 1 pint of water, and cook for 2 hours. In the meantime cook 2 pounds of prunes in 1 pint of red wine, 1 pint of water and a little sugar until the liquid boils away. Add the prunes to the veal for the last half hour. It sounds wonderful. I'm adapting it for Ruth Dubonnet[1] to use with her own liquor instead of the red wine. Also for her, a duck with Dubonnet, Dubonnet jelly in a ring with fruits and whipped cream, and a Dubonnet version of strawberries Romanoff. Or does that all revolt you?

Love,
Jim

---

[1] An American who married into the Dubonnet family and did promotion for the apéritif.

                                                    Pasadena
                                                    September 12, 1955

Jim dear,

   Damn it, I have been literally starving for three weeks and what
happens. I . . . find I'm fatter than ever. I really have been living on
tea, chicken breasts, tomato aspic, steak and berries. . . . Where
shall we go for dinner in Chicago?

                                                    H

                                                    36 West 12th Street
                                                    New York
                                                    [September 14, 1955]

Dear Helen —

   I suggest you eat once in the Pump Room if you have not been
there. Then I think the Cape Cod Room of the Drake is very
good. It has excellent seafood and a pleasant ambiance. I like to
go to the rough and ready little old Corono for one thing alone. I
have antipasto, usually, and their pork tenderloins. Chicago is
one place where you can get them. They grill them or sauté them
there, and I have always felt they were very good. I do suppose
you should go to the Stockyards Inn just to see the place and
the decor. It is a really startling restaurant, and they do it
well.

   Louis Vaudable may be here for your party on the 4th. He
is really sort of a sweet guy in his way. He wants to be generous
and grand and big and sometimes misses the point — but don't
we all?

   I am trying to rack my brains for weird and wonderful rum
drinks and things to serve them in. I am now doing something
with banana and pineapple in it, all done in the Waring Blendor
and all icky goo, and served in a pottery pineapple. And I shall do
a rum and champagne thing, and a rum Alexander of some sort
with cream, rum and Grand Marnier. What I'm going to do with
all this I really don't know.

Had lunch at "21" yesterday. It was mobbed. Would you like me to order our lunch ahead when we go there?

I have two tickets for the fabulous new Spanish ballet on the 9th. I didn't get one for Philip because I know how he feels about such things, so he can get a date for something else or sit home with his feet on the desk and smoke a pipe or a cigar.

I turned the Bloomingdale's job down flat. They wanted me to do two full-hour shows a week for them, with no guests, and pay me $25 a show. Not for baby.

If you drive through Iowa, for heaven's sake stop at the Amana place and have some of their country food.

Love and kisses,

J

36 West 12th Street
New York
[November 1, 1955]

Helen, dear —

My radio program starts on Thursday the 10th — at 10:30 here. It is the Weekday Show with Margaret Truman and Mike Wallace on NBC. I shall have a regular spot.

We had a delightful dinner at Cecily's. She made Country Captain but differently from her usual recipe. She served the sauce and rice separately. We all liked it very much. And Alice McComb[1] made fabulous squares of frozen strudel dough filled with fresh crushed strawberries and baked for 5 minutes, served with a cold sabayon sauce.

This week I go to Denver and fly back all night long, arrive at eight or something in the morning, and go on the air at ten-thirty. They wanted me live for the first day's show. That afternoon I have to have everybody in to taste ice cream the day before [Maxfield's] opening party.[2]

You, too, will be hearing little from me this week, next week and the week after. I guess we'll just have to get rich and have secretaries and make long distance calls.

My love to you both,

J

---

[1] A caterer and chef who later worked closely with the food authority Michael Field.

[2] An ice cream parlor with snacks for which JB had helped style the menu. Michael Field was one of the owners.

36 West 12th Street
New York
[November 13, 1955]

Dearest Helen —

I acquired the worst sinus cold of my life in Denver and this week has been sheer hell since my return. I have had to give a great deal of time to the ice cream restaurant, and, I'm afraid, most of it in vain. They are completely inexperienced and won't take the time to iron things out. At any rate I'm through now and have my money, but I am heartsick over it all.

Isn't it nice about the bean article [for *Collier's*]. What would you have me do — the foreword, plus some of the recipes?

If you get a letter from Marvin Small[1] — who invented Arrid — asking you to become a member of a cookbook writers society, turn it down. Cecily, Ann, Myra,[2] Jane, all the people I love most here are in accord. We don't want to standardize cookbooks. We still want our own personalities to come out of them.

The coffee-cognac ice cream* I invented for Maxfield's is the sensation of the year — outsells vanilla, even.

I love you all.

J

---

[1] Nutritionist and author of diet cookbooks.

[2] Myra Waldo, food consultant and author of guidebooks and more than forty cookbooks.

* Recipe.

Pasadena
November 15, 1955

Jim dear,

Thank god for the bean story deal. Yes, send me your favorite recipes and follow the outline, but remember it is Beans, U.S.A. Also send any bean anecdotes you can think of. Better do a foreword in the rough. I will add my two cents' worth and do some polishing. . . . I am sure you realize that this is very important to us both and must be our very best.

Love and kisses,
H

[36 West 12th Street
New York
December 1955]

My dear Helen —

I am sending you a few notes on beans. This is not a subject on which I have the great store of knowledge that you have. My real bean love has been for the foreign things made from beans, and so I feel rather helpless about it.

I think the recipe of Miss Beecher[1] is important, for it establishes the fact that there were baked beans without the loathsome addition of sweetness. I also like her idea of boiling corn on the cob with beans for what she so charmingly calls "succatosh." And the Hotel Plaza recipe is a wonderful one. Then we very often had a delicious version of succotash made with dried corn — to me, the acme of corn flavor — and what we called shell beans, which were in reality pinto beans. This was delicious in the way my mother prepared it, with the beans cooked with ham and then the dried corn added at the last and bits of ham slipped into the mass to make it even more intoxicatingly delicious— this, a dish so wonderful that we always begged to take it on picnics.

I should like to include the kidney bean, ham, red wine, and onion dish,* which is definitely an American adaptation of a

French dish. It is even better when a little chili is added to it, so it could be classed as a Southwest dish.

I don't know whether it is American or not, but I love plain boiled beans with plenty of garlic, butter and chopped parsley with my leg of lamb, in the French manner.

My mother did a baked bean dish with the same loathing for molasses for sugar that I have. The beans were boiled and combined with onion and pickled pork in rather thick slices. Then a good deal of English mustard was added with the cooking liquid from the beans, salt and pepper, and some caramel for coloring. This was dotted with bacon fat and baked in an open pan till there was no liquid. The beans were soft and separated, and there was a lightly crisp layer atop them. They were quite good, and cold they made a wonderful salad. Sometimes they were eaten with home-made chili sauce, heated — because my mother didn't like the idea of cold sauce on a hot dish.

We also had boiled beans with ham hocks and cabbage, boiled separately. This was served with English mustard in quantity and a salad of hard-boiled eggs and lettuce, and sometimes with a sour-cream dressing.

And we had bean salad. Although it is primarily French, it can be called an American adaptation. White beans with vinaigrette.

One of our favorites in summer, which a farmer raised for us, was the asparagus bean, the long Chinese bean you use today. This was cooked and served with bacon nearly always although we often had it cold with vinaigrette sauce.

And scarlet runners — these were shredded paper thin and cooked crisp, as you like them, and served with either butter by the ton or bacon and bacon fat. And I must say, they are delicious when picked at their prime and eaten as they should be. Of course you know they are considered poison by some benighted folk.

Do you think we should include the Burgoo and Brunswick Stew recipes with their large quota of beans?

I have never yet seen a recipe for kedgeree with beans. I have seen an Indian one with lentils, rice and seasonings.

The recipe in *Key West Cook Book*[2] for bollas, those little balls of fire made with black-eyed beans, is wonderful. This is a sensational hors d'oeuvre when correctly made. I add a bit of cayenne to them.

The black bean is a difficult one to find in eastern markets except for the great metropolitan centers. Sometimes called the turtle bean, it is traditionally used for soup in the U.S.

However, you and I, Helen, know the joys of cooking black beans for what they are. You have several ways with them, and I have the feijoada. I also do them with beef and an onion stuck with cloves to give them flavor, and add cabbage just before serving. If possible I boil some pork skin with it so the juices become thickened a bit.

I have used black beans for a vinaigrette with great results — this, when I had them left over and it was easier to do a vinaigrette than to think of ways to reheat. And I gave them lots of hard-boiled egg and chopped onion. I see no reason why a version of Beef Salad Parisienne couldn't be made into a truly American dish with black beans, bits of beef, hard-boiled eggs, chopped scallions, parsley and vinaigrette sauce, with perhaps a little shredded green pepper and capers.

Also, hot black beans with oil and bits of pork, covered with shredded pork cracklings — garlic, onion and parsley for flavorings — should be a good buffet dish.

And of course there is your wonderful black bean dish with sour cream and rum.*

Dried lima beans I have never cooked, and they are not my favorite idea of bean.

The fava [broad] bean has never been greatly prized here except with various national groups. My mother adored them, and there was always a small plot of them for her benefit every year. I never shared her love for them and don't to this day. I have eaten dried salted ones, which I thought were very good, but the oily, unctuous taste of the beans in other forms really doesn't take my fancy. They do make a good salad if you like them.

One summer — in 1942 or 1943, I guess it was — just after leaving the army and before going into the United Seamen's Service I raised about two acres of various beans at Riveredge Farms near Reading, Pennsylvania. There, all the beans had to be cut undersize. The limas were picked and shelled when they were infinitesimally small, cooked quickly and served with butter, double cream and lots of ground pepper. The shell beans were dried, and the others were frozen in great quantities. I don't know how they came out, but I can imagine, perfectly, for they were such tender little morsels.

This about covers my great bean repertory as far as the 48 states are concerned.

Love,

J

---

[1] Catharine Beecher, author of *Miss Beecher's Domestic Receipt Book,* 1846.

[2] By the members of the Key West Woman's Club, 1949.

* Recipe.

36 West 12th Street

New York

[December 7, 1955]

Dearest Helen —

I know what you mean about being a dead bunny. I have one more thing to finish for *House and Garden* before I leave for Europe and then three pieces to do there for them, besides a Bordeaux food article.

There is a Feijoada recipe in my *Fireside Cook Book* — Brazilian Bean Dish, I think it is called. I like it better with black beans but they are so difficult to get. And I put pigs' ears into it when I make it and serve it with quantities of rice. You should mention that it is not meant to be a dinner dish but a luncheon dish strictly. You cannot buy it in the evening in Brazil.

Two new dishes: Bits of sautéed Virginia ham and shallot with vermouth, soy sauce and whole mushrooms. Covered and sautéed well. A bit of arrowroot and seasonings of salt and pepper and a dash of Worcestershire.

Chicken, cut in pieces, dipped in cornmeal or tamale meal, sautéed crisp and flamed with you-know-what, with a bit of heavy cream added and allowed to boil down after the grease is poured off.

You are a honey.

[JB]

S. S. *Independence*
[December 15, 1955]

Dear Helen,

I have slept till nine o'clock nearly every day — something unheard of for me. They have given me the special treatment — their publicity guy worked with me during the war, and I have known their purchasing agent for a long time. So Saturday morning I find they have given me a large outside cabin with two big picture windows. There was champagne, Scotch, a huge bowl of caviar and a large terrine of foie gras waiting for those who came to see me off — plus all the rest of the champagne that trickled in from here and there. Everyone turned out in force, and it seemed that I was giving my annual cocktail party. I'm carrying enough liquor to Bill Veach to see us through the holidays.

Tomorrow we have a full day in Lisbon. I have to buy my Christmas cards and try to get them addressed before we get to Gibraltar. Also going to lunch at a hotel where they make, for one thing, what is supposed to be the most fabulous smoked duck. The maître d'hôtel on the ship buys it and takes it back to New York with him.

I have eaten simply but exceedingly well. The tiny racks of lamb are delicious. I had a chateaubriand one night, and last night I invited three people for dinner and they gave us two double entrecôtes that were perfection. Started us with lots of caviar, then on to the steak, with broccoli, and topped it off with a Grand Marnier soufflé with a zabaglione sauce. Let no one tell you American ships cannot produce good food. This one does. There is a Chinese baker aboard who makes the most remarkable pumpernickel I have ever eaten. It's nutty, smooth, and velvety in texture and medium brown in color, and no molasses flavor that one gets in so many of the heavy breads nowadays.

Love and kisses,

J

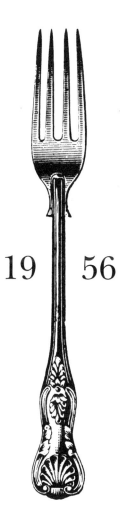

19 56

JB was in the South of France at the beginning of January, traveled up to Paris, then toured Cognac and Bordeaux, where he was made a Commandeur de Bontemps de Médoc. He returned to Paris for a week and enjoyed several days in London before sailing for New York on January 30. In late March he went to Los Angeles to do food demonstrations and continued north to Bakersfield, Menlo Park, San Francisco, and Seattle. He spent some time in Portland and Gearhart and on his way back to New York stopped off in Detroit for a party in his honor. He was in Boston and on the Cape in mid-May and visited the New York State wine country around Hammondsport on May 21–22. On June 29 he flew to Madrid, proceeded to Barcelona, and spent the rest of July and part of August on the Costa Brava, working on a book with the wine authority Frank Schoonmaker. In September he rented a second apartment at 36 West 12th Street for his new companion, Gino Cofacci. Cooking classes with André Surmain began on October 8. Later that month the J. Walter Thompson advertising agency offered JB a job for French's mustard, styling food for ads and creating new dishes. He spent Christmas Eve in New Canaan with Cheryl Crawford and Ruth Norman.

Dearest Helen —

Of course my typewriter went on the blink this morning & no Olivetti in Nice!

A wonderful week with dear Bill [Veach]. Our big Christmas party was a sensation & our tea for the dowagers a minor triumph. Such ricketty old girls some of them were, and they adored the tea & mulled wine & the potato cake Bill made — and his new specialty, tiny hot biscuits with just a dot of butter and ice-cold foie gras.

A wire from *House & Garden.* They want a fish article for April, so I did most of it in longhand for poor Isabel this morning. I interviewed three different Italian families for the Italian piece for *McCall's* and collected about fifty recipes.

This morning while wandering I came upon a bar at the Old Port, and there was a little shop next door where they make only pissaladière & onion tarts. You buy squares for 25 francs, about 5 cents, & take them to the bar to eat with your drinks. The pissaladière was superb. I had a square of onion — chopped finer than fine, sautéed in oil, then spread on light, crisp, tender bread dough just before it comes out of the ovens — with tiny black olives on top. Then one with tomato purée, anchovies & black olives, on the same dough. Then a two-crust onion tart with a rather thick crust on top & bottom — really wonderful.

I went to bed at 10:00 on New Year's Eve & traveled all New Year's Day. We were invited to a party, but it was just too much, and besides, Bill's Mario wanted to spend his New Year's Eve with his family. So we went to bed instead — not that we didn't imbibe well beforehand.

And on the train I had a beautiful lunch that Mario packed for me, with a bottle of wine, & John Ferrone gave me a flask for Christmas, so I had Scotch along the road and took in the scenery. The dining car is such a nuisance. You go through a million cars.

Sorry you have to wade through this scratch. Love & kisses anyway.

JB

[Paris
January 10, 1956]

Dear Helen —

Goodness, how much there is to learn about food. Each time I am here I realize how small my knowledge is. Someday I hope to know something. It's the truffle season and I have been lucky enough to have had almost my fill of them. I still like them best with potatoes and secondly with eggs. Scrambled eggs with truffles the other day at the de Lavals' were wonderful for a hot hors d'oeuvre. I can't explain what has happened to me, but I cannot eat an oyster anymore. I am revolted by them — I, who used to adore them.

Love and kisses,
JB

[Paris
January 19, 1956]

Helen, Dear —

I have just come back from Cognac and Bordeaux, where I was made a Commandeur de Bontemps de Médoc. You can just call me Commander from now on. The luncheon Saturday in Pauillac after the ceremonies was quite elegant, for sixty persons. We started with a soup of vegetables in cream to heat us up after the really cold period in the cellars, then foie gras of duck — fresh, with Madeira sauce and raisins — guinea hen with a truffle sauce, potatoes and tiny green beans, cheese, a wonderful cake with ices, and then fruit. The wines were impeccable, being the choice wines from seven different vineyards in the district. Afterwards we had cognac and coffee and such things until late in the afternoon.

Then back to Lichine's after some vineyard visiting. Bettina Coffin, who used to be with *Vogue,* and Henry McNulty of the Gottlieb office are here with me. We had a big dinner party at Prieuré that evening and went off to [Nicolas] Trambitsky's, Lichine's business manager, afterwards to a party. The Trambitskys have just moved down from Paris and have bought a small château. They have only finished the bedrooms, bathroom and kitchen, so they had the party in the kitchen. Bettina is a darling and quite as nice as you or Helen McCully, and they all loved her very much. She speaks very good French, and so that endears her as well.

Tonight we are going to dine with Sandy and Grete at a new bistro, tomorrow my friends from Mexico, the Palominos, are having a real do, and one day we are lunching with Alice B.

Love and kisses,

J

[Paris
January 20, 1956]

Dear —

I just sent you 200 grams of truffles by air express — about six brushed ones — which should arrive in good condition. I would do them with potatoes. Slice potatoes very thin, sauté in goose fat, and add the truffles, sliced thin. Also make a Poulet Demi-Deuil — steamed chicken with truffles under the skin and a cream sauce. We had it last night in an enchanting little bistro [Alliance] Sandy has found. Bettina and I started with cochonnaille. They bring a huge platter of every kind of pork charcuterie — sausage; pig's feet stuffed with sausage; pig's tails, pickled and boiled, served cold; pig's ears the same; and cold jowl. They slice off a little of each for an hors d'oeuvre. The others had quenelles with red sauce — lobster and shrimp in the sauce. Then the poulet with rice. We finished off with ice cream molds they make there. One was a rich vanilla, almost like a mousse, with candied fruits in kirsch in the center. The other was a coffee with coffee mousse in the center. Elegant.

Sandy went down to Brive with one of the restaurateurs with whom he had been working on his new book — spent the whole weekend at the truffle fair and ate them till the truffle became, according to Grete, something she didn't want to see for a year. This is a good year and they are selling for about 8,000 francs [about $16.00] a kilo for the brushed ones.

We had to go to the knife place today to pick up what I had ordered. So we went to a Jewish delicatessen down there in the very heart of the ghetto and had a wonderful lunch. We had chopped chicken livers with goose fat and great mounds of chopped egg, good old boiled beef with kasha and vegetables, and almond strudel. I bought some Rillons d'Oie — goose done in cubes like carnitas, skin and flesh.

What they do on trains here is amazing — in a kitchen about as big as mine in New York, with a coal stove, and sometimes four sittings. Wisely enough they have only one menu. Going to Bordeaux, the four of us had a Pullman compartment, and they served our lunch there — hors d'oeuvre, with five different vegetables in sauce Grecque, stuffed eggs, sardines and sausage. Then trout amandine, an excellent tournedos Rossini with chip potatoes and haricots verts, a salad of endives, cheese, and a fruit ice cream with wafers and coffee. And a large choice of wines. Coming back, they served Henry McNulty and me at the fourth sitting at quarter to ten at night — soup, quiche Lorraine — fresh and hot as it could be — rare roast filet with Lyonnaise potatoes and braised endive, salad, cheese, and fruits. I think they do a fantastic job. Imagine that meal on the 20th Century, served the way it is. They used to serve food beautifully on the Union Pacific years ago, but I don't think they have kept up that standard. And we had hot plates for hot things, cold for cold, and silver for each course.

Glad that *Collier's* have taken us and that they want more. I hope it is the fish stew one, for I have documentation on it, and I have a Tahitian stew.

Love and kisses. I leave here Tuesday night for London.

J

Gore Hotel
London
[January 28, 1956]

Helen, Dear —

I adore this hotel. Tonight Ned Bradford,[1] his wife and Margaret Fiddest Watt, Sandy's sister, are coming to dine in the Elizabethan manner with me. I've lunched with Robin Howard[2] twice in the regular dining room, which serves good English food. He had a luncheon on Thursday for Sir Malcolm Sargent[3] and femme and one of the Hennessy [cognac] gals, the English branch. We had caviar in honor of Sir Malcolm and potted shrimp for the two ladies. Then breast of chicken with mushrooms sous cloche with Armagnac and cream — and awfully good. We had a quiche Lorraine for a combined dessert, cheese and savoury course. Good Bordeaux all the way through and brandies and coffee.

Otherwise I have been eating straight English fare, and good it is if you go to the right places. Wonderful roasts and grills and fish. And the English are still the only people who make good toast that stays crisp and has body. As a matter of fact, they make good bread generally.

Yesterday Jim Finney of Pimm's invited me and André Simon[4] for oysters and champagne before lunch at Bentley's, and the brown bread served with the oysters was heaven— good heavy whole wheat, simple and unadorned. I then had lunch with Mr. Kennerly of Faber and Faber, who said they wanted to do everything we publish. Our book comes out in April.

Went to the Hotel and Catering Show yesterday morning, and what the apprentice schools and the Royal Air Force schools are doing here is unbelievable. I saw an R.A.F. class giving a demonstration in which they were using the finest French techniques. They know all the intricacies of classic cookery and decoration as well. Some of their displays were as fine as the Salon Culinaire itself, and that includes the Great. England has certainly come along.

Today I lunched with a chap from Lemon Hart rum — I'm doing something on them for Julius Wile.[5] We went to a pub [Prospect of Whitby] — the oldest one left — right in the dock section, with the river at your feet. The service and clientele upstairs has become elegant and smart, but down in the pub you see quite a cross section. In fact there were more French there than anything else, and the menu is strictly English — potted shrimp, soup, oysters, joints, chicken and duckling, and apple tart or cheese. I guess I must still have a hell of a lot of English in me — I love Brussels sprouts.

Lyons, which is practically the biggest food operation in the world, has huge ready-to-eat shops in their restaurants. Here you can buy, among other things, 8-ounce packages of puff paste for 2 shillings and packages of regular short pastry for 1 / 6. Wonderful idea, no? And all kinds of meat pies, turnovers, little tarts, sweet and savoury, and bridge and tea and cocktail sandwiches in little cellophane packets. We have nothing like it. In Paris, also, in the elegant tea shops you can buy thin sandwiches of chicken, pâté, tomato and egg, cucumber, ham — wrapped individually in wax paper and as good as you would make yourself. Several times, when people were dropping by for cocktails, I would buy wonderful salted almonds and some Rillons de Vouvray — a French version of carnitas — and could have a very pleasant gathering in my little old Second Empire drawing room at the France et Choiseul.

The secret of French bread is yeast and flour. It is nothing but yeast, water and flour with a little salt baked in a brick oven with steam. It is heavy and chewy, the crust is crisp, and it has big holes in it. It gets stale quickly.

Love,

J

---

[1] Editor-in-chief of JB's publisher, Little, Brown.

[2] Manager of the Gore Hotel.

[3] Conductor of the Royal Choral Society and the BBC Symphony Orchestra.

[4] President of the Wine and Food Society and author of *The Art of Good Living* and other books on food and wine.

[5] The wine importing firm.

Pasadena
January 28, 1956

Jim dear,

I was wakened this morning ... by a special [delivery] from John. It was to tell me that *Collier's* wanted the picnic article by the middle of February! ... Please send me any hot ideas that follow the outline. They want, thank goodness, interesting breads for the sandwiches. Wouldn't it be nice if *Collier's* gave us about four of these assignments a year?

Love and a hug,
H

36 West 12th Street
New York
[February 9, 1956]

Dearest Helen —

I am hoping to rent my apartment and go to Spain for the summer to work with Frank Schoonmaker. Or I may give up the apartment right off the bat and hunt till I find a big kitchen. I am literally bursting at the seams here and cannot even store what I have.

I make a galantine with turkey instead of chicken because I like the final flavor better.* You can use one of the small, compact ones. I bone it carefully and take the thigh and leg meat and a little of the breast and cut it into strips. Also smoked tongue in strips, and if I have it, some good ham in strips. I make a farce of 1 pound of lean pork, ½ pound of veal, and 1 chicken breast seasoned with salt, pepper, nutmeg, a tiny hint of thyme and really mix the hell out of it. This is spread over the boned chicken or turkey, and then I make a crazy pattern of the tongue, ham and turkey strips, slice a truffle very thinly and distribute that, and add plenty of pistachio nuts. I roll it well, tie each end, and sew the seam. Then wrap it in cloth and tie it at each end and twice in the center. About 1½ hours' cooking in broth, made with a veal bone, a calf's foot, and the carcass of the bird. I usually rest it on a rack or an inverted plate. I weight it pretty well when I cool it. For a picnic there is no reason why it could not be unrolled into a long dish and weighted and cooled that way. Then covered with broth to jell.

I had a most fascinating terrine in France made with thinly sliced calf's liver, thinly sliced ham and fresh pork siding, done in layers, with finely chopped onion and parsley — similar to the veal and ham terrine I do. White wine or cognac poured over and baked in a slow oven for about 1–1½ hours, then weighted and cooled. You must fill the terrine well and put a thin layer of pork skin or salt pork on the bottom.

I also like huge ripe tomatoes with a cold poached egg, tarragon and a hunk of cold lobster, served with a green mayonnaise to decorate and flavor.

I think we should suggest biscuits — such as the Romary wheaten biscuits in a tin — instead of bread. Easy to carry and not sticky starchy.

And please don't forget my favorite thin onion sandwiches, preferably on stale homemade bread, with salt and plenty of black pepper. And chicken or turkey slices well bathed in English mustard mayonnaise, rolled in paper-thin slices of prosciutto, and served with cucumber fingers that have been packed in a jar with a sweet vinegar and herb sauce to marinate them well.

And great big artichokes, trimmed and filled with shrimp mayonnaise, so that you can have the shrimp for an hors d'oeuvre and there is enough mayonnaise clinging to the artichoke to make it either an additional hors d'oeuvre or a salad course.

And carry along an immense cabbage filled with cole slaw with a really bitey fresh horseradish, sour cream, mayonnaise sauce. The cabbage carry-all is economical and easy to dispose of after the picnic.

Try blending 1 cup of sugar and 1 cup of butter, adding about 2½ cups of flour, 1 teaspoon of cinnamon and a little cream if necessary. Work it well and let it stand for a few minutes. Spread thin as you would with shortbread on a cookie sheet, brush with egg, sprinkle with chopped almonds and granulated sugar and bake as you do shortbread. Cut in squares while warm and leave in the pan to carry to the picnic.

Of course a real English pork pie with the boiled crust is heaven, but I suppose it is too involved for this article. And I adore ham and egg tart, with thin slices of ham and hard-boiled eggs in a double crust with salt and pepper.

Have you used veal and onion sandwiches with anchovy butter?

Smoked salmon with onion on thin pumpernickel? And cucumber and fresh salmon with mayonnaise? They are delicious on good white bread. And Niçoise sandwiches — anchovies, shredded pepper, onion, seeded and chopped tomato, and sliced black olives on French rolls? Of course you have included sausage rolls with puff paste?

And strawberries with powdered sugar — this, with a pound cake or with pound cake in madeleine molds.

And just plain old-fashioned sponge cake split in two and spread with jelly or raspberry jam — what the Scotch call jelly sandwich. Nothing is better for a picnic.

Another thing — crisp celery and a cheese board — but no bread. It is very British that way. Three or four cheeses and plenty of celery, crisp and large, with plumes left on if you will.

I hold no brief for Cornish game hens. I think they are for those who don't particularly like flavor. I agree they are best broiled, and I don't like the little ones that are stuffed with wild rice and such.

Bettina writes that they had a Helen Brown dish at Alice B.

Toklas's. She said it was a low oval casserole soufflé with sweet-breads and mushrooms. Is that yours?

Love and kisses,

J

---

* Recipe.

[36 West 12th Street
New York
February 17, 1956]

Dearest Helen —

I have an offer from Seattle to do a lecture on the 10th of April. Mary Hamblet wants me for her fiftieth birthday on March 17. Maybe you could come up for that and I return with you and then come back to Seattle? That would give us about two weeks' time. And we might do a good West Coast travel article. And who could do the West Coast better than we? Mary is going to have a real shindig, with all the Irish overtones.

I have always admired Frank Schoonmaker and feel he has done more for California wines than anyone. I also think he is a great writer. And he has taught everyone. He is considered in France to be probably the world's greatest authority on wine, and French restaurants consult him for their wine lists.

I'm having Helen and Ruth and Cheryl tomorrow night, and we are probably going to the theatre afterwards. I'm giving them roast pork from the Italian market, with fresh basil, Italian parsley and garlic rolled into it, sautéed apples, braised endive, and roast potatoes — then cheese and fruit. They are not hors d'oeuvre people so I shall skip that. Ann comes on Sunday for choucroute — what else? I have tails, ears and hocks for it, and sausages.

Night before last, André and Nancy Surmain were here. I made "beef with a spoon" — rump, larded, with a calf's foot, cognac, vermouth, spices and onion, cooked nine hours in the oven, with carrots and leeks added after five hours. It was superb. I talked to a fine chef this year who insisted that anything like a daube or pot roast or à-la-mode should never be cooked less than six hours and that it was better after seven or eight. Certainly this had a texture and concentrated flavor that no similar thing could have. Had it with Elena's rice and chilies, and a celery salad with LOTS of mustard. The leftover rice I made into a casserole-do with sautéed chicken hearts.

I think the bean article is swell. I think you are swell. I think Philip is swell. I think I shall end with love and kisses for all.

J

[36 West 12th Street
New York
February 1956]

Dearest Helen —

The truffled potatoes are done as follows. I use Idahos and sauté them well — raw, in slices — in either goose fat or butter until some are crisp and some just tender. Then I heat the truffles, sliced, in butter or goose fat and combine them with the potatoes at the last minute. It is sort of galette potatoes with truffle slices. The girls[1] nearly lost their minds over them on Saturday night.

I go to Spain the first of July and stay into September. If you and Philip could come over then, I would go to France with you. I think you should try all the angles. See if you can't make a deal with TWA or Air France. At any rate there is a special rate for two together — husband and wife. Then write to Bill Kaduson and Philip Klarnet[2] and ask them what can be done. I'm sure you'll get trips to Cognac and to Champagne with all the trimmings. And I feel reasonably sure that in Bordeaux you will get the treatment. I'll see to that. Also I can arrange that we go to Burgundy together.

I think you can do it on $1500–1800 plus your fares for a month in Europe, with car rental and all.

Had to have my robes made for the Commanderie de Bontemps. I appear on the first and the fifth at all the ceremonies.

Love and kisses,
JB

---

[1] "The girls" were usually Cheryl Crawford and Ruth Norman, though sometimes JB's nearly life-size pair of terra-cotta figures.

[2] Philip Klarnet, like Kaduson, was a vice president of Edward Gottlieb Associates.

[36 West 12th Street
New York
March 2, 1956]

Helen, dear —

At the Bordeaux tasting I met the Home Show chef, who is evidently doing the food for our *Collier's* [picnic] article.

He said, "Why do you tell people it is simple to make a galantine? It took me four hours. Nobody could do it unless it was demonstrated." So I said, "I am sick of thinking the American housewife is dumb. She can do anything if she wants to, and the reason she doesn't is because too many of you think everything has to be done for her. I know plenty of people who learned to make a galantine without a demonstration. After all, if you can read and know cooking there is nothing you can't achieve." Boom. Period. I suppose they think I'm nuts, but we both learned to cook without having anyone show us all the difficult things. If we couldn't do something, we struggled till we had it. And no mixes either.

I must go. I have a goose in the oven, a tongue on the stove, along with two pots of broth, a turkey ready to make a galantine, and stuff to come. There will be fifteen tomorrow night. I surely don't mind crowds if the menu is easy. And these folk are all congenial.

Just got the Little, Brown royalty statement. *Fish Cookery* sold 87 copies in six months. It makes you sick, what with the notices that book has had and the things people have said about it. One's favorite child is always the backward one, I guess.

Love and kisses,
J

Pasadena
March 6, 1956

Dearest Jim,

It was funny about the chef and the galantine. I taught myself to make them many years ago. I don't remember ever having seen a professional make one, but mine come out fine. I agree with you

that anyone who really wants to cook can teach himself. We might
do an article on that.

Love,
H

[36 West 12th Street
New York
March 14, 1956]

Dearest Helen —

I went to Philadelphia yesterday and got home at three a.m. —
up at seven, to the doctor for my head, then to the Lexington,
where I worked with Albert Stockli[1] and a photographer. One of
the assistant photogs got snooty, and I said, "O.K., work it out
yourself. I'm only used to second-raters like Breuhl, Ellisofon and
Lazarnick.[2] I shall stand around and watch the master at work."
That finished my day of photographing.

Tonight I have Bill Kaduson and Alvin and Peter coming for
dinner. They are getting nothing exciting — chicken flambé, a
fresh corn sauté with mushrooms, salad, and some wonderful
schnecken which were sent to me today. Tomorrow night I am
having deviled crab and a pot-au-feu — the latter, by request.
Chicken, fresh tongue and beef, with leeks, onions, cabbage,
carrots, turnips and potatoes.

I have spent about five hours with the boy from *Collier's* on
research for our bean story. In all my life as a contributor to
magazines I have not been through such a third degree. They
wanted our sources for every fact we mentioned, and I think I got
most all of them. They have written you for some I didn't know.
They called Washington about the bean soup, and I gave them
permission to change what we had because the Senate said we
were not right. They tell me that if they don't check facts the mail
they get is terrible, so I guess they are right.

Love and bunny hugs. I must order another kimono while I'm there with you. They are superb for traveling.

J

---

[1] Executive chef of Restaurant Associates.
[2] Anton Breuhl, Eliot Ellisofon, and George Lazarnick.

[36 West 12th Street
New York
March 19, 1956]

Helen —

With this storm I don't know whether this letter will get there before me or not. It is the old blizzard of '88 all over again. The snow has hardly stopped for two days. It is simply amazing what happens when people think spring is here too soon. I plowed over to Fred Shrallow's[1] to a party last night, came home about seven and went to bed.

I got up at seven to make a batch of bread. Then I had to perfect a recipe for a do of codfish, cream and potatoes which I had eaten in Lisbon — and which turned out beautifully.* We can try it if you get good salt cod. I had two people in for breakfast to eat up the things. Next time I do it I think I shall put the codfish in the Waring, with cream, instead of in the Kitchen Aid. It is cod with cream, butter, garlic and mashed potatoes, whipped to a frothy blend, then formed into a pyramid, buttered and crumbed, and baked till brown. It is my thought that this is probably the father of the New England codfish cake. But the taste is far more wonderful.

I understand through the underground that *Collier's* is really happy with our bean article. I only hope this is going to lead to a permanent attachment.

If all goes as it should I shall see you at the Biltmore about 6:30 or so on Saturday.

Love, in the meantime,

J

Monday, in the deep snows

---

[1] Interior decorator and friend of JB who lived in the neighborhood.
* Recipe.

36 West 12th Street
New York
[May 10, 1956]

My dear Philip and Helen —

What a week of celebration. Paul Bernard and Harry Marinsky[1] gave a huge birthday party for me in the country on Saturday, and it was, thank God, a beautiful day. All your friends were there for drinks and a choucroute supper. Naturally, I made it. Then on Sunday I was a guest for dinner and the ballet, and on Monday night André and Nancy christened their new house with a party for me — they had eighteen sitting down for dinner. A simple but beautiful dinner. Eggs en Gelée, Tournedos with Sauce Madère, ratatouille, salad, and a chocolate cake that Nancy made — heavy with nuts, very chocolaty, with a creamy frosting.

Then Albert did a big birthday cake — two tiers.

I'm leaving for the Cape tomorrow, for the weekend. Alice McComb is going to be chef up there this year, and I have to make some changes. Monday I go to work with Albert, as they have engaged me to do new dishes for the Paul Revere room they are doing in the Lexington. We are also trying out new summer dishes for them. Everything is to be on wagons, with either heat or ice, limited menu stuff, so it should not be too hard. By the way we are getting wonderful frozen crawfish tails from Chile, which they are using in a salad with rice and vegetables in the oriental style.

JB

---

[1] A sculptor and close friend of Paul Bernard.

[36 West 12th Street
New York
June 22, 1956]

Dearest Helen —

I'm living on Miltown and 1000 calories a day. It all got to be too
much for me. I leave on Friday the 29th for Madrid. Four days
there, then to Barcelona, where I drop all my bags and fly to Paris
for two days to do an interview with Vaudable and collect material
and money for another booklet he wants me to do. Back to Spain
to work with Frank [Schoonmaker] till the 4th of August, when I
go to Portugal as a guest of the government.

Francis Guth has been here from Mexico. I had to sit at a long
lunch at "21" with him and Jane [Nickerson] and count calories,
and I did. I ate one spoon of caviar and a broiled filet of lemon
sole. Me!

We have been having the most wonderful berries, canteloup
and beefsteak tomatoes this year. I have practically lived on them.
The tomatoes are huge and hothouse grown but simply fabulous.
Sometimes they weigh over 1 ½ pounds each.

We had our O'Quin luncheon on Monday.[1] The jellied eggs with
O'Quin [Charcoal Sauce] were good, and the filet O'Quinned was
excellent on parsley bread. Then the biggest strawberries of the
season and the largest cherries, and a simple little wine with it all.
On Tuesday we sent the baskets around — charming baskets with
a small tablecloth and two napkins of gingham, which Nancy
made by hand, two hens, the O'Quin sauce, all the stuff I mentioned, and the story of the sauce, written up in beautiful longhand by André.

We wrote a letter to Whirl, telling them we would do the
booklet, providing we could segregate the recipes and not be
credited with those which we feel are done better with butter —
that we like Whirl for certain things. I cannot see myself selling
it. It looks like something for artificial insemination when it
comes out of the can, and I am sure it is going to have that effect
on most who see it.

Did you know that Perdita Schaffner's third child was born? — a girl, Elizabeth Bryher, and I am the godfather.

I love both of you.

Bye Bye,

J

---

[1] JB had been hired to promote O'Quin's Charcoal Sauce.

[Palamós
Costa Brava
July 6, 1956]

Dearest Helen —

This is the most heavenly spot you can imagine. My little house — three bedrooms isn't so little — is high, open and breezy, and the terrace faces the sea. I have a maid who is supposed to be a good cook. The Schoonmakers are coming to my place for dinner tonight, and we'll see. I'm giving them the shrimp of the sea here — cold, with mayonnaise and chicory, then squid à la Romana, beans and carrots, a salad of romaine, and fresh fruits. We have wonderful apricots, peaches, figs and wild strawberries and tame ones.

In Madrid we had the most wonderful raspberries I have ever eaten, and the white asparagus is still in season there. You know me and white asparagus — I had it nearly every meal. And such fish! Here, the boats go out every morning at six and return at six at night for the fish auction. Whiting, sometimes sole, rascasse, rouget, baby mackerel, fresh sardines, squid, baby octopus, shrimp, langoustines, langoustes, tiny clams, mussels — a wealth of fish that is fresher than fresh. The veal and pork and lamb are quite good, but the beef is not much to rave about.

My kitchen has a coal stove, a charcoal stove and an electric plate.

Something I didn't realize before is that the Spanish never, never use pepper. It is almost impossible to find unless you buy it from a butcher who uses it in sausage-making.

We went to the famous Los Caracoles in Barcelona, where they have spits turning, with chickens and other birds, right on the narrow sidewalk. The street itself is about six feet wide. There are tables on the sidewalk, practically in the street. But wonderful cooking — good fish and good chicken, perfectly roasted with charcoal. And much gaiety and good living — all this right in the middle of the whore district, but everyone loving it.

Frank and I are almost at the point of getting an outline made for our book. We didn't have one when we started out. We only know that it is to be wine and food.

Think of me trying to keep my weight down and more or less succeeding. I have a little fruit in the morning with tea and one piece of crisp toast. For lunch I usually have fish and fish, or fish and chicken, with vegetables and fruit. Dinner, about the same — with a little wine.

Love and loads of it,

J

[Palamós
Costa Brava
July 14, 1956]

Dearest Helen and Philip —

I go into the water at seven-thirty in the morning, come back to have my tea, waiting for me on the terrace, and bring my type-writer out. At noon or a little after we usually go swimming up the beach about two miles and then have lunch at my house. We work through till eight or so, have cocktails at eight-thirty or nine and dinner around nine-thirty or ten — rather early for Spain, where almost everyone gets down to dinner at eleven.

We eat fish by the ton because it is the best thing we have. Tiny baby lamb chops cut thin and broiled over charcoal are definitely the best meat one can get. But we have wonderful squid, fresh sardines and rougets. The melons are coming now. Little arti-chokes no bigger than your thumb are here, and we eat those by the pound, and good beans, zucchini blossoms, eggs and chicken.

Yesterday we brought some fine cheese from France, so we can be happy for a time with that.

Our charcoal burners are two in the kitchen. They are about twelve inches square and four inches deep, and all in tile except for a small bowl of iron. Little racks are put over them. Mercedes cooks some vegetables in saucepans on these burners and broils the fish, shrimp and chops over them — very slowly, and they are really delicious. The wood stove does a good job of roasting chickens. And toast made over the charcoal is wonderful.

Three nights ago there was a Catalan street dance, which was enchanting — must have been five hundred people dancing in great circles and circles within circles.

Love and kisses,
Don Jamie

[Palamós
Costa Brava
July 18, 1956]

Dear Helen —

Your letter arrived last night when I got back from two days in Barcelona. I had to have shirt fittings, and I ordered a new suit and a camel's-hair coat — these last two made by the best tailor in Spain and one of the three or four best in Europe, costing me less than the coat would cost ready-made in New York.

Had a wonderful time, for I bumped into a friend of mine [Jack Raglin] who is as much fun as Philip. We ate two marvelous lunches at the Ritz, one of the best-run hotels in the world — and my charming room at the back, with a huge bath and perfect service, costs $3.50 a day.

One night we went to Caracoles. We had a fish stew of Barcelona, with loup de mer, merlan, langouste, langoustines, mussels, squid and octopus in a sauce of oil, tomato, salt and a touch of garlic. The chicken, which I think I told you about, is cooked on a spit in front of charcoal, and the spits overhang the sidewalk so that you have to go out of your way and walk in the street. Funnily enough five people we knew passed while we were having dinner, including Tennessee Williams.

Due to the freeze one can't get good olive oil in Spain, unless you smuggle it in. So if you still get the good California oil, won't you buy me a gallon or two and ship it to me?

Today we had a delicious lunch — to begin with, a salad that is more of an hors d'oeuvre, with romaine, curly endive, cucumber, celery, onion and tomato. I make the dressing at table. Then we had baby pig's feet and lamb's feet, sautéed in butter, tiny aubergine and young cabbage.

This is the day of Our Lady of Mt. Carmel, and the saint's day of the fishermen, so there was a great procession in the harbor this noon. The Virgin is carried from the church and put aboard one of the fishing boats, and then the parade starts, zigzagging and all that sort of thing. So we started with a bottle of champagne to celebrate the day.

Love,

J

[Palamós
Costa Brava
July 23, 1956]

Helen and Philip, dears —

We have just finished dinner, it is almost midnight, and I feel the need of some exercise. I have been tense all day. Frank fell ill yesterday and is forced to stay in bed for several days. Bob Lee,[1] whom you met at Eleanor [Peters]'s once or twice, is staying with me for a few days, and tomorrow George and Helen Lazarnick come.

Mercedes made us a paella in my new pan today.* It was lovely. The rice from around here is blunt, short and deliciously flavored. In it she had chicken, the large local shrimp, squid, whiting, gamettas — which are like the French langoustines — crayfish of a pale pink color with strange claws — then a few peas, a little tomato, onion, cognac and water — cooked on top of the stove.

No saffron and no glutinous mess, as is often true of paella. I shall buy you a paella [pan] when I leave, and you can make a better one than you have ever eaten.

I have discovered the most wonderful breads here. One is called coca and is made in oval loaves about 14 by 10, and like a pretzel, rather, with open spaces. It is something between lavash and sourdough French — not light and not crisp but very chewy. Another bread, flutes, which are about 1½ inches in diameter and crisp. And strange whole-grain rolls about four inches in diameter, two inches high at the center, very grainy and delicious with butter — without butter they are terrible. And rolls made in the shape of chickens, with wings, as in coq en pâte.

The wild strawberries are wonderful, and now the yellow plums, the Claudias, are coming in, and the apricots, figs and pears — all better than you have eaten for years. But fish has increased in price over one hundred percent in two weeks because of the tourist season. Isn't that shocking? Squid, which we love so much, is almost a dollar a pound, and the big shrimp are the same. Sardines remain cheap and they are one of the best things in the market.

Philip, I should like a Fannie Farmer [*The Boston Cooking School Cook Book*] of the era before she died. I have the last two or three editions, but I would like an early one.

This is the next morning — and one of the most beautiful ones you have ever seen. Frank is better and ready for work. I just had the joyous news that Bettina and Henry McNulty[2] are coming down to take the house for the rest of the month of August after I leave.

Love,

J

---

[1] Robert Tyler Lee was a TV set designer and head designer for CBS.
[2] Bettina Coffin and McNulty had married.
* Recipe.

[Palamós
Costa Brava
August 10, 1956]

Helen Dear —

Will you please send me your cioppino recipe when you get around to it so that I can have it when I get home? We will do a little story about you, that this is your favorite recipe for it, and all that.

Only two more days of this paradise before starting back to New York. I am loath to go, in some ways, but very happy in others. It has been a most rewarding summer. I loved a great deal of it and learned a hell of a lot.

I think squid is the most wonderful of all seafoods as to flavor. The nearest thing to it is abalone, if well cooked, and next to that, razor clams. I can't have enough of it. It is superb dipped in egg and flour, sautéed in oil, covered for a while, then uncovered and put in the oven for a few minutes. It is just maddeningly delicious.

Did I tell you we have the best bacon here I have had in years?

Love,

J

[Palamós
Costa Brava
August 12, 1956]

Helen, dear —

We have finally finished our hundred menus that go into the book, and I think you will feel that they are distinguished and typical of both of us.[1] You and I are so closely in tune about certain things that we know almost instinctively what to say. Frank and I have worked into that now. We had a rather long time getting together, because we had been friends without being intimates, and in our ways, we are both perfectionists. I must say that his knowledge of food is almost as vast as his knowledge of wine. I'm a very lucky person to have two such collaborators as you and he.

Today there is a plethora of people. In addition to all the

holiday crowd there are four tremendous buses from Barcelona, full of trippers with food and bathing suits, who will leave a trail of litter.

Made a wonderful curry last night with the fabulous shrimp here — used Bill Veach's recipe. I added hot chilies to it and pepper because there is no ginger available. Used eggplant, which Bill uses for the body of the sauce, and used broth made from the heads of the shrimp for liquid.

I'm sending you three packages because we cannot mail over a kilo. Your paella is in one, a kilo of the native rice in another and a huge box of the wonderful sardines in another. Mercedes puts her paella in the oven for a few minutes at the end to dry out the rice. Cooks the chicken first, then her onions, till they are almost black, and tomato — and she uses several gizzards in it, with langoustines or shrimp, mussels, a firm white fish, sometimes langouste or lobster, and squid in rings — previously cooked a bit. She adds the fish and shellfish according to the time they take, while the rice cooks.

Love and kisses in Spanish,

J

---

[1] The book was never published.

36 West 12th Street
New York
[September 4, 1956]

Helen, dear —

I had your newsy letter, en route, and wanted so much to be with you all for the holiday in the Northwest. Some of that country appeals to me as much as any place I possibly could imagine.

I had a pleasant weekend at Cheryl's, tending our vineyards and cooking a hell of a lot. I made the best sourdough French bread I have ever made, on Sunday, which was even better when we made herbed bread with it on Monday. I used a cup of sourdough and a yeast cake in 1 cup of warm water, 1 tablespoon of sugar and 6 cups of flour. I kneaded the hell out of it twice and gave it a short rising before doing it into loaves. Baked it at 375. Brushed it thoroughly with water before putting it in the oven and added a tiny bit of water during the baking. The crust was crisp and thick.

Sunday I made a fine sukiyaki and last night a huge roast of beef on the General. And for lunch yesterday, a quiche, which all and sundry ate with great good will.

I am cutting down on my activities with André because I am being given a great deal more to do with Gottlieb this year, and more money. So I am doing only the most important work. I go to the Cape on Friday for a week and will help Steve[1] go over his summer, do a class, and get a small bit of rest. Then back into the whirl — with a daily rest each day, however. I am going to take care of myself.

I am taking the apartment downstairs, in addition to this one, and sharing with a friend of mine, Gino Cofacci,[2] whom you haven't met. I can use part of the downstairs for an office, and Gino will have his bedroom and bath there. The difference in rent is not so much, and the space is wonderful. Then if I entertain I can have cocktails and hors d'oeuvre downstairs and coffee and liqueurs as well. This, I decided, was a better move than getting a much more expensive apartment and then buying a lot of stuff that moving takes. I'm hoping to get painted by the time I return from the Cape — and I have weakened and am buying an air-conditioner.

Love and kisses,

J

---

[1] Robert Stevenson, the owner of Chillingsworth.
[2] A young Italian architect JB had recently met.

36 West 12th Street
New York
[September 1956]

Dearest Helen —

I am so glad you had the sort of time you did, for I know what fun the Northwest can be if you are on the hop all the time. And Mary [Hamblet] is one of God's most anointed creatures in that way — she really gives it a going over.

I'm just back from a week on the Cape and Nantucket. On Monday Steve entertained thirty women and men, with a demonstration by me and then cocktails and luncheon. I did a pasta with the native clams — the clams steamed open with white wine, chopped and combined with garlic, oil and parsley. I did a Mexican chicken,* with chilies and almonds, a variation of the mole theme which I developed for Steve last year. With this, polenta, and I made a huge Greek salad with everything in it — and for the cocktail hour, seviche. I finished off with bourbon peaches.

Did you ever hear of the Arm of the Gypsy? Spread cold mashed potatoes on a damp cloth and spread with mayonnaise, anchovies, pimientos, capers, tuna, cold peas, string beans and onion. Roll like a jelly roll and make pointed ends. Decorate with pimiento strips and capers and mayonnaise, and cut in thick slices. Incredibly delicious.

The school seems to be lining up so that we shall have about four classes. We are giving a complete menu with variations. For instance, one will have a Canapé Marquise for a tidbit, a spinach and cheese soufflé for an hors d'oeuvre, three different kinds of duck with accompaniments, a vegetable, and, for dessert, another type of soufflé, such as the lemon one with no flour or a regular ginger one. In this way the soufflé question, the duck question and the vegetable styling will all be covered with one lesson. In another we shall have turkey, capon and goose with various stuffings. Everyone works every different station. Then when one sits at dinner it becomes a seminar.

It is a great enlightenment to me, after sixteen years, to have more room than the rather tight little island I had before. I don't know where I put everything.

Love to you both,

J

_____

* Recipe.

[36 West 12th Street
New York
October 7, 1956]

Darling Helen —

Well, we are all set for tomorrow's opening blast. We have forty paid students, and the first lesson is an hors d'oeuvre table, chicken three ways, corn bread, salad and a plain layer cake. Not exciting but the right thing for a beginning class where everyone is getting accustomed to one thing and another. For some reason I am looking forward to the classes — because I am such a ham, I guess.

Friday we did our scallop luncheon for the New Bedford Scallop Association. They were to send us forty-five pounds of scallops to arrive at seven in the morning. By eleven o'clock nothing had come, and guests were bidden for twelve. We bought scallops here and between eleven and twelve-thirty I did all the hors d'oeuvre, including two quiches, scallop seviche, scallops sauce verte, potato salad, cucumber salad, tomato salad, and two other dishes — and made arrangements to buy more scallops. When the guests arrived I served the hors d'oeuvre on time, with the help of two waitresses, then sautéed — in plain sight — scallops amandine, scallops Provençale, and scallops au Xérès, and did rissoles, délices, broiled marinated scallops and scallops in champagne. And talked with the guests. In the middle of luncheon the original scallops arrived and were promptly sent back to New Bedford.

Helen and I are working hard on our dinners for the Florence Crittenton League.[1] We both are sold out, and our joint dinner is almost sold out. Mine is next Sunday, and Helen's and mine the following Friday. And with four nights at the school and all the rest of it, you can see where my time is going.

Today is so beautiful. There has been a brilliant sun, the leaves are falling and turning, and there is a brisk something in the air.

Love,

J

---

[1] Annual benefit dinners for a philanthropic organization founded in 1883 to aid destitute young women.

Pasadena
October 9, 1956

James dearest,

Home economists! . . . Nothing I do is right any more. . . . "Lovely is not a word to apply to food." "Don't say paste or pasta, say macaroni products." "Don't say stale bread, say day old bread" etc. See what I mean? I am so self-conscious about everything I write that I can't write. . . .

How did you ever get signed up for so many F[lorence] C[rittenton] dinners? Lord, man, you need someone to tie you down.

Lots of love,
H

Edward Gottlieb & Associates Ltd.
New York
[October 1956]

Dearest Helen and Philip —

This is soufflé week. Last night's class of nine succeeded in preparing eighteen soufflés — spinach and cheese, cheese, spinach, ginger, cherry, Grand Marnier, five lemon soufflés without flour, etc. I don't ever want to do one again. Then this morning I was looking for something in the *Holiday* [*Cook Book*] or *West Coast*

[*Cook Book*] and what did I find to make it even worse — that Brown woman's recipe for a cranberry soufflé.

I had such a snotty letter from Nicholas Roosevelt about cooking trout in bacon fat[1] that I have not even bothered to look at his book [*Creative Cookery*]. I have plenty of intelligent French authorities he might read. As for the other book you mentioned [*The Birth of a Cook* by Ernest Mundt] — I have not heard about it, but that's not surprising, for I never get a chance to read. I have never found a book so fine as the Doctor Edouard de Pomiane for basic cooking.[2] It revolutionizes half of the things you do in the kitchen, and you know why you do them.

Saturday night in the country I did some of the quick-cooking beans with a little soy and apple cider, mixed, which had been used to baste the pork roast we had, along with an onion, some garlic cooked in butter and a touch of tomato sauce. With thinly sliced sautéed apples and the pork they were a fabulously good dish.

Start reading up on regional dishes for your trip to France and get a Michelin and start marking restaurants which specialize in things. Or shall I do it for you as part of your travel kit?

[JB]

---

[1] A recipe that appeared in *James Beard's New Fish Cookery*.

[2] Possibly *La Cuisine en Dix Minutes ou L'Adaptation au Rythme Moderne* (1930).

[36 West 12th Street
New York
October 21, 1956]

Helen, dear —

Well the two Crittenton dinners are behind me. Simply a hell of a lot of hellish work, but I guess they were worth it. Sunday's really looked beautiful. I had chrysanthemums in the lavabo and red oak leaves around them, white roses here near the desk, and candles by the ton. My new — last summer — candelabra, tall silver ones with triple arms, were on the table. In the downstairs apartment I had Helen's candlesticks and huge pink chrysanthemums, and also a big bouquet of my favorite eucalyptus. We started there and had big bowls of nuts with champagne, Scotch or vodka. Then we came up here for snails — with them, I served a Savigny-les-Beaune, chilled — and the bourguignonne, for which I used 23 pounds of beef. Pommes vapeur and endive and watercress followed. Then Crêpes Amoureuses. I served a very interesting red Burgundy with the beef, a Fixin. The crêpes were flamed with cognac and then drenched with Grand Marnier. We went downstairs for expresso and liqueurs.

Friday night Helen and I had our party, at the apartment of Bush Barnum.[1] We had a wonderful collection of people, beautifully dressed. Most of our food came from restaurants.

For the cold buffet, green eels from Quo Vadis, chicken chaudfroid Véronique from Chateaubriand, ham balls with pineapple filling from Albert Stockli, and a very inferior pâté from Gaston. Then for the hot buffet, stuffed duck with plum sauce from Albert, veal from Maxim's, shrimp à l'Armoricaine from Maxim's, and green fettucine from us. We had a Lascombes rosé and Château Lascombes '53 from Lichine. For dessert [Joseph] Bugoni of the Baroque gave us one of his inimitable Jambon au Madère cakes — génoise made into the shape of a ham, with butter cream and currant jelly between the layers and a marzipan icing the color of a ham basted with Madeira.

The school is going great guns. Last week we gave them bread and rolls; Terrine de Body; scallops Provençale; scallops with sherry; scallops soaked in soy, wine, garlic and ginger and grilled; breast of veal stuffed with sausage, veal and spices; saltimbocca; and veal in papillote. Also potatoes fondant and cabbage and noodles, and for dessert, Diplomate au Grand Marnier with sauce Anglaise. They eat themselves into bliss when they finish. This week is beef, three kinds of gnocchi, Pommes au Lard, chocolate mousse, Cuban bread and Tartine Marquise.

I have been offered a stupendous job by J. Walter Thompson for French's mustard — styling all the food for their ads and creating new dishes. And then Green Giant has finally come through and may put me on a retainer for a year. They want new flavor development and new ideas in canning.

Tonight Ruthie [Norman] is coming for dinner. We have clams to make into a spaghetti sauce, we're having a salad, and I'm making apples Bonne Femme — basting them with butter and sugar — served on a piece of fried toast. I adore them.

Love and many embraces,

J

---

[1] Public relations representative for the Glass Containers Manufacturers Institute.

Edward Gottlieb & Associates Ltd.
New York
[November 1956]

Dearest Helen —

Hibben gave us a grand write-up in *The New Yorker* about the school this week. Wonderful.

The first semester of the school ends this week, and a large percentage of the students are coming back. They are up to their necks in goose and turkey. I tried a goose on the Bartron, but must say the one I cooked in the oven was a hundred percent crisper and better tried out. I shall do it again. The turkey I did on the Bartron last night was much better but took a hell of a long time to cook. I had done one earlier in the oven, with cheesecloth saturated in butter, and it was the most perfect turkey I have ever cooked. 450 for almost an hour and then 350, and it was basted constantly. We are doing Mabelle [Jeffcott]'s[1] graham bread* this week, too, with great success. We finally have a source for fresh yeast and get it five pounds at a time and keep some in the freezer.

I'm having home economist battles. I couldn't use tarragon in the mustard sauce I did, so I substituted rosemary. The home economist sent word that since a housewife would have to have a mortar and pestle for rosemary, she was changing the herb to oregano. I also had called for grated onion, and she said it should be minced because a housewife had no Mouli, which she presumed I had used. I said I was being paid to create flavor and that she should keep rosemary — it didn't need any mortar and pestle — and that I grated onion because I wanted the juice, and it was done on a dime-store grater. Then she found fault with the cayenne pepper, which I used because I wasn't allowed to use dry mustard. I tell you these people have no regard for flavor, only for how many steps a housewife has to take.

Love and kisses,

J

---

[1] Mabelle Jeffcott and her husband, Ralph, lived on a farm south of Portland and were old friends of JB. Both were fine amateur cooks.
* Recipe.

Pasadena
November 26, 1956

James dearest,

We had a lovely lunch with M. F. K. Fisher. All wished you were there. Wine of the country, a salad that was like a Niçoise but called by her Provençal. Cheese and fruit for dessert. Very fine, all of it. And she is really fascinating. You must meet her.

Love,
H

[36 West 12th Street
New York
November 1956]

My dear Browns —

Thanksgiving was different for me, for I cooked dinner for the first time in years. Rhoda and Francis [Adams][1] were here, and we had Agnes and Bill White as well. I had a pound of fresh caviar, which Gino and I dug into the night before. So I had smoked salmon and caviar on my crazy fish plates, which I found just before I went to Spain. The center is just the color of smoked salmon and the other bits are blue.

Then I had the best turkey I have done in ages. Cooked it with cheesecloth and loads of butter at 450 for 1½ hours and then down to about 300 and finally to 200 to coast. Filled it with my crumb of French bread, butter, parsley and shallot stuffing, flavored with tarragon. The turkey had eight unborn eggs in it, so I cooked them with the giblets for the sauce. Had mashed potatoes, peas with tiny glazed onions and — don't faint — crystallized cranberries,* and even I liked them. They were rich, didn't taste like cranberries, and were crisp, runny, and gooey, which pleased my taste buds. Gino, who loves cranberries, didn't like them.

For dessert, Alice B. Toklas prunes in cream,* which I think are superb. We drank champagne all through. Agnes and Bill don't drink, so they had Perrier.

Up to my ass in mustard right now — doing a whole menu on Friday for J. Walter Thompson with mustard rampant. An Easter dinner, a ham leftover dish, and a main-dish salad. They will be Frenched to death. Mustard bread, too. I'll be glad when it is all over.

Frigidaire is installing a kitchen for the school with their new range — two ovens and a rotisserie in one of them — and a new refrigerator. This is on consignment. I'm thinking very seriously of getting an electric stove for home since they have installed that horrible natural gas — what a stinking thing it is. We had more temperature trouble with it in the school than I can possibly explain.

Love and kisses,
[JB]

---

¹ Portland friends.

* Recipe.

36 West 12th Street
New York
[December 1, 1956]

Dear Browns —

The mustard home economist came down on Friday, and we gave her the works. My leftover ham dish: line the bottom of a double boiler with ground ham and cup it along the sides. Make a heavy cream sauce with 3 tablespoons of flour and butter and 1 can of evaporated milk, add ¼ pound of grated cheese, 3 tablespoons of French's mustard, and six eggs, beaten in one at a time. Pour into the double boiler top, steam for 1¼ hours and then dry in the oven for 10 minutes. Unmold and serve with a tomato sauce. Or bake it in a pan of water for 1½ hours at 325. Also did a salad for them and a molded salad. They were enchanted.

I'm getting to like the stuff. And I sneaked it into a dip for Bill Chapman's[1] party. It was a dream party, for the guests were fascinating and the tables looked like a picture. I had done a fresh ham, boned, on the spit till the skin was crunchy. There were bowls of our lamb meatballs* with a French's dip, a huge copper container full of bagna cauda, and two great brown bowls filled with brilliant vegetables sticking out of ice. A bowl of shrimp nested in watercress. There were tostadas, buttered pumpernickel, bread sticks, Genovese toast, and homemade French bread, and a lovely fruit arrangement.

We are about to dine on a small two-rib roast, which we are broiling in the rotisserie, some turnips and rice, and baked apples Bonne Femme. I think it will be distinguished. Gino is having a cookery lesson and is a damned good pupil.

Love and kisses,

J

---

[1] Senior editor at *House and Garden*.
* Recipe.

36 West 12th Street
New York
[December 30, 1956]

Helen, Dear —

We had a quiet weekend in the country. Gino and I went up on Sunday. Thornton and Isabel Wilder[1] were there, and then Mary Martin, Dick and Heller[2] came by, and we sat around the fire. Monday we all sort of went our ways and then had our Christmas Eve dinner — steak Diane, petit pois, stuffed baked potatoes and cherries Jubilee. Christmas Day I made a quiche for lunch, and we drove into town in the afternoon. Gino and I ate cold Virginia ham and salad for our Christmas dinner. I never felt more pleased with not having feasted and drunk to excess, and the spirit of Christmas was nowhere to be found in any of us this year.

Got the usual commercial things. But wonderful liquor — a case of champagne, a case of cognac, a case of Bordeaux, a case of good Burgundy and a lot of odd bottles. And for the first time in years, loads of candy.

Eileen Tighe[3] has come to life again at *Woman's Day,* and I am doing several things for her. My first one is on cheesecake. Is there any famous one in Los Angeles now — one that would warrant a picture of the place and the recipe? The Victor Hugo, in the old, old days, had the best one I ever ate, and then I think the Gotham had one, but I have lost track by now. Would you tell me please? Is there one in the Farmers' Market?

I've got fifty or sixty coming in on Tuesday for your milk punch — with full credit. It seemed a good way to do the holiday thing with the least amount of fuss and fume. Peter Carhartt told me again that you are the most copied cookbook writer at *Gourmet* — I'm second.

I guess we have about finished up the mustard series now. They have given in on some points and I on others. Whew, it was a job to put the home economics down my throat.

Love, and the biggest New Year's ever.

J

---

[1] American novelist and playwright, and his sister.
[2] Richard and Heller Halliday, Mary Martin's husband and daughter.
[3] Editor-in-chief of *Woman's Day.*

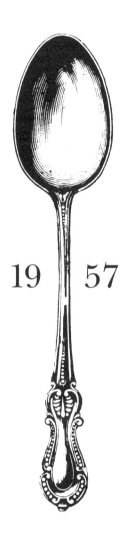

19　57

Failing to buy an old Greenwich Village restaurant, the Grand Ticino, in January, JB continued to look for a suitable place in the Connecticut countryside. He also became a consultant for a new restaurant in Philadelphia, owned by Helen and Charles Wilson. In March he began cooking classes with Florence Aaron and Paula Peck, who would become a food authority in her own right. On May 8 he flew to Paris on Air France, went to Cognac for several days, and returned to Paris for a week, during which he picnicked with Alice B. Toklas and the McNulties. After a few days in England and more time in Paris he departed for New York, on June 2. In the meantime the Browns were planning their first trip to Europe, with advice from JB on their itinerary. In August JB went to Le Sueur, Minnesota, to present new dishes to Green Giant. The same month he started wine classes for the staff of Restaurant Associates, and in September did a series of cooking classes with Albert Stockli at the Lexington Hotel. He went to Dallas in October for cognac demonstrations and continued on to Los Angeles, San Francisco, Portland, Seattle, and Detroit. On his return in mid-November he moved to a new apartment, at 86 West 12th Street. A few weeks later he had a bad fall at the apartment-house entrance, injuring an ankle and keeping him out of circulation for the holiday festivities, but he spent Christmas Eve with Cheryl Crawford, Ruth Norman, and Gino Cofacci at a new Restaurant Associates showplace, the Forum of the Twelve Caesars.

[36 West 12th Street
New York
January 12, 1957]

Dearest Helen —

I have just had a bitter disappointment. I heard that my darling little Grand Ticino restaurant, which I have known for years and years, was for sale. I made up my mind I wanted it, Gino was all for it, Bill White made the overtures, and it seemed right in the bag. Suddenly the owner decided she would die rather than give it up. So there it is. I really want to do a small restaurant, Helen, worse than anything in the world. You should weaken, after your trip to Europe, and do it with me. I would even give up all and go to California.

Did I tell you that I have been approached to play Nero Wolfe on TV for an indefinite number of weeks? If it happens we may never have to work again, any of us. But that is just another of those things which may or may not come along. I only believe things now when they are in my hand in the form of checks.

J. Walter Thompson accepted my recipe for mustard bread. They had Breuhl do a picture of it, and the home economist at Breuhl's called me to ask for the exact dimensions of the French loaf I used. Then she made a larger loaf and overcooked it. They couldn't find me, so they called André. He went down, doubled the recipe and cut the size of the loaf, and it came out pale as a virgin. Now after about twelve transparencies I have to go up on Monday and do another couple of loaves for pictures. Isn't it unbelievable? Do you know, though, I'm beginning to like French's mustard for certain things. For it is not mustard at all but a turmeric cream.

Their home ec gal sent down a recipe using Worcestershire sauce. Cook one bunch of broccoli. Drain. Arrange on a dish. Cover with hollandaise sauce. Then combine ¼ cup of Worcestershire sauce, ¼ cup melted butter and 1 cup of crumbs, and pour over the hollandaise sauce!!!!!! Then cover with ¼ cup of grated Parmesan cheese!!!!!!!!!

Needless to say, I love exclamation points.

Love and kisses,

J

Edward Gottlieb & Associates Ltd.
New York
January 18, 1957

Dearest Helen —

Did I see you praise *The Mistress Cooks* somewhere? I think the author [Peter Gray] is filled with misinformation. I fight his feeling that he is the Escoffier of America, for he has not even bothered to read Montagné and Ali-Bab[1] and some of the others who *know* what they are talking about. If you could only read enough gastronomic French to get through the de Pomiane book you would know why I consider this man stuffy. Besides which, I am getting to the point where the esoteric food people give me a pain. Pomiane gives a real reason for everything he does and brings things down to earth so that everyone can do them. His chapters on technograstronomie are superb.

Our Commanderie de Bontemps de Médoc dinner was delicious and simple. We had some Cramant Blanc de Blancs with cheese pastries, light as puff paste can be. Then they passed trays of oysters with lemon. We drank a Domaine de Chevalier with that and went to table to a very small cup of triple consommé, perfectly roasted pheasants, a chestnut purée, and braised celery. A couple of good 1928 wines with this and then a cheese board with an 1886 claret. And to finish off, a Cordial Médoc soufflé.

Love and much kissing,

J

---

[1] Auguste Escoffier, the great French-born chef and culinary writer, who practiced his art at the Savoy and Carlton hotels in London. Prosper Montagné, also a renowned French chef, was the author of the monumental *Larousse Gastronomique*. Ali-Bab (Henri Babinski) was a French mining engineer who turned to food as a second profession and wrote the famous food treatise *Gastronomie Pratique*.

Pasadena
[January 1957]

[Dear Jim,]

As for *Mistress Cook* I did not say that it was a great example of classic cuisine. I did say, and still mean, that it was an idea book. . . . Of course I don't agree with you that the only people who know anything are Ali-Bab and Montagné. They may be tops in French cuisine — that I wouldn't deny — but there are other people who know something about cooking even if it isn't classic. I believe there is room for both in this badly fed world of ours.

We love you,
H

36 West 12th Street
New York
[February 1957]

Dearest Helen —

I didn't say that the only people who knew anything were Ali-Bab and Montagné. I think Gray has charm and wit and other fine attributes, but I think he has the great fault of not bending to modern developments. He is a scholar. I think Mundt has a more delightful quality although some of his recipes are terrible — but then so do people feel that way about me and you. They are both engrossing reading. MFK still holds the key to that kind of food writing, though — in this country, anyway.

But I'm getting tired of the esoteric, and I'm coming down to earth with a great bang and finding the simple things by far the best of all — our Commanderie dinner, and the dinner I gave the boys the other night — a wonderful antipasto platter, a capon flamed with cognac, mushrooms and green rice, and a Grand Marnier mousse — what could be simpler? Gino's and my menus here are the quickest things in the world, but good. Last night, for example, we ate a halibut steak with butter, onion slices and thin lemon slices, baked at 425 for 18 minutes. With this, merely a salad and cheese. The night before, we ate a flank steak with rice, salad, cheese and fruit. Tonight we are eating tongue, spinach and fried rice. We get wonderful little tongues in packages all cooked and skinned, which heat in ten minutes in hot water and are delicious. Well, this is not peasant food, but it is good simple food. That is what I want people to realize — that natural foods without embellishment taste wonderful if they are well cooked. Maybe I will write a book someday soon and say all those things.

We went to the country over the weekend with Agnes and Bill and looked at places till we were red in the face and destroyed in the fanny. Nothing. Agnes wants us to take a great barn in Sharon [Connecticut], which could, with the indulgence of great numbers of people, become something, but what I want is a restaurant that is small and good and expensive — not a place where I have to rent rooms to people and all the rest of it. The right one will come one day. I could cry when I see the Grand Ticino and know that the old lady will never give it up. But then I guess it wasn't for me.

I went to Rochester today to interview the Bernz people, who are bringing out a grill with ceramic tile and a propane gas tank. We cooked 3-inch pork chops, steaks, 3-inch lamb chops, fish and chicken on the thing, and the flavor and texture were sensational. It is portable, simple to operate and clean. It is revolutionary. I am going to do a short booklet for them and probably do some of the promotion work. One more tedious job, but that seems to be what pays the money.

What can I do to help you about the European jaunt?

Love and kisses,
JB

[36 West 12th Street
New York
February 5, 1957]

Dearest Helen —

Did I tell you that Mrs. Martin is putting her Nantucket place up for sale? I wish to God we could have it and run it, the three of us. It is three months of real work, but it is gratifying, and then you have time for yourself.

Helen's omelet party at the church on Sunday was a tremendous success. Stanish made over 400 omelets, and there were wonderful brownies and all manner of things to make a delicious brunch. Though you know, I can no longer put a forkful of omelet into my mouth — they have become so rich and cloying to me. And this was the day that Rudolph presented me with one of his omelet pans, the heavy cast aluminum ones which he has made specially.

This morning, after all the French's mustard things had been set, they changed their minds again. I blew my top and said they had taken twice as much in value for recipes created for them as they were paying and that I was absolutely fed up with it all.

Kiki's birthday party was fun. I roasted a turkey but could only get an eviscerated frozen one. I tell you, they toughen when they are frozen. This is the second one I have done. I roasted it with cheesecloth and butter at high heat for an hour, then down to 350 and then to 300, and after four hours it was tough, and there was practically no turkey fat in the pan. I was bitterly disappointed with it, for there is nothing as uninteresting as a tough turkey, unless it is an overdone one.

I found a different cheesecake this week in a little Viennese shop. They make a rich sweet pastry and roll it thick. This goes into a square pan, which is filled with cottage cheese, raisins, currants, sugar and eggs, with strips of pastry across the top. It is swished with melted butter and baked. Try it if you're in the mood.

I also found a most obscure French one, which is mashed potatoes, to which you add 1 cup of sugar, 3 eggs, 3 tablespoons of flour and 1 cup of curd cheese for each 3 cups of mashed potatoes. Form it into a cake and bake, brushing with butter.

Just did my first travel article ["Costa Brava"] for *House and Garden.*

Love and kisses,

J

[36 West 12th Street
New York
February 6, 1957]

Helen, dear —

I'm redoing my Costa Brava piece. Seems I didn't get enough thunder in it. Also doing a quickie on restaurants for *Harper's Bazaar,* and so it goes.

Had lunch with Irma Rhode and her mother today, who at 82, having lived in Germany through two wars, is really wonderful — and looks like Bill, who was handsome as hell.[1] We ate Esterhazy steak, broccoli, carrots, rolls and cheesecake — as German a lunch as you could imagine, with coffee and cake afterwards in another bedecked corner. I wanted Irma's old recipes for cheesecake and got them all. She does the typically German ones, with either a kuchen dough or a Meurbe Teig and pot cheese — the dry, raisiny kind so many people like.

Did veal chops on the propane-gas grill tonight. They were 1½ inches thick. Seared them in the flame for two minutes on each side, then put them in foil with butter, tarragon, salt and parsley. Ten minutes on each side and they were superb. No dirt, no utensils.

Yrs., with fatigue,

J

---

[1] Irma Rhode and her brother, Bill, both born in Berlin, started a catering service, Hors d'Oeuvre, Inc., with JB in 1939.

[36 West 12th Street
New York
March 29/30, 1957]

Helen —

I had luncheon with Myra Waldo yesterday. She really doesn't deserve the criticism she gets, because she can cook like a fiend. She had a simple but delicious luncheon, and we discussed a plan she has for our mutual benefit. She has tremendous respect for you, by the way.

I have started my small class with Paula Peck and Florence Aaron[1] on Tuesday mornings at Paula's apartment. This woman is probably the finest cook I know and the most brilliant technician, and Florence is fast becoming the same. We are going to do just one thing each time we meet. For example, next week we are doing aspics. Fish and vegetable. It is a most intelligent approach to the question. I am really looking forward to this.

I was offered half-interest in a restaurant this week to use my name and remake the place according to my ideas, but I decided it wasn't for me at all, at all. It isn't the type place I want, and it has no challenge. I just couldn't be less interested in making what is a steak and chop house more profitable than it is now.[2]

Saturday: Went to Nom Wah today for lunch and had a wonderful time. We ate tea lunch till it came out of our ears. Then the owner sent us a huge dish of lo mein and after that little custard tarts and steamed sponge cake. And sent us home with boxes of cookies and cakes.

I'm doing sukiyaki and such for fourteen tomorrow night in three electric skillets. I have pork and beef and shall use fresh asparagus, Chinese mustard, and both fresh and black mushrooms in it, with long rice and some of those wonderful pickled scallions on the side. To begin, I'm having French bread with anchoiade, made with figs, almonds, anchovies, herbs, oil and garlic, spread on the bread and toasted. Then I shall give each person an infinitesimal cup of strong turtle soup while the sukiyaki cooks. I just found about six quarts of turtle broth I bought ages ago for nothing at a sale and will use it to gain space. For dessert, for this international meal, Alice Toklas's prunes with whipped cream. I hope they can stand it.

You will have the time of your life.

Love,

JB

---

[1] Paula Peck, a self-taught cook, became a virtuoso pastry chef and an instructor in JB's cooking classes. She wrote the highly praised *The Art of Baking.* Florence Aaron was the wife of Sam Aaron, of Sherry Wine & Spirits.

[2] This was probably the Philadelphia restaurant run by the champion golfer Helen Sigel Wilson and her husband, Charles. JB changed his mind, became a consultant for this restaurant as well as for two others, and, according to Julie Dannenbaum, brought good food to Philadelphia.

Paris
July 8, 1957

James darling,

You must stop being so unhappy in your work. If you hate it so much, for God's sake quit the jobs you don't like and go into the restaurant business. I am almost convinced that you would be happiest in it. And I have discovered that the great chefs around here have, for the most part, very limited menus. . . . Perfect a few dishes and have them as your specialities. . . .

You're sweet to think I could do Jane's job.[1] But remember, dear boy, that we live in California.

H

---

[1] Jane Nickerson was leaving the *New York Times.*

[36 West 12th Street
New York
July 12, 1957]

My dearest Helen and Philip —

Welcome home.

Green Giant has come through, the Philadelphians [Charles and Helen Sigel Wilson] are starting the place in the park next week,[1] and I am getting set for the fall. I just had a long session about training work with wines I am to do for Restaurant Associates. Teaching their staff and having once-a-week tastings.

I go to Dallas on the 19th of October, then to you on the 26th. Bill [Kaduson] and possibly Gottlieb will join me there, and we want to do the cognac and coffee party at your house and garden as soon after that as possible — Halloween?

In Dallas at Neiman's I have to do flaming foods one afternoon, cold foods for a buffet another, and then one afternoon on table settings, glassware and how to use it, and all that sort of crap.

They want me three days a week in Philadelphia, but that is just not in the picture at this writing. I am going once and possibly twice until the place gets started. It is only supposed to be a summer deal. We are going to run a nightly buffet till theatre time and then have three great specialties after that. If this works we may keep the thing going till Thanksgiving. Funny, the things that catch on in a restaurant. Do you know what has become the most popular dish in Philadelphia? — lentil salad — and everyone is trying to imitate it. Just as the beans with tuna have become something that Chillingsworth on the Cape cannot live without.

My Green Giant work is all niblets and wax beans. Any ideas on the latter? I have done a wonderful quiche with bacon, niblets and Switzerland cheese. For wax beans I am thinking up new things to be done in the can — flavors and textures which will hold.

I ordered the blowtorch to be sent to you.[2] Paula Peck tells me she is enchanted with the one I let her have to try, and I have used mine a number of times with great success.

Helen, you are probably right. I feel that a restaurant is the thing for me after this year, when I want to settle. I want it to be on the ocean and have been thinking of somewhere between Monterey and the Mexican border. I agree with you — a limited menu with specialties, and almost the same thing every day, with some seasonal changes. It must be a place where people will come especially. Wish of all wishes, that you had the same idea. It could be the Pyramide of this country, with both of us. I want to look for a place when I am there. See what you can come up with. But the ocean must be in the picture.

We still may be moving to the corner [of 12th Street]. If so, and we do decide to go to the Coast, there will always be a little income from renting the place furnished — at least a hundred dollars a month can be made that way, and you don't need to leave all your best furniture.

Welcome, thrice welcome, genii of the stomach and gullet.

Love,

J

---

[1] Belmont Mansion in Fairmount Park.

[2] In connection with a promotion campaign to use the blowtorch in cooking.

[36 West 12th Street
New York
July 1957]

Helen, dear —

The main reason for moving is that I can no longer cope with the sink I have, and the landlady will do nothing about it. And as far as investment is concerned, everything I have is movable. I think one of the magazines — either *House and Garden* or *Woman's Day* — will do the kitchen for me, so that I have very little to do. Also, I want an electric stove. This gas is terrible, and the less I have to do with it the better.

The restaurant in Philadelphia got going on the hottest day in thirty years. It was cool on top of the hill, however, and we had about one hundred the first night for the buffet. We had homemade madrilene, gazpacho, with a tray of things to add, cold halibut with sauce verte, lentil salad, onions à la Grecque, a vegetable bowl, mushroom salad, cold crown of pork with horseradish cream, French potato salad, country ham (from Great Valley Farms), tiny veal rolls, roast filet, rissole potatoes, tomatoes Provençale, and risi e bisi. The desserts — fresh plum parfait, lemon tarts, and peaches with raspberry sauce. The buffet is $4.85 and the desserts 70 and 90 cents.

Everyone seemed quite content, and the food did come through like a million, though it was well laced with sweat. Both Saturday and Monday we had workmen underfoot every second.

Well, work piles up and I don't know when I shall get any rest. I am taking five days around Labor Day, and I'm not going to do a bleeding thing but sit on the Nantucket beach and bask in the water. Mrs. Martin's good food will do me for sustenance.

[JB]

[36 West 12th Street
New York]
August 1, 1957

My dearest Browns —

Last night Florence Aaron and Paula Peck gave me a dinner party. The menu reads "Prepared by two gastronomic disciples of James Beard." The menu —

Coquille en croûte — and what croûte!

Boeuf à la Tuscany — thin slices of raw filet in oil, lemon juice and seasonings, marinated for 24 hours

Cuban bread

Tomatoes stuffed with spinach, garlic and sorrel

Zucchini stuffed with rice, pine nuts and a bit of seasoning, cooked in a sauce à la Grecque and served with a sauce made with egg yolks and some of the Grecque

A delicate mousse of duck livers

Peaches cooked in old port and served with homemade sour cream and millions of little dry petits fours — fabulous ones

The homemade sour cream is superb — 5 tablespoons of buttermilk to each pint of heavy cream, stir and leave for 24 hours. Stir again and refrigerate for 24 hours longer, stirring once in a while to prevent separation. This cream is twice as heavy as the other and will whip. An old Department of Agriculture recipe, and it is wonderful.

The wines — Corton-Charlemagne 1955
                    Clos de la Roche 1952
                    Latricières-Chambertin 1952
                    Champagne Reserve Rainier IV

Then some of the new framboise that Frank Schoonmaker buys for Sam [Aaron], which is delicious. It was a delightful evening, with the Pecks, the Aarons, the Masons, the Herb Alexanders,[1] and Jane and Alex [Steinberg], as well as Gino and me. I was very proud of my two star pupils.

The Philadelphia place is going very well. I work awfully hard to get it into the state it's in, I can tell you. You show the cooks how to do something and get the flavor right, and still they will go and do it another way the next time. You just have to stand over them with a whip. However, they have learned a lot in the time they have had. We can give people a perfect Poulet à la Crème, trout in port-wine jelly, several different pâtés, a good ratatouille, and risi e bisi (you are right, rice and peas). Also, the fresh plum parfaits and fresh plum tarts are good, and the peach Melbas with fresh fruit. The cold salmon and halibut, the pork tonnato and such dishes, they really do with a flair. But Jesus, then they'll go and make veal rolls so thick they look like sewer pipes and send out filets deliberately overcooked. And breakage! My restaurant will have two robots and me and one other person. But I love it.

Albert and I are doing six classes in September in the new experimental kitchen at the Lexington Hotel. They are going to do wonderful things at the new restaurant in Rockefeller Center [Forum of the Twelve Caesars], but you'll be here for that opening, probably. And for the new apartment.

Love and kisses,

J

---

[1] Herb Alexander was publisher of Pocket Books.

[36 West 12th Street
New York
August 24, 1957]

My dear Helen —

I am just back from Le Sueur and Chicago. It seems that my six niblet recipes upset the whole organization [Green Giant]. They had never thought of doing any of the simple things I did with corn, and now I have to do the same things with peas. The setup in Le Sueur is wonderful in its way. The whole town is Green Giant. The board of directors are professional board sitters — Pillsbury, General Mills, American Can, Continental Can, etc. I did a report on wax beans, and we had some cans of green beans with various seasonings — small whole ones, sweet and sour, and green beans canned with a small amount of dill, which only shows up in the aftertaste. I am hoping this remains a good contact for a few years. They seemed to appreciate what I had to say about the products and took my criticisms nicely.

I don't know spaghetti carbonara. Neither does Gino. Give the recipe at once so that we may try it. Tonight Gino made a tomato soufflé to go with some wonderful skirt steaks we had. My butcher gives me really elegant skirts about once a week — better than flanks lately.

I must say that the Middle West this time added but little to my gastronomic memories. We did have superb smoked spareribs at the country club last night, along with great platters of freshly cut ears of their prize Goldkist corn.

I have a private lesson with young Arthur Vandenburg, son of the late senator, who said he has to take back a few new French recipes to Florida with him. I'm hoping the winter will bring a goodly number of private students. The class is full already, with no announcements whatsoever. People call every day out of the blue to ask if there is going to be a class. This one will tell whether or not there is to be any profit in such an enterprise. Please God there will be.

I'm tired and want the joy of my own bed after one night on the train and the other in a hotel.

Love to you both,

J

36 West 12th Street
New York
[September 1957]

[Dear Helen —]

How about you, Paula and I doing a Mexican buffet for Florence Crittenton the week you are here? We can have Pierre d'Argout's[1] apartment or Ruth's and Cheryl's and could do a grand one.

Jane's successor [at the *New York Times*] is to be Craig Claiborne, who has worked with Ann for so long. Jane and I had a long talk about this last night and both agreed that you were the only person who could have done the job as we feel it should be done. But that is in the family and never breathe it.

Nantucket was a bitter disappointment. However, we had beautiful food at Mrs. Martin's [The Mad Hatter] and did get some rest, and the beach thrown in. Had her really wonderful cheesecake one night, which is the best I have ever eaten. And her wonderful clam bisque. And a good pâté en croûte, for which she uses mostly beef! And fresh bluefish out of the sea less than an hour before it is served. Wonderful Portuguese bread for breakfast, toasted and drenched with butter. This is a restaurant of greatness run entirely by non-professionals, all but one being students. With the executive ability of Mrs. Martin. Friday night there were three hundred dinners, but she was calm, and nothing ran out. And practically everything has some last minute preparation attached to it.

Last night I did a tenderloin of veal with port and tarragon, which proved to be right delicious. I am doing some port work and felt this was a good try. Browned the veal, added tarragon and port, and braised it covered for a while, then added cream for the last ten minutes or so. Try it.

I know what you mean by a thing not coming. I simply get out of the house, take myself somewhere for lunch, and either go shopping or to a movie. I usually get an idea and rush home and start working. This is what I call the period of gestation. Or buy something you shouldn't and your conscience works on you and gets you started so you can pay for it.

I'm doing a tiny leg of lamb on the spit tonight — and beans — that's all.

Love,

J

---

[1] Of the architectural-design firm d'Argout, Ferguson, Inc., which did promotion, packaging, and windows for clients such as Baccarat and Chanel.

Pasadena
September 12, 1957

James dearest,

Certainly I will do a Mexican dinner for Florence Crittendon. Please tell Helen so. . . . Can you buy tortillas in New York? . . . As for Paula — won't too many cooks spoil the mole?

H

[36 West 12th Street
New York
September 16, 1957]

Dearest Helen —

We had a lovely weekend with the girls and hated to leave. We tried spaghetti carbonara with smoked loin last night, and it was delicious. Also Cheryl made a wonderful antipasto, and I added to it with real imported prosciutto — delicious. For lunch today I made an eggplant parmigiana with sausage on top — with eggplant from the garden.

The school went over with a bang. Albert got started demonstrating sauces and couldn't stop. We had too much on the menu and they ate themselves into oblivion. It's nice, though, to have a room in the hotel where they can sit down and have a waiter take care of them. This week is Viennese, and we are doing a croustade with egg and pâté, champagne cabbage,* goulash and all the rest of it.

My wine course got started on Wednesday. I have fifteen, and they know nothing of wine at all. This is for six weeks only and may start again when I come back.

Going to four parties for Jane this week. She leaves next week for Florida, and how we all hate to see her go. She has done more for dignified food coverage than anyone. Everyone will miss her keenly, and I more than most, for she was a good friend and a most amusing person always.

Love and kisses,
Jim

---

* Recipe.

[36 West 12th Street
New York
September 22, 1957]

My dear Helen —

The Nickerson Farewell Social Season is almost over. The Farnols had a beautiful party, with smoked trout in jelly with horseradish cream, chicken Kiev, and a fabulously good raspberry soufflé with fresh raspberries and cream. Then came my and Bill Kaduson's party at the Italian Pavilion, with the most beautiful antipasto table you ever saw, stracciatella, veal with mozzarella, thin strips of zucchini with crumbs, deep fried, spinach, and a zuppa inglese which was a dream. Sam brought a magnum of La Tâche 1949, which proved to be liquid gold, and so the party really had éclat. André had a party on Friday done by his French chef, with vichyssoise, a cheese soufflé, cold striped bass with green aïoli and Salade Russe, and the chef's special sherbet, made with a purée of melon, heavy syrup, orange and lemon — the most beautiful frozen dessert it has been my privilege to eat. Helen's party comes next, on Tuesday.

The Crittenton dinner is November 19 at Cheryl and Ruth's. They have practically sold it out already to their friends — it will be a very theatrical crowd — and Cheryl is having a guitarist hidden somewhere to play soft music. Ann is going to do the Thanksgiving one with me. Pierre d'Argout has given his house, and we shall do it for twenty. Cranberries and all!

We went to *Carousel* this afternoon and then had dinner with a publicity gal who is always hounding me for dates and whom I see about twice a year. She is sweet and has a hard time, and I feel we should be nice to those people who struggle for existence.

Did I tell you that Myra has done a pasta cookbook for *House and Garden,* which ruins your chances of same, damn it. Why not try *House Beautiful* now that they are accepting some free-lance work? Or why not try *House and Garden* with an Italian travel piece and bring in the pasta?

> Love and all that,
>
> J

> Pasadena
> October 14, 1957

James dear,

What the hell is all this talk about staying at the Green? If you did, Ward and Marka would be deeply hurt, and I don't blame them. They have been most cordial in their invitation to you, and I cannot for the life of me understand why you have decided not to stay with them.

> [H]

> The Statler Hilton
> Dallas
> [October 17, 1957]

Helen —

For God's sake, I didn't mean to upset you — I was only making plans. I don't mind staying with the Ritchies[1] only I am not a very good guest unless I feel completely at home, as I do with you and Philip or a few other people. It is not that I have anything against either Ward or Marka, merely that sometimes, believe it or not, a certain shy quality comes out in me — or didn't you know that I occasionally have to beat myself into going to parties and dinners. My stomach turns over seventy times seven. I cannot help this silly thing, but it has lasted all of my life. That is why I go through tortures every time I make a public appearance.

The first show [at Neiman Marcus] went off with a bang. I am almost touching the ceiling on a runway they use for the fashion show, with red velvet draped all around me. Stanley Marcus gave me a big introduction, and I think everything went well. At least one woman wants to come to New York for a week and take four hours' private work a day at twenty dollars an hour. Also wants me to come back here and give her maid private lessons at the same price.

I did a fish flambé, a Poulet Flambé with sauce, stuffed butterfly steaks, cognacked sweet potato fingers, and broiled flaming peaches, and I did a baked Alaska with the blowtorch and eggshells filled with cognac for a finale. This, in fifty-five minutes flat!

Have had the most awful food most places. Today's fashion group lunch reached a new low. Chicken stuffed with bread, cooked three days ago, and overcooked. It fell apart when the knife hit it. And fruit cup, a fruit salad in Jell-O, and fruit with ice cream for dessert.

Love and kisses,
Jim

---

[1] Ward Ritchie owned a small press in Southern California and published a number of HEB's cookbooks. Marka was his wife.

36 West 12th Street
New York
[December 1, 1957]

My dear Helen —

The Crittenton Thanksgiving dinner went very well, although it was a hell of a lot of work. Irma Rhode came to the rescue, and we used her oven for one bird and the d'Argout for the other. Two different stuffings — one with toasted Italian bread crumbs, tarragon, chestnuts, onion and butter; the other, with apples, nuts, raisins and butter by the ton. The apples in ginger syrup were a sensation, and our mincemeat. Had a pound and a half of caviar to start off with and then turtle soup with Madeira. The turnips with mushrooms were loved by all. The pumpkin pie, we covered with brown sugar and chopped pecans and glazed it.

Reading galleys of a book by Waverly Root to be published by Knopf soon, called *The Food of France,* which is the book to end all on French food — absolutely superb. Have Philip find out when it is to be published. You'll want it at once.

Love to Philip and all,
J

86 West 12th Street
New York
December 12, 1957

Helen, dear —

I am laid up in the hospital with a bad ankle. I slipped on the sidewalk and fell down the two entrance steps of the new house and tore the tendons in my left foot. It is nothing serious, and I am lying in a hospital bed trying to catch up on all the things that need doing.

I expect to be home Monday or Tuesday at the latest, and although I will have to keep a foot off the ground, I can accomplish more than sitting or lying here looking out at the East River.

Love,
Jim

86 West 12th Street
New York
[December 1957]

Dearest Helen —

I am still incapacitated to a degree. I just cannot walk around without pain. I have to shape my life for the next month or so to going one place a day and staying close to a stool for most of the time. It's a bloody nuisance but perhaps I shall get some more work done.

I love my stove. Why I used gas for all these years, I don't know. It bakes perfectly and is fast and efficient, and with two ovens I can do anything. It even broils well and browns things. It has an electric meat thermometer which rings a bell when your temperature is reached!

The new Forum [of the Twelve Caesars] is open and simply beautiful. I think Albert is overdoing it again with richness, which is his greatest fault and one which is not alone his.

I am having to forgo most of the parties on the Christmas spike but hope to get in one or two. Christmas morning Cheryl and Ruth come here for breakfast, and then we may drive around the park and have supper in front of the fire at their house.

Love and all that.

JB

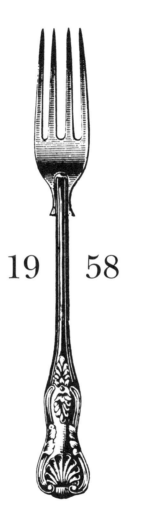

19 | 58

JB went to the Home Economist convention in Chicago in February. On April 15 he sailed for France on the *United States* and in Paris lunched with Alice B. Toklas. He visited the wine country of Alsace and the Moselle Valley, went on to Geneva and the Auberge du Père Bise in Talloires, where his favorite restaurant was located, then traveled to Barcelona and Madrid. In Jerez he was a guest of the sherry producers. He returned to New York on the *Independence* on May 24. In June he once again was a judge at the chicken festival in Maryland, and during the rest of the summer he searched the Eastern Shore for a restaurant site. In August, Clare Boothe Luce became a pupil. For several months JB had helped develop a series of sauces for Nestlé, and at a final presentation in October ten were chosen for a marketing test The same month JB traveled to Richmond, New Orleans, Boston, and Chicago. On November 15 he went to Los Angeles for a week and then north to San Francisco, returning to Pasadena to spend Thanksgiving with the Browns.

[86 West 12th Street
New York
February 3, 1958]

Dearest Helen —

I had a wonderful time in Chicago, and for the HEWIB [Home Economist Women in Business] benefit we had over 325 persons. I worked for two hours and did the usual gamut, and they wanted more. A very nice audience it was, too. I like the gals from Armour, who are really pretty solid. I was treated beautifully and had service from all sides. Mary Burke[1] from *House and Garden* was there. We gave out the "Pork Cook Book" and some of the "Corkscrew" columns, and Mary and I had a riotous trip home on the Century.

I had a day with Green Giant doing corn in foil for summer and planning another year's work. They are nice and don't fuss and stew and worry the way the others do, and really get to work. Their, or rather, their PR agency's [Leo Burnett] home economist, who is a glamour girl of the first water, was my assistant on stage the night of the demonstration, and a real darling she is. The next day we built charcoal fires in the Leo Burnett kitchens and grilled corn in foil with several different combinations, including a hot corn relish that is quite wonderful.

Jessica and Milt[2] came to lunch yesterday. They brought me a wild goose, which I shall have tonight. I gave them some ham — I had bought one at Christmas and just got around to cooking it, one of the Pennsylvania Dutch ones. Then we had corn with Gruyère, Parmesan, cream, eggs and garlic butter baked with ripe olive rings in it — one of the things I did for Green Giant niblets, which I like very much. Brioche and peach preserves, champagne, and coffee, with hazelnut macaroons. Simple as hell. As yet I can only have four people unless it is buffet. The new table is not in place yet, and so I stick to the kitchen table.

Got my professional Waring, and it is like handling a skyscraper.

Love and all that,

J

---

[1] Merchandising editor at *House and Garden.*
[2] Jessica McLachlin, who did public relations for the Wine Institute of California, and her husband, Dr. Milton Greengard.

[86 West 12th Street
New York
February 13, 1958]

Dear Helen —

For classes last night we did two different coq au vin recipes — white and red, and one with a brioche crust. Then we did four hors d'oeuvre, one of them sausage in brioche. Then omelet soufflés — four different versions. Albert works hard and so do I, and we all have a wonderfully good time.

Crazy about my new Blendor. It is a dream, that big one, for certain things. For soups, for meats and for quenelles — superb. You must have one sometime soon.

Helen and I had lunch at Quo Vadis today — really my favorite restaurant in New York — simple and delicious food, in the right amounts and perfectly served. More and more I turn to Helen for the advice I want and find she is nearly always right about it.

I'm in love with Portland [Hoffa] Allen.[1] She is a darling pupil, with great interest in what she is doing and a pride in her accomplishments. Couldn't be nicer.

[JB]

---

[1] Actress on the Fred Allen radio program and Allen's wife.

86 West 12th Street
New York
[March 8, 1958]

Dearest Helen —

Tuesday morning a class here with six advanced gals and John Clancy.[1] We did a saddle of veal Prince Orloff — 18 pounds — and Blendor hollandaise — and of course the two sauces for the veal. And a soufflé which is a triumph — lemon, macaroons soaked in Grand Marnier, then a Grand Marnier soufflé mixture, and more soaked macaroons on top of that. It comes up like a mountain, and the two flavors together are superb. That finished after three, and I had the evening class at five.

Thursday, a class of six for puff paste, with Paula helping me. I had to leave that to go to my wine class at the Forum, and then home to dress and back to the Forum, where I had to host a party. Home at twelve, took the nine-thirty to Philadelphia Friday morning, and got back to meet Gino for dinner at eight-thirty. A slightly full week.

I am doing a stuffed breast of veal tonight, with fresh asparagus and corn with almonds. I am on a new kick for Green Giant — twenty-five recipes throughout the year — any ideas?

The big news is that Bettina and Mac are on the way back. They sail April 17 and will be here indefinitely. Mac will be with Gottlieb and Bettina will free-lance. I am sick, for I may be going to Europe on the 15th for a month and will just miss them. I sail back on the *Independence* on the 19th of May. A month with practically nothing to do seems the answer to all my problems at this particular point, and I shall just loll and be a fool tourist once my little chores are done.

[JB]

---

[1] John Clancy later cooked at Chillingsworth on Cape Cod and at The Coach House in New York, and was test kitchen chef for the *Time-Life Foods of the World* cookbook series.

[86 West 12th Street
New York
March 23, 1958]

Dearest Helen —

Returned from Washington and Philadelphia this morning at two. Went to Washington in the worst snowstorm of the year, on the only plane to arrive for twelve hours — a miracle. Was three hours late but got there. This was for Gottlieb's Puerto Rican rum account. Did three radio shows and presided at a party for 200, then took the train for Philadelphia at nine, arriving around midnight. Had dinner and a good night's sleep and spent the day at the Wilsons' restaurant getting ready a buffet.

We boned legs and shoulders of lamb last week and kept them in a red wine marinade for a week, then roasted them and served them with polenta squares and a sauce Diable. We boned turkeys, rolled them with shallots, parsley and thyme, roasted them and served them with a sauce Suprême. I'll never roast turkey any other way. We had lentil salad; peas Piedmontese — done with thick bacon, mint, garlic, olive oil and a touch of vinegar; roast filet and potatoes Anna; an antipasto and tomatoes with lobster. All this for the Saturday-night buffet. Despite the weather we had 125 people.

Craig has just been accepted at the *New York Times* on a permanent basis and given a raise. He loves it and is doing a fine job.

My cassoulet party was such a success that Helen used the same menu when she had a big party on Thursday night.

Love,

J

[86 West 12th Street
New York
March 29, 1958]

Dear Helen —

Sidney Reich has written me that he is anxious to have a recipe booklet for the blowtorch and thought I had made overtures to you. I shall have to say I did and that he can call you about it, if you think you want to do it. Why not? You have all the stuff at hand.

Had a fine time in Boston. The party was the right size, and I did four dishes. People tasted and stayed forever. Went over to the Cape for a day, and Steve had asked twelve people for dinner who wanted to do a course with me. So he said they could come and cook dinner under my direction. We started with my favorite new appetizer — crabmeat sautéed with onion, green pepper, tarragon and a little sherry and then flambéed with cognac. After that, steak au poivre, tiny new potatoes, asparagus with Blendor hollandaise, and baked bananas with kirsch — the bananas baked in their skins. They ate like fiends and worked in the same temper. One of them owns a big restaurant and is dying to have food as good as Steve's. He's building a buttery this year and wishes we two could run it together for the summer.

Green Giant seem to be pleased as hell about my stuff this year and tonight I have to make corn fritters for another thing they are doing.

I guess, unless I can rent my apartment furnished for a fine price, I have to stay here. It has cost so much already, and it is so perfect, if it were not for the noise, that I should hate to move. It is beginning to take final shape now and is really going to be smart. The kitchen is most convenient, and how I adore the portable dishwasher — get one, dearie.

Yes, my European trip is still on and something is added. Instead of spending a week in Paris I am going to the wine country of Germany with Frank, which is what I have wanted to do for a long time and swore I would never do until I went with him. I shall meet him in Strasbourg and go to the Rhine and Moselle country. I shall fly to Geneva and Annecy from there and thence to Spain. How I need those days on the ship to rest.

Just tried my corn fritters. They are the kind we used to have at home, not deep-fried. This is for an advertising tie-in with Aunt Jemima. I used 2 eggs separated, 1 cup of Aunt Jemima, 1 cup of niblets, 1 cup of milk, and 3 tablespoons of melted butter, and then folded in the egg whites. The fritters were surprisingly light and fluffy. The recipe Green Giant had been given produced greasy, horrible things. These were like light little pancakes with corn. With bacon and maple syrup they would be wonderful.

We're having a strudel class on Monday. Six eager beavers are coming along, and I think they will leave a trail of strudel all over the place. Tuesday we are having just three in the class and doing Poulet Espagnole, chicken Mexican and chocolate mousse — could anything be more confused? I have a final class the day before I sail — with matelote [d'anguille Normande], pauchouse [Bourguignonne] and paupiettes of sole.

Gino and I are having a little roast of beef, some potatoes in the pan and a salad — and a bottle of Lascombes '52. We won't starve on that.

Love,

J

[86 West 12th Street
New York
April 1958]

Helen —

The strudel class met on Monday, and we had strudel over the whole house. We made cabbage, fruit and nut, two kinds of cheese and crabmeat strudels. I find the dough made with only whites is so much better than the one with yolks. It is more crisp, and the texture is different and a hundred percent more delicate. I made the cabbage strudel again last night to go with a beautiful pheasant one of the pupils brought me and which I have had in the freezing compartment. It was fat and tender and juicy — so different from the usual run.

Today I'm trying to get a cabrito [kid]. I'm going away over Easter to Philadelphia, where we are going to have baby lamb for the buffet on Saturday night. We got fifteen-pounders, and they should turn out to be sheer heaven. Also doing Easter eggs in aspic and a pea pie. And Coq au Vin Rouge.

Monday night I'm having Peggy and Kiki, John Ferrone and his friend Johan Theron, and Irma Rhode for supper. Crabmeat strudel, chicken Mexican with olives, chilies and almonds, plenta of polenta (I couldn't resist this), raw asparagus and endive with green mayonnaise, and savarin with strawberries and whipped cream. I'm ashamed that they haven't been here, but we still aren't settled. No dining table yet and no curtains, but I guess they can live through that.

Alice Petersen[1] had me to dinner on Monday, with Al and Dora McCann.[2] She is an amazing cook but has no sense of how to build menus, an art that I fear is ending. We had millions of canapés — good pâté, but I feel it needs crisp toast and butter and not a smear on a cracker. Then a fruit cup, roast beef with little Parisienne potatoes, asparagus cut in rounds, a huge endive salad with Roquefort dressing, and a sponge-cake-type strawberry shortcake. It was a hell of a lot of feeding, although I must say her beef was wonderful and her cake. And the dressing was superb for a Roquefort, because it was so subtly blended with the olive oil. Helen's dinner the next night was so different. Blanquette de Veau with green noodles, French bread, raw asparagus and endive, and her baba, made with leavening powder.

Monday, went to the Chambord with a group from Browne Vintners and had the most atrocious luncheon I have ever eaten, at those prices. I'm certain, for eight of us, it cost well over $300. The broiled lamb kidneys en brochette I ordered I am certain were tenderized, and they were overcooked — after I asked for them pinky — and they were cold. The smoked sturgeon was dry enough to be called jerky. And the service was appalling. This is the end of what a famous restaurant should be. I now understand why I enjoy eating at home or at my friends' more and more.

Can you tell me why I crave cottage cheese lately?

Love to you and Philip,

J

---

[1] Food editor of the *New York Daily News*.

[2] The McCanns had a radio program, "The McCanns at Home," on WOR and reported on food and fitness.

86 West 12th Street
New York
[April 6, 1958]

Helen —

Came home from Philadelphia this morning — a rainy, sloppy Easter with no letup all day. We had a nice buffet last night, and they ate baby lambs like mad — had one with its head on with a big bow, and mixed Easter eggs and golf balls, out of deference to Helen and her golf prowess. Had country hams with sherry-raisin sauce and plenty of mustard and a fabulously good coq au vin.

I leave on the *United States* on the 15th and arrive the morning of the 20th. Direct to Paris and the France et Choiseul for the first few days. I can't get a place to stay in Brussels so will go back and forth [to the World's Fair] by helicopter. I got money from the olive oil and sherry people for my trip to Spain. They will take me around as well — Seville, Madrid and Jerez, and they get me to Algeciras for the sailing.

Love and kisses,
J

Hôtel de France et Choiseul
Paris
April 23, 1958

Helen —

I just returned from a day with Alice [Toklas], who seemed to me to be brighter and gayer than ever. We had a lovely lunch at Allard — cucumber salad and radishes and Loire salmon, grilled, with a very thin hollandaise that was over the potatoes as well. More of a beurre blanc than a hollandaise. At any rate it was delicious.

We went afterwards to my knife people in the rue de Rosiers, and she bought herself some knives and brought me here in a taxi.

I watched them making soufflés at Allard, for my chair was right by the kitchen, and it seemed to me they made a meringue with the whites before they folded, and they folded with a whisk. The soufflés came out like great clouds — wonderful.

The crossing was absolute heaven, and I slept at least twelve hours a night and three or four during the day. The food was superb. I ate good caviar — they buy it here and it has no salt — the best steaks I have ever had, good European and American asparagus, excellent squab, good chicken — poularde de Bresse — fine cheese and so much fruit you couldn't begin to eat it all. I ate simply but well and just did nothing.

I'm lunching with Mapie Toulouse-Lautrec[1] on Saturday at Maxim's to discuss several things. I think she is going to do a Maxim's cookbook for Alfred Knopf and then teach in a sort of charm and housekeeping school that Maggie Vaudable[2] is considering opening here.

The hotel is being painted and is fuller than ever with Americans.

Love to you both,

J

---

[1] "Mapie," the Countess de Toulouse-Lautrec, was a household name in France. She was food editor of *Elle,* a contributor to *Réalités* and director of the cooking school of Maxim's Academy.

[2] Wife of Louis Vaudable, director of Maxim's.

[Hôtel de France et Choiseul
Paris]
April 26, [1958]

Helen dear —

Alice is taking me to lunch on Monday at a little spot in Montmartre she likes very much. Yesterday the Aarons [Jack and Frieda] and I had a perfect lunch at Chataigner — wonderful crevettes and I had Brochet au Beurre Blanc. Then we went antiquing a little, and I found one of these old pottery chicken roasters with the spit — it is a real honey and I'm thrilled with it.

Last night I had Phil Klarnet, Genevieve Seznec and Lucie Cambernous, who works for cognac here in an official capacity, for dinner Chez Pierre, where I don't think you ate. Place Valois. We started with beautiful quenelles — I think he makes the best in Paris — then Poulet à l'Estragon, perfectly roasted, with pommes frites and fresh string beans, cheese and one of his fabulous omelet soufflés — au cognac with a bit of rum and vanilla as well. We ate ourselves happy and stayed very late, drinking the best marc de Beaujolais you have ever tasted.

I'm off to Maxim's and the Countess Toulouse-Lautrec.

I'm back. She is a great person and works as hard as we do. We lunched at Maxim's with Louis Vaudable's assistant, Mlle. Boyer, and I heard more of their proposed cooking school here, with three-week courses, and Mapie de Toulouse-Lautrec as the head teacher. But Helen, we can teach French cooking to Americans because we can explain and they cannot.

Love,

J

Hotel Ritz
Madrid
[May 1958]

Dearest Helen —

Waiting for a call to Jerez to come through.

Madrid is beautiful but it is not Barcelona. Met some acquaintances from New York [the Wittys] and we have done many things together. Had a wonderful day at the flea market yesterday and bull fights in the afternoon. Then we had a dreadful dinner — horribly expensive — at the Jockey, with the most insolent maître d'hôtel in my experience. We asked for a soufflé, and he told us that we just plain couldn't have it because it took twenty-five minutes and why did we want it anyway. So we sat out the twenty-five minutes and sipped coffee. I am dying to write a piece showing how the *Holiday* awards can ruin a good restaurant and make a bad one worse. Funnily enough it is the bistros and the small country places that keep things going.

I have learned a great deal this trip. If we really believe in food we must do something about it, for our voices should be raised above the rest.

At Horcher's the other night I ate a very good baby lamb, but they are so German they put pimientos and all sorts of glop into their pâté en croûte, and it tastes like a fine Wurstgeschafft. It was packed with Americans from the time we arrived at about ten till well after twelve when we left.

Well, the call to Jerez is taking some time. I guess the Spanish telephone system is not as inquisitive as the French. I always feel that French operators are so anxious to hear what you have to say when you make a long-distance call that they put it through in double fast time.

Love,

J

[Auberge du Père Bise
Talloires
May 6, 1958]

Dearest Helen —

Your long newsy letter arrived in time for dinner on my birthday. I had been in the bar for a couple of drinks, and the concierge handed it to me just as I left. Earlier I had been watch shopping, for mine went, as I think I told you, and I simply cannot sleep without a watch. I lie awake wondering what time it is. Fortunately the France et Choiseul has those clocks in the courtyard, and in Strasbourg I could see the clock at the station.

Frank [Schoonmaker] met me there and we had a good lunch before starting out to Hess, who produces the great white alcohols. We sampled them for about an hour after sampling some of the Hess wines. They are as overmade as his alcohols are perfect. We next went to the Mullers'[1] near Colmar for a tasting and then for dinner with them in a fantastically good spot nearby, where they made us sample too much. As a result we couldn't walk at all.

Frank and I spent a night in Les Trois-Epis — were you there? — high in the Vosges overlooking Germany. Where the Queen of Holland hides out. We left the next morning for Germany, and I

won't go into all the details now, but I only wish I could have stayed
there another week with Frank. You have no idea how much I
learned and what a complete revolution took place in my thinking
about the wines of Germany. As you begin to know them they
become the most exquisite things in white wine bottles, and the
greats — which we can never afford in America — are so great
one is struck almost dumb.

We ate surprisingly well in the little hotels, but of course we
knew what to order — smoked salmon, eel, trout, fresh salmon,
and another fish of the Rhine unlike anything we have, cold meats
and salads, and that was about it. One night we did have wonderful
chicken, and we had asparagus at every meal, practically, and good
potatoes; and the bread and butter are superb.

And here I am at Père Bise. My room overlooks the lake [An-
necy] and the lovely garden. The leaves are just breaking out, and
the fruit trees are a mass of bloom. I lunched magnificently on a
hot pâté of sweetbreads, truffles and a good deal of grated carrot
in a delicate crust. Then an omble chevalier, the superb fish which
comes from the lake, and a chicken with morilles, gathered this
morning on the grounds. I am eating only asparagus and an
omelet tonight — then sleep and a lazy day tomorrow. On Thursday, Barcelona. I have a very heavy week next week with olive oil
and sherry. And I swear I am not going to eat a thing on the ship
but eggs and vegetables and fruit.

Alexis heard that I was going to Germany with Frank and was
worried over that. Jesus, there are just as many prima donnas in
the wine business as there are in any other. I like both of them and
don't want to fight. I still think Frank taught Alexis all he knows
and that Frank is incredibly fine. I watched him taste over three
hundred 1957s in four days, plus some 55s and a few 53s, and his
technique is sure and swift and really amazes some of the producers themselves, all of whom have a great respect for him.

Yes, Knopf sent me the galleys of the Waverly Root book last
winter. Alfred still says he'd like to have done *Paris Cuisine* — why
didn't he speak up then? Root is a correspondent who has lived in
France for about twenty years. I think it's very, very good. I did a
jacket blurb for June Platt's book at their request. Funnily enough
they didn't ask me to do one for Sandy's *Paris Bistros*. I told you,

James Beard doing a pitch for cognac in his 10th Street kitchen

Beard at the Jeffcott farm near Portland, Oregon, 1954; and with Helen and Philip Brown during the same visit. *Courtesy of Mary Hamblet*

A food demonstration in the 1950s.
Copyright © B. A. Bakalar; courtesy of Caroline Stuart

Ready for a television broadcast, 1950s. *Courtesy of Caroline Stuart*

Beard's work corner in the 10th Street house, and one of "the girls."
Courtesy of Mary Hamblet

36 West 12th Street; James Beard occupied a second-floor apartment at the rear of the building. *John Ferrone*

Beard's house at 119 West 12th Street.
John Ferrone

The 10th Street kitchen, with its famous pineapple wallpaper and
"grand piano," where Beard held cooking classes and entertained.
*Copyright © 1970 by The Condé Nast Publications Inc.;
courtesy of* House & Garden

Picnicking with Bettina McNulty and Alice B. Toklas in a meadow at
Montfort-l'Amaury outside Paris, July 4, 1957. *Henry McNulty*

Wine tasting in Pauillac.
Photo-Médoc; courtesy of Caroline Stuart

Cooking with Mercedes in Palamós on the Costa Brava, 1956.
Bettina McNulty; courtesy of Caroline Stuart

Beard with his friend Mary Hamblet on "Strawberry Knoll"
in Gearhart, Oregon, 1967. *Courtesy of Mary Hamblet*

With William Templeton Veach in Bonnétable, Sarthe, 1964.
Courtesy of Mary Hamblet

Helen dear —

The *nth* chapter in the comedy is that due to cancellations & all that sort of thing we arrive on the same day in New York. We had to take the *Queen Elizabeth* and arrive at noon on the 10th or some weird hour! —

Hope your trip is fun — Amuse to see you —

love

A note to Helen Evans Brown written in October 1963

Philip and Helen Brown, James Beard, and Bettina and Henry McNulty toasting in the Browns' Pasadena garden, November 1958. *Courtesy of Henry and Bettina McNulty*

didn't I, that Knopf is doing Elizabeth David's Italian book [*Italian Food*]. I think it is delightful.

Have you read the Thomas Jefferson memoirs that came out last year? Frank says there is a great deal about wine and some about food in it — including his story of a journey through the Rhine and Moselle. I must get to that when I get back, also find Ausonius's poem about the Moselle. The Forum should go in heavily for Moselles this year.

When I get home and have a typewriter that I like I shall write a great deal on a favorite subject — food. I have many things to say right now and want to go on record. As it is seven-thirty by my new watch I think I shall dress, go downstairs and have a large double Scotch. Happy Mother's Day, if this reaches you in time. They had a piece in the Geneva papers this morning on how this American custom was reaching Europe. Why not? They are rapidly getting all our worst habits and losing some of their own lovely ones.

My love to the Browns.

J

---

[1] Jules Muller, wine producer, in Bergheim, Alsace.

[S.S. *Independence*
May 22, 1958]

My dear Helen —

Just finished doing my customs declaration, and my God how simple it is now compared to the old days, when you had to list every little pin you were carrying with you.

I've been reading the biography of Alexandre Dumas by André Maurois, and it is lusty and wonderful. Also a fascinating Spanish book on eating, which is, as far as my Spanish deciphering goes, a real treasure. Full of criticism and real sense. *La Casa de Lucolo* by Julio Camba. I'll send my copy on to you to look over.

This ship has been like coming home. I know all the personnel from before, and I love its sort of ambling speed over what has been, so far, a mirror sea, with deck buffets every day. Several military men and some women have come and asked me if I am that Beard. I gather the men love to cook very much. One Lt. Commander told me that his children, at table, ask who prepared the food and if it is their mother they refuse to eat it because she hates to cook and does it so badly. However, she is a good baker.

We have eaten simply, this trip, but we had a beautiful roasted pheasant the other night and asparagus — tiny wild green ones from Italy, baked with butter and layers of Parmesan and Romano — elegant.

The bartender in the smoking room is a good cook. He it was who taught me the wonderful salad of salt codfish. He made me a dish of tripe, cut into tiny shreds, with just enough tomato, onion and brown sauce to lubricate, then layers of chopped parsley and a bit of oregano, and topped with Parmesan. Today he has promised me a risotto made with veal, Virginia ham and olives. All the steward's staff come up to see what he cooks every day and beg for a bite or two. But the waste on these ships is beyond belief. The other night two people next to me had duckling bigarade, and the waiters came with two ducks, cut off two tiny helpings and threw the rest away. I had Escalopes de Veau the other night and they brought enough for six persons, easily. And the buffets. They do a full buffet at 11:30 at night with a turkey or two, pastrami, ham, whole roast filets, tongue, pâté maison, hamburgers, frankfurters, salads, and a huge bowl of fruit, with sherbet — and even though some people have only just had their first belch from dinner they down a plateful. I found myself eating the best roast beef sandwich I ever ate because it was so beautifully rare and crusty that I couldn't resist.

Did I tell you about my trip to Jerez de la Frontera? If not, I want to, for I feel that next time you and Philip should start in Portugal and get your way paid by the port, sherry and olive oil people. It is all so lovely — sort of an idealized California, between Seville and Jerez. And the people in Jerez are delightful. Everyone is related to everyone else, and there is such a pleasant social life, something that no other wine district has. The mixture of English and Spanish is so old that everyone speaks the most perfect English, with a pronounced British accent, and they use Spanish for work. The bodegas are lovely to look upon, with whitewash and flowers. And if anyone ever tells you again that sherry should not be chilled, tell them to go to hell. They keep bottles cooling all the time — all varieties — and I will say that I am beginning to love sherry after spending the days drinking it like water, and that is exactly what they do. The workers may drink as much as they want, and they come into the bodegas and draw off a glass just as others would go to a fountain. I'm certain that the last day but one I was there I drank at the very least fifty glasses of chilled sherry and had wine with both lunch and dinner, besides, and drank brandy after lunch and dinner and Scotch before dinner — but no trace of its being too much.

There was Ascension Day to be taken care of while I was there so the Beltrán Domecqs — he is married to the daughter of Guy Williams of Williams and Humbert and related by blood and marriage to everyone else — took me out to their little farmhouse, where they live with five children, English and Spanish tutors, and servants. Lunched on a fabulous egg dish with rather thick onion rings, almost caramelized, and one of the typical peasant dishes — great big beans, like haricot beans, cooked with a bit of onion, sweet pepper and chorizo, which was sliced on the platter just before serving. Then a braised piece of veal with tiny young carrots, tiny potatoes and a crisp salad. I must say, the Spanish make better salad than the French, usually, for they really use good oil. Finally, the most heavenly quince jelly, which the nuns make for them and store in rather deep white bowls. It is very heavy, clear as crystal and rich. You slice if off as you do quince paste, which they also get from the convent.

We went to the races that day, along with all of the Gonzálezes and Gordons and Domecqs and Williamses and all their children, governesses and tutors. They raced their own horses, and between races you were invited to sherries or brandies. The races were over about eight-thirty, and I went to the hotel to rest and wash before we went to dinner.

They paid all my expenses in Jerez and were really hospitable. I laid the groundwork for you, and they would be delighted to have a California person come and see the bodegas. I would like to go back for the fair in the spring or the harvest in the fall, both of which are times of great festivals.

Home Saturday morning and jury duty starts on Monday morning. I got out of it three times this year but cannot again, I am sure.

I dread the getting-home part. I am being sensible for once and taking a Carey Cadillac from the ship rather than fighting and tipping through the batch of longshoremen. It will cost less, and they come right into customs to meet you, and all your baggage is in the car. Old age teaches us a few things, and that is one of the things I've learned — avoid confusion and crowds of people who are bent on getting somewhere. The Americans and the Germans are the worst, almost equalled by the French and Italians.

Love and kisses,

J

[86 West 12th Street
New York
May 30, 1958]

Dearest Helen —

`Just back from Philadelphia where we started the second season of the park restaurant [Belmont Mansion] with all the Bartrons. We have three of them going and will probably have two more by the end of the year. Steaks, chicken, and king crab legs. Then we have a potluck dish every night on the buffet.

I have been on the jury the whole time and have next week again — so far one rape case and I almost got chosen on a narcotics case. Been eating nearby in Chinatown every day because I like the food and also because it is less fattening.

I'd like to use your Dumas [*Grand Dictionnaire de Cuisine*] for a couple of weeks this summer or until Philip can get me one. I want to do some research for the book with Frank. Did I tell you I was given a copy of that beautiful book on sherry by González Gordon? It is breathtakingly beautiful and should be translated. I also have a copy of the famous old Spanish cookery book — 1728 — and a lovely thing it is as well.

What is your conception of a croissant? Can you give it to me in one succinct paragraph. I'm having a great argument with three persons on this subject.

Had lunch with Craig and Ann. Craig just moved into a new apartment yesterday and had us there today. Prosciutto and melon and a very good cold salmon with dill sauce and cucumbers. I'm very fond of Craig and want to see him get ahead on the paper, hard though I know it is.

Ta ta,

J

Pasadena
May 31, 1958

Jim dearest,

Did you ever hear of calling cocktail choux "profiteroles"? *Gourmet* does this month. All my authorities, including Dumas, say they are sweet.

Love,
H

[86 West 12th Street
New York
June 1958]

Dearest Helen —

Jury duty goes on.

I wanted to make one of my favorite dishes over the weekend — rabbit with mustard spread on it for 24 hours and then roasted. The butcher had nothing but frozen California rabbits, two of which I bought, and meaty and lovely they looked. But after being cooked they were so tough that no one could cut the meat from the bones. I am trying it again with some other rabbits. I am on a croissant binge, too.

In answer to your query about profiteroles. They do use the term with soup; I have never seen it used with hors d'oeuvre. But a consommé aux profiteroles is quite the thing.

We had a lovely seasonal dinner tonight. I was on the radio at

6:30 so it had to be a quickie when I got home. We had shad roe —
the last of the season — in foil, with lemon, parsley and butter;
mustard greens steamed in their own water; sautéed mushrooms;
sliced beefsteak; and strawberries with port. I adore strawberries
this way, and when I think I can afford it, calorically speaking, I
smother them in cream, à la Romanoff.

Did I tell you I am judging the chicken festival again? It is really
fun, and I enjoy the days down there — one of my favorite parts of
the country.

Jesus, I have to have some people here for supper — a series of
suppers is more like it — and I just have to wait till Agnes gets the
curtains done and I get the new dining table. I'm hoping for July,
with three suppers planned. One with salmon as the pièce, one
with a galantine of turkey, and another with a stuffed breast
of veal with a chaudfroid. I'm going to do a mussel salad with
the first, a rice and lobster salad with the second, and a wonderful white-wine potato salad with the veal, and a corn salad
as well.

If you go over to Los Angeles someday not too far distant, would
you pick out two materials for kimonos for me, a silk one and a
cotton? The raw silk one I have is full of holes, and the cottons are
just about worn out. I find them the most comfortable ones in the
world, and she [Miss Akita] does make them nicely. I am sick to
death of thinking up ways to use rum.

Love and kisses,

J

Blowtorch — you've used gratinéing, singeing, plucking, searing,
browning. Paula used one for cooking thin bits of fish. Buttered,
spread with seeds, and browned with a torch, the fish was
more delicate than if baked. What about using the torch on
peppers, for skinning, instead of the usual? And on tomatoes, for
peeling?

Pasadena
June 6, 1958

James dear,

Thanks for the blowtorch ideas. I had thought of them but I think I am going to have a hard time dreaming up enough for the booklet. . . .

Is it correct to say bonnes bouchées? Or bonnes bouches? Our French dictionary gives the latter and it seems wrong.

Love and kisses,
H

[86 West 12th Street
New York
June 8, 1958]

Dearest Helen —

I'm through jury duty. I got called on every case possible, but many sat out their whole two weeks and were not called at all. What a waste the whole thing is. Now to work. I have a date with Nestlé on Tuesday for what may well become a really big job. Then we are probably starting a class in Mildred Dunnock's[1] house in a couple of weeks with about ten students, and another a little later with about fifteen.

Yesterday I had this lovely person from Dallas for a whole morning of soufflés. We made six in every kind of container you can imagine, and she was the proudest person in the world when she walked out, having made them all rise to perfection. I gave her soufflés without flour, without egg yolks and with the traditional things. She is the type of student one adores having, for she is so thrilled and grateful when things work that her joy is contagious.

Last night I had Polly Dick — one of the owners of La Cuisinière — and Bud Williams to dinner. Had the Hamblet deviled crab. I have so much frozen king crab, it has to be used, and it is delicious in that recipe. Then I had one of the veal tenderloins, such as I gave you, with a soubise sauce, and some wonderful Italian bread, with crisp bits of pork in it, that I get down near the jail — made in a wreath. I had planned strawberries with raspberries, but there were no good raspberries, so I finished off with strawberries Romanoff — the old recipe.

Today we went out to lunch at André Surmain's air kitchen, where he has wonderful chefs and you see the process of readying a meal for the plane. We had a delicious sauté of beef jardinière, cucumbers smothered in butter, tiny potatoes, a good salad and cheese, and little apple tarts with apricot glaze.

Another use for the blowtorch — loup flambé or whatever fish you can think of with herbs. Also, why not do that same thing with steaks, with dried herbs piled on and flambéed with cognac?

Had dinner with the darling McNulties on Friday in their dream apartment, which they have for six months — a view of all New York is theirs, and it is breathtaking. Bettina had huge shrimp with a lemon butter, steamed in the shell. Then a roast of beef with truffles in its center, zucchini in sour cream, cheese and fruit. We had a whirl of an evening.

Love and kisses,

J

---

[1] American stage and film actress.

Pasadena
June 14, 1958

James dearest,

Charlotte Jackson (Mrs. Joseph Henry Jackson) was here for dinner last night. I had already planned it so she had to take potluck. It was Boeuf à la Ficelle. The soup was superb but the meat tasteless. First time I'd ever done it and I was disappointed. Could it have been that the meat itself wasn't properly aged?

[H]

[86 West 12th Street
New York
June 1958]

Helen, dear —

I think the secret of Boeuf à la Ficelle is its quickness and rareness, as well as its quality. See that you get a very well-aged piece, and give it a slight rub with rosemary before you sink it into the pot. Plenty of gros sel and a pickle.

"Bouchées" — if you mean the tiny little puff-paste ones, it is spelt with two ees. If you mean "Amuses Bouches" or such, it is another thing — also "Bonnes Bouches" — which relates to the mouth rather than the small vol-au-vent.

I am not taking the Nestlé job. Too much supermarket and too much testing. I'd have nothing left for myself. I feel very relieved. Maybe I'll die in the poorhouse, but what the hell if I do. I can always use the kitchen to cook goodies my friends send me.

The rum party was a great success. The five punches went over well, and they fell for the coffee-vanilla-rum ice cream, as I knew they would. All the food gals were mad about it and judged it the tops. Get things rich enough and gooey enough, and they love it.

Tonight I go to see Beatrice Lillie in *Auntie Mame,* which should be a panic.

[JB]

86 West 12th Street
New York
[June 24, 1958]

Dearest Helen —

The Home Ec convention [in Philadelphia] was something. I had a small party at Belmont Mansion on Friday night with Louella Shouer,[1] Helen McCully, Eleanor Noderer, Kate Titus,[2] Ruth Seltzer of the *Philadelphia Bulletin,* the Wilsons, and the Green Giant boys. Connie Wolf[3] spent the best part of two days gathering wild strawberries and brought them in as a surprise to me. The Vitello Tonnato was elegant and jellied of its own accord, and the trout were superb. We had a filet and corn. They stayed for hours.

Saturday the Green Giant party was in my honor, and I was Home Ecced all over the place. Several people wanted to know when you would be back, they so much wanted to know you. Ten of these girls have asked me to do a ten-day seminar course for them, where they will work all day for ten days and do good restaurants at night. I shall have to go away for a vacation when that is over, but it will be a stimulating time.

The party was good. I had corned beef, hams, vegetables and smoked-fish platters, and wonderful two-colored rye bread. We had a chef carving all the time, and it was a relief to the guests, for they get so many little turds. I made over a gallon of corn relish, and they ate that with the corned beef. And most of those gals are two-fisted drinkers.

Nestlé called me after I sent them a letter more or less refusing the job and said, We want you more than ever. I just can't refuse. Twenty thousand the first year and expenses is what they are talking about, for a job as consultant. What do you think?

Having Bill and Gloria Kaduson to dinner tomorrow night. I still have part of one of my Tallmadge hams, so I shall do some fried rice. Then probably good skirt steaks marinated with soy, garlic and sherry and broiled quickly. And perhaps a strawberry soufflé. Easy and quick and light enough for anyone.

Did I tell you what Irma told me about croissants? Anyway, it is to add potato flour to the mixture and a bit of finely chopped beef suet to the dough. It does something fantastic to the finished product. She says they were taught this in the Grand Duchess of Baden School when she went there.

Love and kisses,

J

---

[1] Associate food editor at *Ladies' Home Journal.*

[2] A partner in the public relations firm DAY (Dudley Anderson and Yutzy), which gave JB work with a number of their accounts.

[3] A champion balloonist.

86 West 12th Street
New York
[June 30, 1958]

Helen, darling —

The Chicken Festival has been and gone. I had to judge the
men's barbecue all by myself. There were twelve entries, and they
set up their own equipment, from specially built grills to just bricks
and concrete blocks — which one guy used well. He removed
bricks as the cooking went on, thus adjusting his fire. All of them
took a long time over slow fire, and none of them had ever seen
any of our stuff. The winner, I chose because what he had tasted
good and was simple. The other entries were overcooked — some
men took two hours to broil a chicken, with slow fire, of course,
and much brushing. But I have never eaten so much dry chicken
in my life.

The senior contest, for which I was one of the judges, was
something different. This year, 196 entries. The three who received prizes deserved it. The first prize was a simple tarragon and
mushroom job which showed off the broiler-fryer as it should have
been and was good to the palate and not overcooked. One judge
felt that tarragon was too exotic for the housewife, but we all
frowned at her, and she came through. But, Helen, some of those
recipes called for cooking tender little chickens 1½ to 2½ hours!
Some had the world's worst mixtures. Second prize was an excellent paella with minced clams and clam juice. It came in a fish-
shaped Pyrex dish which was enchanting and fitted into a basket.
Third prize came from a darling little local woman who couldn't
come to the contest because she had to work but who prepared
this real homely fricassee at home — cooked the chickens in
broth, made a rich sauce, arranged it on an old platter and surrounded it with freshly cooked garden beans and tiny white onions. It looked exactly like Sunday dinner at Grandma's. I sensed,
when it came in, that it was prize material, and the flavor proved I
was right. She has a broken-down old range, and so the prize of a
new one must make her happy.

One woman roasted a chicken and sent it in to the judges breast
side down on a platter with a garnish of green apples and apple

twigs with leaves! The old pope's nose was high in the air with an apple crowning it!

The dinner they served us at the gala dinner dance was something to forget in a hurry. First, jellied consommé, then salad and chicken barbecue — this one, with catchup, onion and sugar, glazed with the mess and cooked to death. Then a peach ice cream pie done with a crumb crust, but you couldn't tell for the life of you what the flavor was until you bit into some chunks that looked like peach. Thank God, Al McCann had taken me for mint juleps before that meeting. I love the McCanns — they are so thoughtful and such gay people that to be with them makes any party more fascinating. We need more like them in the food business.

Last night, went to the new Sardi's for dinner. Ordered my pet of the moment, Salade Niçoise, and it was mostly lettuce, with a few flakes of tuna fish, even though the chef is from Monte Carlo. Then we had noisettes of lamb, which were really delicious, with a large slice of truffle, tomato Provençale and an artichoke bottom filled with béarnaise. Delicious raspberries.

Today lunched at the Forum on absolutely perfect gazpacho and a beef salad, with white beans and a rosemary dressing, which was elegant. People criticize that place because they don't know what to order!

They have given Irma Rhode a job as experimental baker for the new place. She will do all the Viennese, French and German pastries for them to adapt.

The curtains went up in the living room today and the house seems to be taking on an air. I think you'll love it when you see it, for it is more mad than anything I have ever had, but it still reflects the funny conservative person I really am.

Love,

J

[86 West 12th Street
New York
July 1958]

Dearest Helen —

I am on the warpath. I may resign from Gottlieb. It seems that one of the cognac people accused me of taking money to use Grand Marnier in making Crêpes Suzette — and who ever heard of that dish without it? We used it in the movie, and they raised hell. Finally Gottlieb asked me in front of a total stranger if I did take money. So I blew my top and told him what I thought for asking such a question. So they are all in a dither.

Henry and I went up to the Culinary Arts School in New Haven this week and they are really doing a wonderful job. I was very cheered with their ideas. They teach the kids to eat as well as to cook. They have about 200 during the winter, and in summer they have two-week refresher courses for working chefs and specialists. The best chefs of the East come in a few times each semester and they have three or four top men in New Haven who teach there.

We had lunch that the students had cooked, and good it was. Marvelous crusty French bread; a jellied consommé that tasted like beef, which it should taste like — cold and no gelatine; a superbly cooked stuffed pepper and rice pilaff; duckling bigarade, with a well-cooked, tender duck and a good sauce, if you like orange; braised red cabbage; and for dessert, a beautiful charlotte russe and two different bavaroises in lovely molds. These guys eat this way twice a day and love it. One of the hopeful things I have seen in this country.

Helen, the Pedlars and Craig were here Thursday night. We had some pretty strange hors d'oeuvre that the new gal who works for me wanted to make. One of them was the beginning of something good — I'll play with it. She rolls bread with a rolling pin, spreads it with a very savory chopped chicken filling, rolls it up, butters it, and rolls it in chopped nuts. It is good, but when it is dipped in a French-toast batter and fried, with the nuts added afterwards, it is sensational — but not pretty. I did a sauté of crabmeat, with shallot, parsley, tarragon and a hint of cognac, on fried toast. Then a tremendous beef salad and homemade mustard mayonnaise. And a raspberry soufflé — all egg whites and raspberry purée — with a raspberry-cassis sauce.

Roasted a boned and rolled shoulder of veal tonight with garlic, fresh basil and white wine — had the bones in the pan and covered it for part of the cooking, really braising. Absolutely delicious, juicy and tender but not dry as most veal is. Had a risotto al pesto with it, and Gino's favorite Gold Cake, which is so damned simple, and a half-bottle of Pouilly-Fuissé.

Out for a short walk before going to bed.

Love and kisses,

J

Pasadena
July 22, 1958

James dear,

Don't quit Gottlieb. That is too nice a connection. Of course you were angry, and rightly so, but just say so and keep your job.

H

[86 West 12th Street
New York
July 9, 1958]

My dearest Helen —

Everything has been going wrong for days now. We set off for Cheryl's on Thursday night and the car gave out halfway. We had to go by taxi the rest of the way. I missed a party at Philippe's on Sunday as a result. Then Gino and I set off for Martha's Vineyard yesterday at noon. We started by standing in line at La Guardia for three and one half hours waiting for the plane to arrive that would carry us to Boston. Today the plane from Boston skipped Nantucket and the Vineyard and we are home. The most expensive trip to dine well at Locke-Ober on record.

But it was a superb dinner, with steamed lobsters and plenty of butter, and before that, clams Casino — I can't eat the raw ones, you know. The lobsters were two-pounders and just elegant.

The editors at *House and Garden* are falling off like flies and not being replaced at this point. No one seems to know what is going to happen or when. And there is no editor-in-chief. I hope they don't decide to fold. Then we'll have to go into the fudge business or something.

Tonight I am giving John Schaffner an experiment — a gratin of salmon and crabmeat with a little Madeira in the sauce. It will be a nice combination of flavors and the sauce will be light. Some sautéed potatoes, a cucumber salad, and raspberries and black-berries for dessert.

Do you get fresh lichee nuts there? I think they are the best fruit in the world and so cooling and exotic to the tongue. Other fruit is terrible this year. Peaches have to be poached, apricots have no flavor, and cherries are dull to the taste. I haven't had a good strawberry since I came home, and the raspberries were good but now are watery and flavorless. Lichees are so much better, for they are ripe and delicious when they come. I buy everything at Mad-ison Grocer, the best and most expensive, but still nothing tastes good.

I must go on a diet of some sort for a couple of weeks. It seems so unjust of God to have given you and me the wrong type of glands so that we can't eat without worrying.

Love to you both,

J

[86 West 12th Street
New York
August 1, 1958]

Helen —

Isabel and Ron were here last night and everything about my dinner went wrong. I had beautiful red snappers and did them in foil with butter, tarragon and onion, and they were just god-awful — part of them cooked to perfection and part horribly. I can't understand it. And my rice got too much herb in it because I was called to the phone at the last minute, and Isabel and Gino dumped all that had been chopped into it. However, the cole slaw was good, and the fruit for dessert — but sometimes nothing goes right in the kitchen.

My class is wonderful. These prima donnas are the nicest bunch I have ever had to teach and love everything they do with a passion. Mary Hemingway[1] is fabulous in her grasp of cookery. This week they made crêpes. Did the piled ones with mushrooms, and spinach ones with ham and hollandaise. Then they did Suzette in the electric skillet and the chocolate ones piled up and served with cream. They also did salmon and dill soufflés and Stanhope soufflés.[2]

Went to the Wheat Flour Institute lunch yesterday for the prize sandwiches, and this was a new low. I shall send you the release on it so that you, too, may throw up.

> Love and kisses,
>
> J

---

[1] Wife of Ernest Hemingway.

[2] Vanilla and chocolate soufflé mixtures baked with lady fingers and served with a sabayon sauce.

> [86 West 12th Street
> New York
> August 14, 1958]

Dearest Helen —

Had to tell you the latest news — I have Clare Boothe Luce for a private pupil. She had her first lesson today and was the most enchanting thing I have ever known — even made me teach her to scrub pots after lunch. She wants Henry to come to dinner on Wednesday, when she will come down ahead and cook. We did three different scaloppine today, a corn and clam soup and green rice. She wants four or five dinners she can do by herself and some she can freeze, when she is in Arizona.

Tomorrow I have the two boys who run Serendipity[1] for an omelet lesson. They are starting an omelet bar in their shop.

There is a chance I may be doing outdoor cooking on the Arthur Godfrey Show next Thursday — I hope not, but I may — so tune in on it and see. This will be for cognac or I wouldn't do it. Gottlieb gave me a bonus, after all our differences of opinion.

Gino and I finished a good dinner. Scallopine alla Marsala, beans and salad from Cheryl's garden, and fresh figs — beauties. And a bottle of Moselle, one that Sherry's have for $1.29 — and really good. I am trying to cut out wine for two months and drinking spirits mildly, but it is such a problem. I must get some weight off me.

Love and kisses,
[J]

---

[1] Calvin Holt and Stephen Bruce, owners of this East Side restaurant and general store.

86 West 12th Street
New York
[August 22, 1958]

Helen dear —

Had both Luces this week, a scene I shall never forget. She arrives any moment now for a lesson scrambling eggs and in codfish cakes. I'll give her a dessert cake, too, I think.

Going to Maryland this afternoon for two days to do some negotiating. The McNulties have become very interested, and I think with Henry and me to run the place and Bettina to do a shop it might make money. We could do it with a fairly small staff, and if HEB came once a year it would be superb. Also, it would give people a chance to come and take lessons for a week or so as they do in the Constance Spry place or the country place of the Cordon Bleu.

Did you see the Arthur Godfrey Show? I gave you a credit line and would have said more, but I had to get cognac and champagne in at the same time.

Love and kisses,
[J]

[86 West 12th Street
New York
August 25, 1958]

Helen, dear —

I was at Nestlé's for my second trip today. So far we have come along swimmingly. We do a good day's work in about three or four hours and taste, and then the sauces are taken to the big labs in New Milford, copied and brought back. We have a long tasting session with them afterwards. It is fascinating.

The Luces are having a complete "do" done on me. They seem to think this is a prelude to offering me a job. I can't imagine what, but this is what they say. They are both quite wonderful to work with. I think I'm going to them after class on Wednesday and stay for dinner and then will be driven back here afterwards. Had dinner with my Dallas student at Quo Vadis the other night. We had string beans in a rich béchamel with almonds on top and a bit of buttered crumbs and grated Parmesan, gratinéed — along with a saddle of lamb, sarladaise potatoes and a praline soufflé. Then the next night, bacon and eggs in a diner on the road. Easton [Maryland] has no decent food. The hotel is elegant and the breakfasts are good, but the dinners stink. Although at Saturday lunch I had some delicious buttered kale which was succulent and not overcooked.

A letter from Alice [Toklas] tells me she had an infected foot and that the doctor wouldn't let her walk on it for a while. She seems unhappy that none of us is going to be there this year. What a darling she really is.

Love and kisses,

JB

86 West 12th Street
New York
[September 7, 1958]

Helen, dear —

Peggy and Kiki are coming for lunch today — a little pâté en croûte, to start, my Portuguese dish with cod, brioche, and wonderful mangoes. Paula and I spent yesterday on pâté en croûte and a fabulous terrine, for which I am sending you the recipe. We had a whirl and made pasta in between. I bought one of the machines to cut it, like the one you bought in Italy.

Madame Luce may call you when she goes to the Coast. She may want to take a lesson or two and ask you about things to buy. I mentioned Balzer's for sending her bits and pieces in Arizona. I am giving her your *West Coast Cook Book*.

The McNulties and I are still bogged down by the price of the mansion repairs. I am glad you feel as you do about Arizona. Madame L presented me with a plan the other day, if we can find a location.

For the terrine — take a small turkey or a large chicken, split down the back, and bone. Remove the filets and combine them with 1 pound each large chunks fresh veal, fresh pork, ham and fresh pork siding. Add 1 large tablespoon spiced salt — shall I make you some? — a teaspoon thyme, a crumbled bay leaf, 1 cup white wine and ½ cup cognac. Mix together ½ pound each of the same meats, ground very fine, and blend with 4 eggs. Remove the filets from the marinade and mix the ground and cubed meats with the marinade and seasonings. Arrange the skin of the bird in the bottom and sides of a terrine or casserole, put ½ the meat mixture in, then the filets, and finally the rest of the meat. Fold the skin over, cover with a slice or two of fresh pork siding and add another dash of cognac. Cover and seal, or cover tightly with foil, place in a pan of hot water, and bake at 425 for 1¾ to 2 hours. Weight down to cool. The slices are mosaical and the flavor divine.

Love and kisses,

J

Pasadena
September 9, 1958

James dear,

What spiced salt? You speak of it for the turkey. Tell me how and I will make some. Or is it a Nestlé secret? . . .

I would like to meet Clare B. L. but I bet she doesn't call.

H

86 West 12th Street
New York
[September 14, 1958]

Dearest Helen —

Sel épicé is the salt the French use in most everything, with a balance of ginger, pepper, cloves, and nutmeg with the salt, and it is wonderful. I thought that since the Nestlé lab mixes it for me up there, it would be easier than your weighing out the formula all by yourself.

Drove up to the Wayside Inn early the other day. Luncheon was good. We had a squash soup with great quantities of mace, then baked oysters — a strange arrangement, I felt — and apple juice to clear the palate, but it only succeeded in filling up those who drank it. Then lovely pheasants with sauerkraut, mushroom caps filled with an elegant stuffing, braised carrots, string beans, and a claret. Then, to my sheer delight, cranberry and raisin pie with cinnamon-flavored whipped cream.

Harper's sent me the galleys of Alice's cookbook [*Aromas and Flavors of Past and Present*]. It is the Gospel according to Alice B. Toklas edited by Poppy [Cannon], who uses Swanson chicken broth and frozen artichokes. There is about as much Alice in it as there is Elizabeth Barrett Browning.

If I go to Mexico it will be the 16th of October, and I shall return on the 20th. Naturally I don't want to go if you don't get there. I have just found my old date book, and here are some of the restaurants. In the old section there is the Acapulco, where the old gents often went for their elevenses — seafood and such things and rich broth in little cups. Trendes is another of the old ones. The Mirador is where they have the most sensational bar; women are not allowed, although they are in the restaurant. They used to do excellent snacks at the bar — the best maguey worms, the best guacamole and good enchiladas Suizas. The old aristocrats used to gather there for games and drinks on their way home and would snack around six or so as a bulkhead against the late dinner.

Of course you know of Jena — their pompano with bananas is wonderful. Also Parador and the Rivoli, which used to be so lovely. If you go to Puebla — and that you must — you will find all the Pobla specialties at the Royalty. It has more of the old Mexican qualities than any of the other cities. The Royalty makes a good mole with pork and one with chicken, and they also do wonderful camarónes with garlic and a good tortilla Español.

If Francis Guth is in Mexico City ask where the shop is that sells all the things made with almonds. It's a Spanish place called the Toledo. They make the most delicious nougat and baked marzipan. If I don't get there, you can send me the toasted nougat — I adore it.

Love,

J

86 West 12th Street
New York
[December 21, 1958]

Helen dear and Philip —

I hope the season brings you peace and joy.

I have just found that the new and wonderful typewriter I bought to replace the one I wore out has keys so close together that I cannot use it at all. I cannot hit a single key — it is always about six, and that makes for difficulties.

Christmas Eve Ruth and Cheryl dine here quietly after which we shall probably go to bed early. Then we dine on Christmas day with Freddie [Rufe][1] and on Friday go to Atlantic City. There I expect to rot for two days and not think of anything at all.

I'm having about ten for a buffet on New Year's Eve, when most people I know hate revelry and want a peaceful evening. I shall have a pâté I have left, a cassoulet with goose, salad, and mincemeat crêpes, which I love, and with homemade mincemeat. The day after New Year's I have two for dinner and the day after that, Agnes and Bill White, then two more dinners and I am through for the season.

I now think I shall go away on the 4th of February and be gone for a couple of months or even longer, depending upon Nestlé. I shall be in England and Scotland, then fly to Turkey and possibly to Madeira. I am planning to give up most of my Restaurant Associates work and change my status with Gottlieb to a per diem arrangement. I have finished with Green Giant for a while and shall finish up soon with Wakefield, and then I can settle into two or three things I really want to do. This year I am going to get myself into working order again and have already started to lose weight.

Love and much of it
Kisses, too,
J

---

1 Rufe, a vice president of Restaurant Associates, helped launch the Four Seasons and managed a number of establishments, including the Newarker and La Fonda del Sol.

Pasadena
[December 1958]

Dear Jim,

For God's sake, how can you take it easy when you take on so many new things? Are you money mad? A new book and a trip to England when you had more than you could do before.

Love,
H

86 West 12th Street
New York
[December 25, 1958]

Dearest Helen and Philip —

It's Christmas, all the mess is cleaned up, and I have nothing to do for five hours. My beautiful box arrived at 5 p.m. yesterday in the biggest packing box Balzer's ever sent out, of that I'm sure.

Cheryl and Ruth were here for supper. We had an enormous hip steak, baked potatoes with sour cream and green onions, field salad, and lovely strawberries with port and Grand Marnier. Then we opened gifts and were raucous. I got a 1905 Fannie Farmer, all sorts of serving stuff, a fabulous Georg Jensen pepper mill, beautiful shell dishes, and an exquisite Minton pie dish — really a great tureen with flowers on the sides and a blue bird on top with feet in the air. Also a beautiful silver serving spoon, an antique one, from the Wheat Flour Institute — this, for judging the goddam sandwich contest.

I love your new book, just love it.[1] It is beautiful, wonderful reading, and completely you, with a great deal of personality in it.

Loads of love,

J

---

[1] *The Book of Appetizers,* with Philip S. Brown.

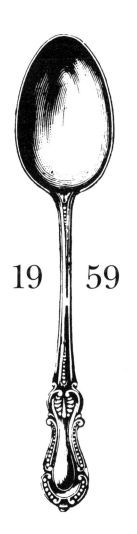

1959

JB started off the year with an irregular heartbeat and a diet. He left on February 5 for Europe, where he visited Scotland, Ireland, and the West Country of England before going to Paris and then to Switzerland to meet with Nestlé executives. In March he did two food demonstrations in Florida, one on behalf of the citrus producers, the other for cognac. *The James Beard Cookbook* was published in April, launched with a party at the Fifth Avenue apartment of George Delacorte. It became a best-seller, and the publisher offered JB another contract. He also began to revise an earlier barbecue cookbook, to be reissued as *James Beard's Treasury of Outdoor Cooking*. In July he started negotiations to acquire a small house on 10th Street, and for the next several months was engaged in renovations and the design of a kitchen that could accommodate cooking classes. In the meantime he was serving as consultant for Restaurant Associates' latest restaurant, the Four Seasons. In September he went to Le Sueur, Minnesota, to work for Green Giant. On October 3 he moved to 119 West 10th Street. Cooking classes started in early November, and JB gave a series of housewarming parties. He appeared on TV on Christmas Eve and entertained in his new house with Christmas breakfast and dinner.

Dearest Helen —

Our New Year's party was a great success. We ate a wonderful goose liver, and I made a cassoulet with canned cannellini beans, goose, lamb, pork and sausages. I put garlic and onions in the Blendor with rum and broth and poured it over the cassoulet, then added parslied crumbs later. Jean Tabaud said he had never had a better one in all his life in France and ate five helpings. Then I made a new type mincemeat tart — filled the scalloped baking dish with my mincemeat, a layer of apple sauce, sliced apples and sugar and baked it that way, then glazed it and arranged little puff-paste bowknots on it which had been baked separately. It looked divine and tasted like the caves of Cognac.

I go to [Dr.] Mack Lipkin next week for a complete physical and so will put my mind at rest if not my body. I have been worried and have not done anything about it so far.

Did I tell you what a beautiful dinner Craig cooked for us the other night? Really elegant.

Dione has brought out a sauce Suprême — $2.00 for 8 ounces, a bit on the steep side. Our sauces seem to be coming along at Nestlé.

Love and kisses from the big city,

J

86 West 12th Street
New York
January 16, 1959

Dearest Helen —

Mack thinks my slight heart irregularity is something that has developed within the last year, and he has given me a lecture and started me on weight reduction and relaxation. He has put me on my honor for one month to see what happens. If all does not go well, he threatens other things. I just have to get to the place where I will not drive myself so horrendously. I have lost weight since Christmas, and last night when I went to the Bordeaux dinner, my dinner jacket almost seemed as if it had been made for me.

The dinner turned out quite nicely. The chef at the Carlton House cooked the saddle of veal as well as I have ever had it. It was juicy, tender and flavorful, a unique experience in veal eating. The soufflés were beyond belief. They were baked in metal, stood at least four inches above the rims and were unctuous inside, with great globs of egg white in them.

Love and kisses,
Jim

Pasadena
January 20, 1959

James darling,

I am worried about you. Do you really think that you will be good on the "honor system"? I think you ought to go to the hospital, and at once. Don't be a nonny. You have only one life, you know. . . .

TAKE CARE OF YOURSELF, STOP ENTERTAINING, STOP DRINKING, STOP GOING PLACES, STOP EATING TOO MUCH, STOP ALL JOBS BUT THE ONE THAT PAYS THE MOST OR YOU WILL STOP LIVING. I am serious.

Love and kisses,
H

The Central Hotel
Glasgow
[February 1959]

Helen, dear —

My Scottish jaunt has been full of distilleries and whisky — and one of the most beautiful dinners I have ever had offered, by a delightful hotel and restaurant man who is sort of a Scotch version of Lester Gruber. Wild boar filets with foie gras, then a consommé of lobster — rich and dark with tiny cubes of lobster in it — then to clear the palate an egg cocotte, followed by Scotch salmon, a rack of young venison, with a soufflé of mashed potatoes, and a feuilletage of Scottish cheese — hot — instead of dessert. You know how unsoupy I am but I have never eaten anything like the consommé of lobster.

Last Friday, before I came up here, I went to a hotel school for lunch and was entertained by a brilliant young guy who is coming up here to head the school — John Fuller. I must say that the English are making great strides to improve their cookery.

Tomorrow I go to Ireland and return on Friday, to be picked up at the airport and driven through the West Country for six days to all the historic inns. Then they drive me to the Paris plane. Fortnum's is the same, and Brown's is the same, and it all has a quality that I love. I have England on the brain this time.

Love,
J

86 West 12th Street
New York
[April 1959]

Dearest Helen —

I'm sending you a copy of Craig's restaurant article, which has cracked the trade wide open. It's a most revolutionary article and one which will be discussed for months.[1]

I went to the doctor today and my weight is going down but the fat around the heart is still there, and my pulse varies like mad—

this morning, from 40 to 70, when I was in the office. I really have to get myself down to nothing at this point and stay there. This is part of what has been bothering me mentally as well, I think. And so does Mack. At any rate, I seem to be dragging myself out of it, for which God be praised.

Next week I'm having all the Nestlé people with whom I work closely. It's a Friday — think I'll have a huge hors d'oeuvre table and then a salmon, sweet and sour, with perhaps a gratin Savoyarde, with some of the lovely celery root that is here at this point. I have to have fish, for I planned this without knowing that some of the guests were Catholics. I might also do a salmon with a clam sauce, which I haven't done for absolute ages.

One night while you are here we shall have a family party of nothing but broiled or boiled lobsters, if that would please you, and acres of good mayonnaise or drawn butter, and that is all except for some good cheese and bread and salad.

I just had to make some cakes and bread for a *Woman's Day* article. Did a currant bread, a seedcake, a Genoa cake and a White Mountain cake, while I did dinner and after. They came out pretty well — however the Genoa is so rich the way my mother made it that I wonder if I should not dilute it for modern consumption.

I hope you like the new book [*The James Beard Cookbook*]. I do think it is simple and easy and basic.

Love and all that,

J

---

[1] Craig Claiborne wrote in the *New York Times* that chefs of leading restaurants and hotel kitchens were leaving for well-paying jobs with fast-food restaurant chains and airlines, and that there were no training facilities in the country to provide replacements.

86 West 12th Street
New York
[April 1959]

My dearest Helen —

They launched the book on Thursday with a party at Mr. Delacorte's[1] twenty-room digs on Fifth Avenue. It was a fun party, with
all the people we know, and the impressiveness of the whole thing
was enough to bowl you over. I had a really wonderful time — the
food was not distinguished but the rest was quite good. Delacorte
took everyone on the official tour and showed everything from his
bust, done by Lachaise, to a photo of his eighteen grandchildren.

Last night I had eighteen people for supper. I invited two or
three and somehow it grew and grew. Had vegetables and a sauce
made with the Nestlé meatless spaghetti sauce; choucroute and
dilled new potatoes; cheese; and a delicious chocolate génoise
with whipped cream and a chocolate glaze. And a heavenly Moselle. Everyone stayed forever. The apartment looked beautiful,
and the bar is now finished. It is fun to have a houseful in this
apartment, for people congregate in all the rooms.

I'm looking forward to sitting down and talking to you for a
long spell when you are here. It is so hard to convey one's thoughts
on paper — at least it has become so for me.

J

---

[1] George Delacorte, philanthropist and chairman of the board of Dell
Publishing Company.

Cincinnati
[May 1959]

Helen, dear —

I'm having a gay and wonderful weekend away from it all with
dear old friends. On to Chicago Monday for the Restaurant Show.

I'm taking over a building, definitely, and remodeling so that I
have a real kitchen and a large apartment. It's going to break me,
but the rent is low and everyone says it is the right move.

Albert Stockli did a beautiful birthday party for me. Then the next night I had Paul [Bernard] and several others who are May people for dinner. The following night, to Paula's for dinner, and now here. As for my birthday, I would love some Chinese bowls — the peach blossom ones or the octagonal ones, about 6–7 inches across, for sauces and for serving fruit and such things.

I guess the book has become a real bestseller — everyone at the Dell office seems stunned that it has had a success so quickly. I only hope the money comes pouring in.

Love,

J

[86 West 12th Street
New York
July 16, 1959]

Dearest Helen —

My house is a small one on 10th Street — a three-story brick building which was completely rebuilt by the present owner five years ago, and which is in good condition. The ground floor is rented to Sutter's, the bakery, for their offices, but they have no sign out and keep their shades drawn at all times. This lease goes on until the year 1965 and the rent increases each year. I will have the two top floors. The second floor will have my kitchen, large enough for ten students, and a salon. We will have the school there, and I will also use it as a test kitchen. Then the top floor will have a small suite for Gino and a huge bed-sitting room for me, a spot where I can have my close friends. There is a small garden, which can be developed, and so I think it is a good move — for living and working over a long period of time.

Paula, Ruth and I did a Mexican dinner on Sunday in New Canaan for twenty-eight. We had Helen McCully, Sam and Florence Aaron, Mary Martin and Dick and Heller, and Geraldine Page and spouse [Rip Torn]. We gave them carnitas, wonderful chorizos you get here now, salsa fria, mantequilla de Pobre, and a fabulous invention of ours — ground turkey, ham, chilies, garlic and onion, mixed with puréed beans, eggs and pine nuts, rolled in rich pastry and then in cornmeal, cut in slices and baked. Then a chili of cut-up meat, black beans, a radish salad, and a turkey boned and rolled with a highly seasoned bean purée, basted with mole sauce, and served with the sauce — simply wonderful. We also had fruit and cookies and coffee and beer. They ate themselves absolutely sick. It began to rain while they were eating, and they stayed out under the trees with the rain coming down gently.

Dell is offering me a contract for a new book on international cuisine, to be done at once. I have so much in that field I have never used that it should not be too hard to do.[1]

Love and kisses

J

---

[1] JB never did this book, and to fulfill his contract he wrote *Menus for Entertaining* (1965).

[86 West 12th Street
New York
August 1959]

Dearest Helen —

Try a veal ragout with pork broth and a pound or so of okra cooked for the whole time, with a little tomato. Then garnish with additional okra cooked in broth — a delicious dish if you care for okra, which I happen to like at least two or three times a year.

I must say, the Chinese-oven-cooked filet of beef at Trader Vic's in Chicago is superb. I would almost like to have a Chinese oven if it could bring forth food that good. The smoked steak slices at the Four Seasons cooked in the Chinese oven and served with ratatouille for lunch are superb also.

Have I told you that I am so sold on the Osterizer now that I cannot see the Blendor anymore? The new model makes twice the amount of mayonnaise or hollandaise, and the removable bottom is a joy. They have sent me their grinder and electric can opener but I shall wait till the new house is ready before attacking them. I shall have so much stuff to work with. But I shall surely be in debt till I die. I have borrowed from the bank to do the kitchen, but am swinging the rest by myself.

This business of Dione styling all the pictures for *House and Garden* does me in. They are shooting my "Wine Cook Book" in December, and José [Wilson][1] called me to say that Dione wanted to do a duck à l'orange! If there is any dish I hate, along with chocolate chiffon cake with lemon filling and cranberry sherbet, it is that one. But Dione says it has such beautiful garniture. So I guess that over my strongest objections we have duck à l'orange. And now I have to include a recipe. Shit.

But I suppose I shouldn't kick, for *House and Garden* gives me a lot of work. I have three cookbooks for next year and twelve "Corkscrews,"[2] which ain't hay, sister.

Love,

J

---

[1] Food and travel editor at *House and Garden* who later collaborated with JB on articles, books, and a syndicated column.
[2] JB's column on wine and spirits.

[86 West 12th Street
New York
September 1959]

Dearest Helen —

I'm just back from Nantucket and the Cape. Mrs. Martin has been after me all year to go up, and I did. Had a lovely time with her and all the oldtimers I know in Nantucket. The weather was heaven, I had a lovely room, and Mrs. M's food is still sensationally good even though her chef is a strange one at this point. Such vegetables you get there — like at Gearhart and Seaside [Oregon] — tender, young and fresh as the dew. There are at least twenty different salad greens every day — oak leaf and Bibb and Boston and romaine — picked moments before you eat them.

Chillingsworth has had a fabulous season, and the food John [Clancy] is doing is really wonderfully good. He has no fear, this boy, and is turning out some fine stuff.

I'm going to a great dinner on the new *Rotterdam* on Friday night — taking Craig with me. Saturday Craig is having a house-warming and offering a Feijoada Completa for the meal. I shall have to have a housewarming before long. I think we shall be in by the end of the month, and I have moved about half my batterie de cuisine over there, in suspense for what will follow. It's going to be a darling house, and I think the kitchen will be the honey of all time.

Of course, just as I get ready to move, all the stuff in the world starts rolling in — two cases of soup, a case of syrup, a case of coconut, pineapple and all manner of junk.

If the *Sunset* breakfast and brunch book will interfere with your Doubleday book, why not make it a book of meals? As a matter of fact, that might be a good title — "Helen Evans Brown's Book of Good Meals." I rather like that. Bring regional stuff into it, and give it your own quality. Not party meals especially but meals for four, six and eight, a few for twenty-five, and a few for two. I'd adore to have such a book. Or make it a double feature of "Helen and Philip Brown's Book of Fabulous Meals."

Craig gave you a plug the other day about something — "the distinguished West Coast authority." He is a sweetheart, really.

Well, I have to go carry a load of junk down to the house so that we can cheat the movers.

Love you both madly,
[J]

119 West 10th Street
New York
[October 3, 1959]

Dearest Helen —

The move came off. Of course it was the day I had to do the Gimbel Cooking School for the second time and the day the aftermath of the hurricane arrived. Gino, who had an abscessed tooth, and John Clancy did a noble job — must have made a hundred trips apiece. Agnes was fabulous, as always, and by eight o'clock at night nearly everything was over. There is no kitchen and the paperhanger has played temperamental, but by the end of next week we should be together. Gino goes out for containers of coffee in the morning, and we have been living at the Coach House[1] for a fortnight, and so it goes. The living room is now papered completely — grapes and an arbor in black and white, almost like a huge etching — lovely — and the same thing is going to be in the hall.

Evidently Dione was the great sensation of all time at the Food Editors Conference. They tell me she put on one of her best shows and wowed the girls. And the Borden dinner seemed to get into an international hassle that simply wound up in insults. Everyone got more for their money than they expected.

I am invited to go out to Pittsburgh in January for the Council of Jewish Women — 2800 gals — all of which is a little paralyzing to me somehow.

Did I tell you about dropping the roast on the floor at Gimbels on Thursday? — just after it had been seared. Roast and baby onions ran rampant. I merely told them it was a new way of tenderizing and let them laugh it off.

Living across from the jail [Women's House of Detention][2] is most enlightening. I never knew how many people screamed up at their friends and families — very dramatic. They have cops to chase them away most of the time.

I love you both.

J

---

[1] A restaurant in the neighborhood, run by Leon Lianides.

[2] A high-rise prison situated behind the Jefferson Market Courthouse in Greenwich Village. It was demolished in 1974.

[119 West 10th Street
New York
October 5, 1959]

Dearest Helen —

I thought you might like to see Craig's review of the Four
Seasons, which seemed to shock everyone except me. I know that
he was being absolutely true to himself and that he fought with
himself before he put his criticisms on paper. But it is honest and it
is Craig, and I think it is a great review. The answer is that on
Friday, a Jewish holiday, when Chauveron had sixteen for dinner
and Maude Chez Elle had fifty, the Four Seasons did a $10,000 day!

Albert and his wife came by last night, and we ended with dinner
at the Coach House, which he seemed to enjoy thoroughly. He is
really a gentle and sweet guy who has been worked to death over
the years.

The oven is in!

Love,
[J]

119 West 10th Street
New York
October 14, 1959

Dearest Helen —

Had a perfectly dreamy time in Cincinnati, where I find I love
the people more than in any other place I've known. Came back
last night to find that some progress has been made, especially
with the kitchen, but we certainly are not going to be ready next
week for classes. Had a bad time with the electricians and with
Con Edison; and with all the millions of yards of wiring we have for
this house, I don't wonder. Haven't been able to cook a meal since
we moved, but I did cook in Cincinnati, and on Sunday I gathered
eight pounds of delicious mushrooms, including morels.

Craig has gone to Europe and I didn't get a chance to tell him
what you thought of his article. However, I don't think he was
fearless at all — in fact, I thought he missed the main point.

Everyone knows Joe Baum[1] likes big plates, but the point is that this is the first really seasonal restaurant, where things are searched out all over the world. To be constructive you have to mention some of the good points, too, and I think that Craig fell down on this.

I hope you are thinking about the seasonal cookbook.

Much love,

J

---

[1] Joseph Baum, executive vice president of Restaurant Associates and its creative genius.

Pasadena
October 16, 1959

James dearest,

Well, sorry we don't agree about the Craig article. I haven't eaten at Four Seasons but I have had reports. And some from people whose judgment you respect. One criticism keeps popping up. Too much food on the plates. And another. The food is spectacular but not classic. But then I do think Craig goes overboard for la haute cuisine. So there are two sides to that coin. Still, as I said, I admire Craig for his frankness. This country needs more writers who will tell the truth about food. We might have fewer gastronomical horrors, don't you think?

H

119 West 10th Street
New York
November 8, 1959

Dearest Helen —

The old Fanny Farmer chicken recipe that you wanted is as follows:

Dress, clean and cut up two chickens (I quarter them). Place in a dripping pan, sprinkle with salt and pepper, dredge with flour, and dot with butter. Bake 30 minutes in a very hot oven, basting every five minutes with ¼ cup butter melted with ½ cup boiling water. Serve with gravy made by using the fat in the pan, ¼ cup flour, one cup each chicken stock and cream, salt and pepper.

Naturally, I have done some variations on this theme with seasonings and with white wine instead of water. This is from the 1914 edition.

The school started this week with the kitchen in quite good condition, and it went extremely well. The cooking unit is very handsome — it looks like a grand piano — and works perfectly. On Wednesday we were thirteen milling around, and there was no confusion. Also, being able to demonstrate and observe from the middle is a great boon. I do think we have achieved something.

I am going to have a housewarming this Saturday and the following Saturday and Sunday. John Clancy offered to do the whole thing, and so it is not going to be a horrible strain. It will be cocktails and about thirty-five people each session. Then that is all over with for a while.

Craig's back, glittering with enthusiasm, finding it difficult to settle into the routine again.

Today the joys of being a landlord are being demonstrated. The furnace refuses to work, and it is Sunday and cold. I have to compose a little ditty on romantic drinks,[1] and I feel as romantic as a toasted flea.

Best love,

J

---

[1] "St. Valentine's Love Potions" for the February 1960 issue of *House and Garden.*

[119 West 10th Street
New York
November 25/26, 1959]

Dearest Helen —

Tomorrow is the day of Thanks. I'm having Craig and Emil Kashouty,[1] who is working for me now, and his friend, Frank Hearne, and Gino, of course. A simple dinner, with caviar to start, a turkey, tarragon bread stuffing, potatoes, turnips with duxelles, fennel, and pumpkin pie, and that is it.

The parties went beautifully, and I'm rather sorry they are over. I'm convinced that giving three in a row is easier than anything else. We made a ton of onion rings each time, and I did a galantine for the last two and a terrine of the farm for the first. I made a new dressing with olive oil, eggs, capers, anchovies, garlic and Quatre Épices to go with the fennel. And did a new shrimp pâté of chopped shrimp added to whipped butter, with mace, Pernod and parsley — like potted shrimp with a hell of a difference.

The house looked lovely. I have a chrysanthemum tree that must have had a hundred copper-colored flowers the size of large grapefruits on it. We banked the fireplace with plants and had pink chrysanthemums in the kitchen, along with the big lavabo full of new potatoes, artichokes, bananas, eggplants and lemons. Looked like heaven, I must say, with a silver candelabra on one corner of my grand-piano stove.

A turkey just came. That makes three I have received. What the hell do I do with three turkeys? Freeze them, I guess, but you know what you can do with a frozen bird.

I must stop and put the turkey in the oven. This is Thursday, and I'm on the jump. Woke up at 5:30 and listened to my tenants load their trucks with millions of pumpkin pies and mince pies and knew the rent would be paid this month.

Love and kisses,

J

---

[1] Assistant to Kate Titus at the public relations firm DAY.

[119 West 10th Street
New York
December 1959]

Helen, dearest —

I'm doing two rum parties for Gottlieb here the week after Christmas. Christmas Eve I'm on TV — "Who Do You Trust?" It is network. We shall probably dine at the Four Seasons, and Christmas morning the Pedlars come for breakfast, and I think Kate Titus and her husband may come for dinner. I am going to have roast beef for dinner, and for breakfast, codfish. I have no feeling of the holidays being imminent.

I just can't get the right person to work around here. The minute they see a house they think they are going to break their backs, but truly, this is simpler to care for than the apartment was. I have an Estonian, a Japanese and a Negro coming tomorrow. We'll see what they want. And can do.[1]

Clementine was down here the other night for her annual story-getting session. She was in fine form and is hoping now to go out for a cruise on an atomic submarine to see how they all eat. She is surely the getting-aroundest person I have ever known, except for Eleanor Roosevelt. She ate pâté and drank champagne like a veteran. I really get quite a kick out of her.

If you don't like your Christmas present, you can forgive me, for I think I did all my shopping in one day and in about three hours of that one.

Love,

J

---

[1] Enter Clayton Triplette, who would remain with JB for the next twenty-five years.

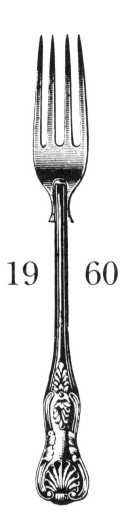

19 60

The year began with JB making plans for a new session of classes, after a good send-off from Craig Claiborne in the *New York Times*. In March he and HEB were together on Avery Island, Louisiana, as guests of Spice Islands. On April 14 JB sailed for Southampton on the *United States,* spent six days in Brighton and London and then went to Nestlé's in Zurich. After a few days in Venice he took a ten-day cruise to Istanbul and disembarked at Marseille on May 10. He remained in France and Switzerland for another week before returning to New York. At the end of May and in early June he was in Los Angeles and San Francisco; in July, in Boston and on Cape Cod; in September, in Chicago, Minneapolis, and Cincinnati. On September 23 he was back in Europe to attend a Colloquium Culinarium in Zurich, where he made a speech. In November he traveled throughout the country doing food demonstrations and book signings, spending Thanksgiving with the Browns and then going north to San Francisco and the wineries in St. Helena and Livermore. He also made appearances in Denver and Dallas, in December, and settled down long enough to celebrate Christmas at home with a traditional dinner of roast beef.

Dearest Helen —

I did the two parties for Gottlieb this week and they came off damned well, I think. I have a new cocktail tidbit or two that I love. One is tangerine sections marinated in wine vinegar and a little oil, rum, onion and fresh rosemary — like the salad, only with long marinating in the refrigerator. It is low-calorie and delicious with drinks. Also, avocado balls in rum, vinegar, garlic, oil and salt and pepper. I did pâtés with rum and hams with rum and an apricot-rum glaze. And we did Jamocha, grog and Russian tea for drinks.

The Christmas ties were a great success. I wore the brightest one with my black shirt on Thursday for the party.

The house has begun to really look beautiful. Have a dining table now. John Clancy gave me an ivy tree for Christmas, and I had some nice ferns. "The girls" had necklaces of Christmas balls, and in the kitchen I had candlelight and a beautiful arrangement of fruit, bread, and a dead pheasant in plumage in the lavabo.

Tuesday, Wednesday and Thursday nights we are having open house for the school. Paula and I are doing demonstrations for the new students and Helen Britt[1] and I for the old. I'm doing a beef Stroganoff and probably a quick sauce or two. Paula is doing a lemon sponge cake, and Helen is naturally doing some lovely chocolate things. I'm hoping we'll get several good classes out of this.

I hope you sent the scone mix, for I have to get this mix book finished for *House and Garden*. There are some good mixes on the market. I like the hot roll mix of Pillsbury and the buttermilk pancake mix of Duncan Hines, and their cake mixes aren't so bad either. And I have achieved some worthwhile things with the oatmeal bread mix and the cornbread mix. I have found lousy stuff as well. That vanillin is poison. I have managed to smother it in a couple of cases with rum and cognac.

I'm beginning to think I would like to have six months to myself late this year and early next. I shall write a memoir cookbook,[2] which is the thing I have wanted to do for the last year or so. I have a lot of good food material around and a hell of a lot of memories. My mother's story, the Hamblet story, my father's deft fingers in the kitchen, the old chef Let, my first introduction to Chinese and French cookery, my war experiences and my experiences since then — all seem to have good makings for a book. After that we should get down to our correspondence as a cookbook — the thing we have always talked of doing. This could be revived with the zest with which we went into it for several years before we became so frantically busy.

This of course will depend on what happens at Nestlé's. They seem to be expanding, and if I go on there another year I shall give up *House and Garden* and one or two other things and cut down to the bone. I have to push, this year and next, to catch up on the house, and then I can be in the clear, more or less.

I got four sets of vermeil dessert service in my pattern for Christmas, which will be very fancy once I get six or eight — knife, fork and spoon, something I have always wanted. Mary sent me the old Hamblet champagne bucket, which I have known since childhood. I was very touched.

Love to you and Philip. It is New Year's Day. I cleaned the basement.

Toujours,

J

---

[1] An executive at Nestlé.
[2] The genesis of JB's book *Delights and Prejudices*.

119 West 10th Street
New York
[January 23, 1960]

Dear Browns —

Craig did a wonderful article about the school, with picture, and
a flood of applications has come in. We have three full classes and
are almost booked for the next course. It is gratifying to have the
reaction, and funnily enough most of the students come from
Dione to us. The dinner group starts next week. They are doing
quenelles de brochet, sauce Nantua, saddle of lamb Bordelaise,
cèpes, a vacherin filled with raspberry mousse and dry petits fours.
Sounds pretty good, doesn't it?

Well, the mix book is finished, and I must say that I have learned
a lot. The hot roll mix is a cinch, some of the new cake mixes are
excellent in their way, the meringue is good, and so on. I think the
roll mixes have a tremendous value for people who would be
afraid to attempt bread. They can get the feeling of yeast doughs
from a mix and then go on to the recipe from scratch. However, I
still see no point in Bisquick or in pie-crust mix, for they do
absolutely nothing that cannot be done as quickly from scratch.
And is my laundress happy? She has taken more cake home to her
children for parties than they ever ate before.

I have a room on the *United States* on April 14th. I want to go to
Nestlé's, and then I think I will either stay in Venice for ten days or
take the boat to Istanbul and back, a twelve-day trip. That way I
would see three new cities and get rest in between, and really be
away from everything.

The other night André called and offered me four dozen
French oysters. They had flown over a mess for the Chevalier de
Tastevin dinner, and he was given the remainders. I took them
over to Lianides [at the Coach House], and we ate them freshly
opened. What a flavor they have — mellow, coppery, with almost a
creaminess when you chew and analyze. I drank some good beer
with them and floated on a gastronomically sensual cloud. Good
food is so sexy in its way. We followed with wonderful veal
kidneys — roasted them in all their fat at high heat and then cut
them and browned them very quickly under the broiler. They had

a crisp crust and a bloody, tender interior. The fat had dried out enough so that it gave a slight char flavor to the whole. This was, to me, a gourmet dinner. I had a little piece of boiled potato, some coffee, and what else is there to want?

Just as a luncheon I had with Albert and Joe at the Four Seasons last Monday was perfect. I had blue trout with a spoon of butter sauce on it, one little new potato, a piece of good cheese and a double expresso. The trout had come that morning and was torn from the water when I ordered it.

And last night we went to a restaurant downtown. The chef is the nephew of a restaurateur I know in Naples. We had stuffed zucchini and stuffed mushrooms, and I had a fritto misto, which was almost all squid and baby octopus, with a couple of pieces of veal and a couple of shrimp, but give me calamari cooked as well as those and I am in heaven.

Love and kisses,

J

119 West 10th Street
New York
[January 29, 1960]

Helen, dear —

Yesterday I had lunch with Ivan Obolensky — the publisher Ivan, not his cousin the champagne person. He wants me to do his father's book with him, with equal billing and an equal publicity buildup, including a series on TV, sponsored by the St. Regis, probably. Then he would like to have anything else I do. Well, he has money by the ton and is ambitious. I think I would rather do a book for him than for Alfred. This might be our correspondence cookbook, if we wanted it. I still want to do my gastronomic memoirs, and he loves that idea.

We are having a time with a sauce on the market called "Aunt Millie's." It has taken Westchester by storm, and while we [Nestlé] are not sold on it, the executives' wives feel it is divine and want us to emulate it. Well, you know the power of a wife in business. I'm just finding out. So I am stewing up evil messes of sauces at the rate of about five or six a morning and feel that I now have it. Helen Britt tried it herself yesterday and was not so sure. Neither one of us ever wants to eat spaghetti again as long as we live. God, the American palate is so immune to flavor that it is sinful to think of putting a good product on the market. The main flavors people want are sweetish tomato and imitation garlic. And sweet mayonnaise and sweet French dressing. Ugh.

Did I tell you that John Conway is coming next week, sans Dorothy. I shall do a party for him, I guess, and make a new beef and pork dish I'm crazy about or that stew in *House and Garden* [Kadjemoula] with fruits in it. Tonight Paul Bernard and Harry Marinsky are coming for dinner, with two other friends, and I'm doing a huge loin of pork, sweet and sour. Opening with an asparagus purée, with cream and cognac. I'll also do another version of chili bread — this one with two packages of mix — Aunt Jemima — 6 crisp rashers of bacon, 1 can of chilies, 4 eggs, ½ pound of grated cheese, 1 can cream-style corn, 1 can white corn and cream. Tabasco and chili powder for seasoning. Good, last time I did it. And I have a beautiful raspberry mousse left for dessert.

At last night's class the quenelles came out beautifully, although they would have been better if they had rested overnight, and the sauce Nantua was divine. Used the quenelle recipe in *Paris Cuisine* but used double the amount of fish and a six-egg pâte à choux. Blended the fish with cream and egg whites, using slightly more than the recipe calls for, because of the Blendor. The lamb was perfection, although it surely was a heller to carve. The Disgustingly Rich Potatoes* I did were so good. And the vacherin looked like heaven when it came in.

I think the students love the idea of sitting down for dinner and having several wines, silver and gold service, and the best china. I found a tureen at the antique show to match the one I have — Minton. This one is like a great woven basket with a garland of leaves around it, and on the lid is a rabbit, a teal and a blackbird, with a rustic handle and more leaves. All in natural colors. It is a sensation! And in Boston I found a pair of Strasbourg geese in perfect condition and had them put aside for me. No wonder I never have any money. But someday I can have a good sale.[1]

Love and kisses,

J

---

[1] The majolica tureen (game dish) was sold at auction after JB's death for $3,500.

* Recipe.

[119 West 10th Street
New York
February 7, 1960]

Helen —

I can't type for a day or two. Slashed my finger trying to make a hole in a can.[1] They took seven stitches in it at the hospital — no pain, though.

Craig was here last night with his friend Henry. Presented them my cut finger and stitches, to start. Then foie gras, roast filet, which I marinated with a little soy and Quatre Épices and served with a large slice of fresh truffle, Madeira sauce with fresh truffles, purée of chestnuts, braised endive, a chèvre cheese that was running, and pineapples with fruits and rum. Drank a magnum of Cheval-Blanc '50 and a bottle of '49.

Tonight I'm stuffing a piece of leg of veal with anchovies and olives and braising it — should be fascinating, with a garlic-scented sauce. And just a rather simple pasta and salad.

I know you'll have a hard time reading this, so I'll cut it short.

Love,

J

---

[1] In the succeeding letter, JB wrote (the passage has been omitted) that he had cut his index finger with a French knife while talking to Claiborne. It is difficult to tell which of these two versions is correct.

119 West 10th Street
New York
[February 1960]

Dearest Helen —

You probably are still trying to decipher the note I sent you on Sunday. I did cut my finger badly, but it has healed beautifully.

Had people here last night and felt like doing an Italian dinner, so I made some lovely antipasto — mushrooms à la Grecque, with parsley by the ton; ripe tomatoes — for this time of the year — with basil, garlic, oil and cognac; my bean and tuna salad; and anchovies, with lots of shallots, parsley and capers. Then I had a piece of veal from the shin of the animal, with a pocket, and made a stuffing of anchovies, garlic, tiny green olives and pimientos. Braised it with leftover Madeira sauce I had, with fresh truffles in it. Added olives to the sauce and served it with green noodles.

I love you both!
J

119 West 10th Street
New York
[April 1, 1960]

Dearest Helen —

I did one of the most foolish bits of food research I have ever done. I was reading — anent the Spring changeover at Four Seasons — that rhubarb tops were used as vegetables in France. So the other day I bought some rhubarb with beautiful tops and thought this was the time to try it. I ate them, sat down to read a folder on fruits and vegetables and read that rhubarb tops were toxic and could be fatal! Well they almost were. All night my whole body smelled like rhubarb cooked without sugar, and I was sicker than I have ever been for an hour or two in the middle of the night. I highly recommend that you leave rhubarb tops alone.

My supper party and ham tasting for the Nestlé group and others was a huge success. I started with mushrooms sautéed with herbs and our wonderful sour cream. The two hams — I shall send

you one of the Pine Plains ones; the other was an Iowa ham —
were good. I roasted them in white wine and Madeira and then
made a mustard, brown sugar, Madeira glaze. For the sauce I
cooked shallots, added brown gravy, Madeira, some of the pan
juices and Quatre Épices, then strained it and allowed it to cook
down. And I did spinach gnocchi. Finished with strawberries
Souvaroff. We drank magnums of the Muscadet 1959, which is a
delicious and exciting wine. I sat the guests down, but after the
first course was cleared I had them come out to the kitchen and
choose their ham. I had set up the Formica buffet tops on the
stoves for the first time. Then Gus and Clayton served the cheese
and dessert. I never had such a good group. They were lambs.

I go to Washington on Monday and do my demonstration on
Tuesday night for the HEWIBs. They have sold 250 tickets, their
capacity. I'm doing shortcuts to gourmet food. Starting with a
Salade Niçoise, then the veal roll, pasta with white truffles, and
crêpes. And as a surprise I think I shall do the Chicken with Forty
Pieces of Garlic — always a success.

I haven't heard from Alice and I am somewhat worried. I think
she may be terribly ill with her arthritis. If I come back from
Europe over the Pole I shall stop a day or two in Paris and see her. I
may ask Carl Van Vechten,[1] who sits in front of me at the Philhar-
monic on Sundays, about her. I have never spoken to him but
might just as well.

Love and kisses,

J

---

[1] American novelist, music critic, and photographer.

M.S. *San Marco*
[April 30, 1960]

Dearest Helen —

This is an enchanting ship and one that you and Philip will love
if you take it next year. You can put your car aboard. As a matter of
fact there are about six on the forward deck. The dining room is

on the promenade deck, with huge windows, and the lounge has long windows looking out to sea. There has been a horrible cold wave, as you have probably read in the papers, but today is by far the worst, for the wind is blowing from the Yugoslavian coast, where they had a terrific snowstorm. However, the feeling is that we shall finally hit some warm weather tomorrow.

I don't remember if you have been to Venice or not, but for food I like it better than any other place in Italy. They use the fish and shellfish of the region beautifully, and the meat is the best of veal and beef. Yesterday I went to Signor Zoppi at La Fenice and had the most thorough lesson in green pasta. They make green cannelloni there, with a spinach and ricotta filling, that is the best pasta dish I have ever had anywhere. It is amazing to see what a restaurant of that caliber achieves with the small kitchen they have. A good kitchen, mind you, but small and without a great number of people doing the work.

Last night I took some good friends of mine from Mexico City, whom I met casually in Harry's Bar, to Al Graspo de Ua for dinner. Signor Lis [of the Gritti Palace] called and asked Signor Mora, who is the most devastatingly handsome restaurateur in the world, to give me the works as far as regional specialties were concerned, and he did. We started with his cold antipasta — shrimp, scampi, tiny calamari, tiny octopus, and crabmeat with nothing but oil, lemon, a bit of parsley and a touch of rosemary. Then cold brandade de morue [bacala mantecato]; a cold salad of beef tendons, with onion, fennel and oil; a risotto with mussels, small clams, much fish broth, a great deal of fennel, and pepper; squid in their own juice with oil and a touch of garlic; tiny fried scampi and calamaretti, with a delicious salad of paper-thin bits of tomato and fennel and good oil and lemon juice. After that, a fascinating do of fraises des bois. Signor Mora did them himself with the artistry of a genius. They came in a silver bowl to which he added freshly ground pepper, sugar, and two dessertspoons of wine vinegar. Then he tossed them well — without spoon and fork — and added more sugar. They were superb. His theory is that they are induced to give their flavor because of the bit of vinegar. I had had strawberries with freshly ground pepper before and had liked them but never with this combination. Well, after that dinner and two espressi and a cognac we were able to struggle home through the winding streets, feeling we had dined abundantly but not to excess, because we were given small portions.

The day spent in Torcello was lovely. I think it should be a spot to go for a complete rest and for air so bracing that it fills you with ambition for the next two years. I was disappointed with the food. In fact, I had the least exciting meal I had the whole time in Venice. I met a charming old gal from Boston and a nice couple from Pasadena. But some of our fellow countrymen are beyond belief. One woman said to her group in the hotel the other night, "Well, we might look at St. Mark's but we don't have to go in." But she knew the depth of the water in the canal and the length of the tunnel coming from Florence.

The menu on the ship is tremendous. You know I cannot resist sausages in any form, so for lunch I had salsicce di Treviso as my single plate, and much to my delight they arrived with the Italian equivalent of finely done sauerkraut. The little sausages had been skinned after heating, cut in half and lightly browned before nestling in their bed of kraut.

Love from the big gondola.

Jim

M.S. *San Marco*
May 9, 1960

My dearest Helen and Philip —

I am arriving in Marseille tomorrow and am sad. I loved this trip and for the first time in ages have been completely away from everything and feel rested. The ship is delightfully clean, it has an ever-changing passenger list, and the food is extremely varied and good. The baker is a genius. I enjoyed every port and only wish we had had more time in Izmir and perhaps in Athens. I had delicious shore times and ate strangely good food, though not quite as good as you or I would make it. This is especially true of Turkey, where they overcook lamb, and while it looks good, it is pot roasty. The doner kebabs, to which I had so looked forward, are never pink or rare, and no one seems to want them that way.

The yoghurt kebab was by far the most interesting one I had in all the trip. And a dish of lamb with artichokes and an egg and lemon sauce I had in Athens makes me wonder if hollandaise is not an outgrowth of that sauce. And let me tell you that Turkish and Greek cucumbers are the absolute end of all cucumbers. They are deliciously crisp and sweet and never have the slightest bit of coarseness that one so often finds in ours. I have been eating them twice a day since Istanbul. I'm enchanted with the things they do with various types of beans for salads and hors d'oeuvre and the number of green onions they use; and the way they serve great heads of romaine, split in half, with salt or cheese and no dressing, much the way we might serve celery. You can have my share of the pastries.

I find I don't want to go home. I am trying to figure what is going to happen next. I am not excited by the things I do. The teaching, yes. Some of the work for Nestlé, yes. But I am so rushed I have nothing for myself anymore. Gino gets increasingly busy, and although we have a delightful understanding, it is not a companionship where things are shared. Ruth and I are on a business basis now. Paula and I are close, but outside of food, there is no common ground, which is also true of Clancy and Emil Kashouty, who is Kate's secretary. I know dozens of people but I am not close to them. I have you and Philip, but good God, you are thousands of miles away. You two are very, very close to me, and I love you both a great deal.

You've heard some of this before, but I have really done some analyzing on this trip. I think I would love to teach and to experiment twenty-four hours a day. That would give me great satisfaction. I would like to be able to train people beyond just the ability to make certain dishes. John Clancy has been a deeply satisfactory person, and so has Paula, for while she knew a great deal when she came to me, she has grown so much and become so much more sure of herself.

Then there is still that idea of a small restaurant I cannot put out of my head. I have Clancy and could have Emil, and I could certainly train a good pastry cook — and serve dinners only, with wines of grand quality. This still burns in my mind.

At any rate I don't think I can stand the schedule I had last year and especially the last two months. I nearly toppled several times, and it was only by being severely careful that I was able to get through. The two weeks before I left were like being at the whipping post, and I nearly died before I finally closed the door on the last departing guest on the *United States* and felt the movement of the ship under me.

I had several wires on my birthday [May 5] but have had no letters for a week or two. I feel I am in space.

My love to you both.

J

[119 West 10th Street
New York
June 13, 1960]

Dearest Helen —

I am going to Boston over the Fourth to be with the two doctors, and then Gino and I and two friends [Emil Kashouty and Frank Hearne] have taken a cottage on the Cape for the first week in August, near Chillingsworth, so that we can dine there or cook for ourselves, as we please. Then in September I have dates in St. Louis and in Fort Wayne. I won't begin a class till about November 1st. So I shall just take it damned easy and not worry about anything.

Chicago went well. Peggy Harvey[1] had a delicious dinner on Sunday. She did a mess of lovely snails and had a Boeuf à la Mode en Gelée, a bean salad, and the most delicious strawberry soufflé. We did a lovely party on Monday for the booksellers, and they drank till two in the morning. I left at about half past eight. Went for dinner to a place Peggy had found — an old whore joint, where the food is sensationally good. They did a chateaubriand with a piece of tough meat, which was cut and put through the duck press to make the base for the sauce.

Emil is sending you the recipe for kibbee, raw, in the next day or two. He had it for an hors d'oeuvre last night, and I loved it again.

He also made another dish with sesame seeds, parsley and lemon that was delicious.

I have guests three nights this week for dinner and a cocktail party next week. Tomorrow night I am giving Steve, who is down from Cape Cod, cold chicken, stuffed breast of veal I made on Saturday, and ratatouille. Wednesday I have the *House and Garden* gals, and I'm giving them sorrel soup, squab stuffed with rice, pistachio nuts and favas, a magnificent Brie, and fruit. Sunday night I have the Pecks, and I'm doing a new pasta dish, with beans — dry ones — zucchini, tomatoes, carrots, bacon and what-not. And a Vitello Tonnato.

Love and kisses,

J

---

[1] A former Powers model; food writer and author of *Season to Taste.*

[119 West 10th Street
New York
June 26, 1960]

Dearest Helen —

I have spent the morning doing dry-freeze casseroles and now feel that I have them licked. They are good to taste, believe it or not, and I know you won't.

Did I tell you that Planter's is having a contest for recipes with peanut oil, and the prizes are five days here next spring for classes? I can go to Europe after it is all over. So maybe I shall see you in May somewhere. I really want to go back to Vienna again, if possible, and do the pastries. That, I feel, is a must for you, for there is nothing to compare with Demel's — to just sit there for a whole afternoon and taste things as they roll out. You'll eat the greatest pastry in the world.

Have you had the new Mobil attempt at a Michelin that Simon and Schuster have published at a dollar? The first volume only covers New England and New York. They have three five-star restaurants in New York — "21," Pavillon, and Chambord, of all horrors. The Four Seasons and the Forum only get four stars each! However, it is an attempt and interesting from that standpoint.

Had Karl Springer and Mateo Lettunich[1] for dinner last night. Gave them figs and prosciutto; a beautiful filet marinated with rum, soy, and Tabasco, which I roasted just 24 minutes; parslied new potatoes with bellybands; and red sweet peppers, sautéed to a crispness, with a bit of my sherry vinegar in them. And Gino made an apricot flan. He has suddenly taken an interest in cooking and made a rich pastry as good as Paula's.

We went to Paula's on Friday with the Aarons and Callverts, and she did a beautiful dinner. Tiny cubes of sturgeon marinated in garlic, oil and parsley and broiled with tiny pieces of ham, toothpicked — also shrimp done that way. Then exquisitely done squab, boned, stuffed with pâté, and coated with chaudfroid; a vegetable à la Grecque mixture, cold; Cuban bread; and a frozen meringue torte, which was beyond belief. We all agreed that squab are too delicious by themselves to be stuffed with pâté and done chaudfroid. It should have been a breast of veal, like that thing I did for *House and Garden* last year.

I have been going over a brunch cookbook for *House and Garden* because someone forgot to put in the wines. Such a mess of stuff. There is actually a recipe for rolling white bread with butter and a sprinkling of Lawry's salt and toasting it in the oven. I nearly popped. What wine you might choose for that is problematic. I would say an old pre-phylloxera Mogen David Concord, with added sugar, myself.

We drove up with Lianides to the most beautiful place for lunch, in Tarrytown. An old mansion high above the Hudson, with a fantastic view and the worst slop for food you ever knew. And crowded to the doors. Does no one want good food in this country? This place would last one week in France or Italy, and here it is packed and overflowing. I looked at the roast duck someone had, and it must have been cooking since last week, it was so overdone, and the skin so flabby. What is cookery coming to anyway? Then I read a recipe in the *Herald Tribune* for lobster parfait, served in a parfait glass like an ice cream, with lobster, mint, sherry, mayonnaise and other bits, and topped with whipped cream flavored with — and get this — parsley, chives, chervil and mint. Who knows what herb is where?

> Love, mixed with fresh herbs,
>
> J

---

[1] Springer was a designer of luxury furniture and accessories; Lettunich, a consultant for the Ford Foundation and the State Department. They were neighbors of JB.

> [119 West 10th Street
> New York
> July 8, 1960]

Helen, dear —

We went to Boston, to the doctors', last Friday and had the most wonderful weekend. They are the two with whom I spent some time in England this year — Annella Brown, a brilliant surgeon, and Alice Lowell, an internist. They have a heavenly house full of eighteenth-century things from France, and a lovely pool. We practically never left the place. Fraises des bois in the garden and good food, and I was waited on.

Annella made a delicious pâté, with plenty of truffles, which I must try. It is similar to the one you and I have done but cooked less. Also had a lovely capon one night and the best leg of lamb I have eaten for years another night. I had lunch at Locke-Ober and ordered a boiled lobster with mayonnaise. They brought horrible sweet mayonnaise which tasted like Mrs. Rorer's[1] fruit salad mistake dressing. I was incensed and told Fred, the maître d'hôtel, as much. Six dollars' worth of lobster almost ruined by a lousy dressing.

We had dinner at Athens Olympia, and it is still madly good. I had squid, and they were tasty and tender. Had ghastly food on the planes, both ways. Didn't eat going up to Boston but had to coming back — rolls of tough roast leg of beef, sliced tomatoes and eggs, and lettuce on two pieces of white cotton bread, open-face.

I did a huge roaster tonight in 55 minutes in a 450 oven. Put bacon strips over it and filled it with about 6 finely chopped cloves of garlic. Then made a casserole of eggplant and zucchini, with an onion, tomatoes and tarragon. And fruit for dessert. A perfect dinner, as far as I am concerned. I never get tired of roast or broiled chicken no matter what else comes along.

Love and kisses,

J

---

[1] Sarah Tyson Rorer, nineteenth-century cookbook writer.

[119 West 10th Street
New York
July 24, 1960]

Dearest Helen —

Today for a change I worked at home all day and accomplished something. Cooked two hams for dinner, to test for the *House and Garden* article. What I am going to do with two, I don't know. Did one braisé au Madère and the other, a canned one, I did in sherry and sugar. The canned one wasn't bad, but the other one was superb. I am amazed at some of the commercial ones you get nowadays if they are not too heavily sagged down with water.

I leave the 23rd of September for Paris, Frankfurt and Zurich. I shall come back just in time to go to Fort Wayne. My speech [at the Colloquium Culinarium] is on the 30th. It is to be a half hour in length, and I shall take big cards with clippings from magazines and newspapers. I wish you would collect some good ones from the papers there for me — from *Territorial Enterprise, Sunset,* and such like. This is a hell of a lot of work, for I shall be competing on an international scale, and I'm a little frightened about it.

Helen, would you ship to us at Nestlé any good pickles you have there — one jar of each — and charge them to us? We are going to have a comparative pickle tasting, with S and W, S. S. Pierce, Crosse and Blackwell, some German ones I found and some French ones.

I must send you a can of the German pickles, for they are

without a doubt the best things I have ever had in a commercial pickle. They are all over 86th Street.

I'm going to have dinner with Ann [Seranne] tomorrow night for the first time in a year or more. She lost her precious dog about three weeks ago and is in deep mourning. We have been friends for so long it seems strange not to see her. Before dinner I have to go to a party for José Wilson — a demi-farewell from *House and Garden,* for she will only be a part-time person there now. And Thursday I'm invited to the 150th anniversary of the Mint Julep. The Bourbon Institute is doing the party and I rather look forward to it.

André Surmain is really going to have his restaurant. More power to him, for I'm sure it will be one of the best in New York.

Love,

J

[Brewster, Cape Cod
August 1960]

Helen, dear —

I had a note from Alice [Toklas], and it seems my damned hotel got messages all mixed up. She was waiting for me, and I was waiting for her, and never the twain met. She is going to Rome for a winter because of her arthritis. She is to be a lady boarder at one of the convents where the sisters care for you.

The Cape is beautiful and our little house amusing. Agnes and Bill White came for the weekend, and we all had a festive dinner at Steve's [Chillingsworth] on Friday, with John Clancy doing his best. I had clams in aspic, chicken Marengo and dacquoise. Saturday we had Agnes and Bill here for dinner because Steve had a big wedding. We had those heavenly ducks from the farm here. They cook in no time at all and have little fat. I did them with olives. And fresh corn from the garden down the road — like butter.

Sunday, cooked in again — except for Chillingsworth there is no place to go, really. Did a leg of lamb which Steve had sent over. Inserted fresh mint leaves and garlic and roasted it at 500 for just an hour and a half — superb. More corn, and I did tiny, tiny new potatoes dug that afternoon. Monday we antiqued, spent the day with John and cooked great hamburgers here for lunch. Peter Hunt[1] gave a supper party for me Monday night, dined last night at Chillingsworth, and today we are going to Provincetown.

I have read my entire book [*Treasury of Outdoor Cooking*] through and feel they have just murdered it to make way for the pictures. I hate it more than ever now and have no interest in doing any publicity for it. It is the most beautifully laid out book you have ever seen. Maybe no one will look at the fluffs they made after I corrected proof. Why they have literary editors for cookbooks, I do not know.

Sandily and sea-airily yours,

Love and kisses,

[J]

---

[1] Provincetown artist who applied folk-art designs to furniture, fabrics, and glassware; author of *Peter Hunt's Cape Cod Cookbook*.

119 West 10th Street
New York
[August 8, 1960]

Dear Helen —

It is good to get back to your own bed and your own bathroom no matter how nice things are in a rented house. But it was fun. And we ate beautifully both at home and at Steve's. John's lobster de Jonghe is as good as any lobster dish I have ever had.

Elena is going great guns at Restaurant Associates.[1] They are all crazy about her. She is Albert's great favorite now and he dances attendance on her. I was up for the tasting luncheons yesterday and today.

I'm having her for dinner on Wednesday and she wants French food. She'll get a beautiful pâté and I'll do the Chicken with Forty Pieces of Garlic and tiny boiled potatoes. For dessert, I think I'll do a peach mousse with cream or a peach and raspberry soufflé.

Saw the new restaurant [La Fonda del Sol] yesterday, which won't be ready till September. It is strikingly beautiful. I think Elena is coming back for another visit after the opening.

They are now bringing brown-and-serve sourdough bread from San Francisco, at two loaves for 98 cents, and selling it fast and furiously. It is amazing to me that the public will fall for that price for bread. Maybe we should have started this years ago.

Love and kisses,

J

---

[1] Elena Zelayeta had been hired as a consultant for Restaurant Associates' new Latin-American restaurant, La Fonda del Sol.

[119 West 10th Street
New York
August 26, 1960]

Dearest Helen —

Next week we have our pickle tasting, with about fifty different ones, which should make for an interesting day. We are making recommendations to Crosse and Blackwell and have all the brass coming for a taste and a chance to blast. Going to give them good charcuterie and breads to go with the pickles.

The Paddleford, Aaron, Britt party was fun, and they all seemed to have a good cosy family time, despite the fact that the air-conditioning wasn't fixed and it was the hottest night we had had. They ate so much of the two terrines we had made that they hardly had any appetite when we came to dinner. However, they brushed off the deviled crab, which I made differently from the old Hamblet recipe — I added much more parsley, some scallions and more butter — and the chickens were good, with plenty of Quatre Épices and a sweetbread-liver stuffing. My peach flan was good, too, but the pastry was too rich. I am not a good pastry maker, no matter what I do.

Love,

J

119 West 10th Street
New York
[October 20, 1960]

Helen —

Fort Wayne was successful and rather fun but hellishly tiring. Two big demonstrations in a day, preparation for them and being nice to people is more than you can take. But I am enough of a ham to love demonstrating. I went to Cincinnati for Friday and Saturday, and we had a big dinner for which we all had to cook. So my holiday was a busman's.

You will see the Beard house in *House and Garden* this month. I think the dining room and kitchen shots are dandy.

The Fonda is beautiful. They have toned down the dishes, but I guess that is necessary for the New York public. But physically the Latin theme is magnificently done. I dined there on Tuesday night and sat late, talking to Joe and Ruth Baum, and Alan and Ellie Lewis.[1]

I'm doing the classes without Paula this year. She is on a sabbatical, as it were. But I find it is not bad at all and that I seem to plough through without hitches. Of course Ruth is around and she does a lot. Tonight we are doing terrines, pâtés and all sorts of things in that department. Flank steaks au poivre and Disgustingly Rich Potatoes. And a salad of fresh mushrooms and Bibb lettuce. They eat quantities of food when they get through. These are people I've had before, so they arc casier and more amusing, although we have one dame who smokes cigars and talks all the time. But she is a fabulously good cook, and her questions are intelligent. The beginning class is delightful, and the time just skips by when they are here.

Physically I am in top form — heart, blood pressure, and all those girls are entirely well — but the brain is wearing low.

Love and kisses,

J

---

[1] Alan Lewis, a vice president of Restaurant Associates, worked with Baum on a number of its dining rooms and later managed Windows on the World and the Rainbow Room.

119 West 10th Street
New York
[December 19, 1960]

Dearest Helen —

I had a wonderful time with you. I feel we have developed a great understanding over the years and that we can travel well together.

I had a strenuous trip the rest of the way. The luncheon in Chicago was swell, and Peggy Harvey did her part beautifully. Denver was good, too, although I will not do demonstrations anymore at big dinners where people have been drinking cognac for hours. It is too nerve-wracking. Dallas was horrendous. Three dinner parties, a couple of luncheons, and a breakfast — with Helen Corbitt,[1] who is marvelous.

I got back on Sunday on the first snowflake. God, did it snow. And today, one week later, we had our first garbage collection. Just awful. Streets impassable and hardly any deliveries — like the Dark Ages.

Peggy is coming to New York for the holidays. I'm giving her a party on the 30th — champagne, rillettes, a ham and Strathborough Paste* with buttered toast. And I'm doing my old smoked salmon, dill, sour cream and caper do. That's all.

Christmas Eve we are dining at Lianides's [the Coach House]. Christmas Day we are here, with Emil Kashouty and Frank Hearne for dinner — foie gras, roast beef, onions, mincemeat flan. Christmas breakfast, caviar omelets, as usual.

I'm doing more work for Joe on the new restaurant [Tower Suite]. He wants me to spend one day each at the Forum and Four Seasons, for the time being. If the Sherry Wine & Spirits thing works out, and this, maybe I can give up all the Gottlieb traveling and be here most of the time. That would be heaven. Saks have made overtures to me about a consultant's job, if they start a food business, but that would be duck soup. Then I could give up *House and Garden.*

Classes did goose last week. Stuffed two of them with grated potato, grated apple and sauerkraut. Delicious. They were both awfully good geese and we did them a full hour at 500 and then at

325. As a result they were moist and crisp but not fatty. Made some good foie gras with the two livers and fat. Real foie gras.

> Kisses and hugs,
>
> J

---

[1] Cookbook writer and director of restaurants in the Dallas Neiman Marcus.

* Recipe.

119 West 10th Street
New York
[December 29, 1960]

Dearest Helen —

Christmas Day was quiet and fun. Monday we worked all day — John Clancy and I, that is — on rillettes, Strathborough Paste and such for tomorrow. Santa was awfully good to me. I received a wonderful shortwave transistor radio on which you get nightly Russian lessons from Moscow and music from Indochina — this, from Jack and Sam Aaron. Gino and I bought a tape recorder for ourselves. I'm going to do my recipes on them for the school and for cookbooks from now on. Freddy [Shrallow] found a magnificent Crown Derby dessert dish and got a group together to give it to me. André and Nancy gave me a beautiful pair of solitaires, deep blood red. And Mary sent me the most enchanting platter of Wedgwood majolica you have seen in all your days. Lianides gave me a beautiful Crêpes Suzette pan and réchaud, which I am so glad to have. Some nice ties and books galore.

New Year's Eve Sylvia and Bill Pedlar are coming over for dinner, and we shall see the year through very quietly. I have a lot of foie gras — gifts — and we'll have a marinated filet, potatoes, a Bibb lettuce salad, and a mincemeat and apple flan.

Monday I shall go to Tower Suite for dinner just to get the feeling of it again. I started classes there this week, so I now have four days a week of teaching for RA. Keeps me going to have a list of things to taste for each group each week. The Tower Suite staff are green for the most part. They don't know wine, and they don't know how to serve it or how to open bottles. But the restaurant is very elegant and the food good. It is, as I think I told you, on the top of the Time and Life Building and overlooks the whole city. Only three entrées each menu, and they are wheeled up and carved at table. A tiny menu and a tinier wine list. It's been a great success. Seven fifty for dinner and wines not expensive. People like to know how much they are going to spend on food.

A darling letter from Alice this morning. She seems steadier as to pen than the last time I heard from her.

Love,

J

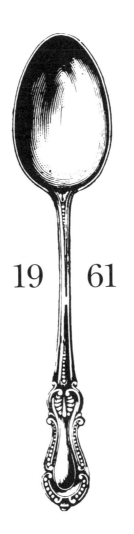

1961

JB's first job of the year was making a series of tapes for Planter's, and Atheneum offered him a contract to do his book of memoirs. He was in Houston for several days in January; in San Francisco and Los Angeles in February; and in Portland, Seattle, Washington, D.C., and Cincinnati in April. On May 12 he sailed for Europe on the *United States*. The Browns were already there, but HEB fell ill and nearly died before being taken by a U. S. Air Force hospital plane from Rome to Germany. JB spent the rest of May and all of June and July in France, Switzerland, Spain, and England. He began his book *Delights and Prejudices* while in Lausanne. He returned to New York at the end of July but was in London again for almost three weeks in September. Julia Child and Simone Beck paid a visit to one of his cooking classes in early November. He spent Thanksgiving in New York and visited Los Angeles and the Browns for a week in December.

119 West 10th Street
New York
[January 9, 1961]

Dear Helen —

Tomorrow I'm cutting twelve tapes for Planter's, and I have been recording all week on my tape recorder and playing back till I'm sick of the sound of my voice. I have a problem, for they are two-minute spots and have to cover a full subject in brief each time. But they are rather fun.

We are having a battle, still, with Dell over distribution of the paperback [*The James Beard Cookbook*]. And I'm doing nothing on the next book till they settle it. People write me every day that they cannot get it. It is just too silly and distressing. Now they say if I let them know when I visit a city they will have books there. A great help. I tell you, the big advance idea is by far the best. They all worked like mad on this one.

I now have an offer from Pat Knopf [Atheneum], and I'm thinking of taking it. If I do, I will stay in Europe for two or more months this summer and get the basic part going. It is just the kind of book I've wanted to do for ages, with plenty of narrative attached, and discussion about what recipe came from where and just why I like it.[1] I think I'd rather do a book for Pat than Alfred at this point, for Alfred is becoming pretty difficult.

Strathborough is the old Scottish paste I was brought up on. Boil lean beef till it is well done. Chop very fine and blend in the Kitchen Aid with chopped anchovies, butter and a hint of thyme. I like it better without the thyme and with a bit of black pepper. Pour into crocks and seal with butter. Spread on toast or use as a toasted hors d'oeuvre or with eggs. Makes wonderful small, thin sandwiches, too, and is less fattening than rillettes or such things.

I have gone completely overboard for the cream cheese pastry we do in the school for upper crust pies, rolled rather thick. I make it in the KA with the paddle. 2¼ cups of flour, ½ pound each of butter and cream cheese, sugar if desired, and ½ cup of heavy cream. An egg yolk if you want it. I know you have one rather like it, but try this one. Made a superb apple tart with it and apples smothered in butter — also a beautiful fresh apricot flan. We have been getting apricots from South Africa, lovely and ripe and full of flavor.

Tonight I'm doing a new pasta dish with chicken, ham, tongue, white truffle, a creamy sauce, made with chicken broth and Marsala, grated Parmesan, and huge macaroni, gratinéed and with chopped truffle on top. It is Parisian style, according to *Cucina Italiana*.[2]

Ask Philip if he ever sees *Les Meilleurs Recettes de Ma Pauvre Mère* [by Pierre Huguenin] advertised. I'd love to have a copy of it. Have you the new Mrs. Beeton?[3] Quite a book, I think. But I'm mad for the new Elizabeth David [*French Provincial Cooking*], simply mad for it.

Going to Paula's for dinner on Saturday to meet Craig's new girl friend, over whom he seems to be completely gaga. It would not amaze me to have him get married.

Love and kisses, many of them,

J

---

[1] *Delights and Prejudices,* which Atheneum published in 1964.

[2] Italian food magazine to which JB and Gino Cofacci subscribed.

[3] Isabella Beeton, author of *Mrs. Beeton's Household Management* (1861).

Pasadena
January 12, 1961

James dearest,

If you do a book, please do it yourself. Let it have that old Beard charm. And yes, more commentary.

H

[119 West 10th Street
New York
February 21, 1961]

Dear Helen —

Everything seems to be pushing ahead. Pat Knopf came through with a contract. The paperback [*The James Beard Cookbook*] is going into hardcover. I didn't go to the Commanderie dinner at André's [Lutèce] but hope to go sometime within the next two weeks for dinner. Everyone at the Commanderie liked it very much.

Had dinner at Dione's on Friday. She doesn't sit, which embarrasses the hell out of me. We had a quiche with drinks. Then borscht, with loads of sour cream and garlic. Then quenelles with a heavily creamed sauce. Then a ballotine of turkey with a creamy farce in the center, and potatoes with dill. Then salad with a creamy dressing and a very creamy cheese. Then a marquise, with chocolate icing over the praline Bavarian, and whipped cream. And fruit compote and Swedish butter horns. Such a sameness. But I am fond of her and wish I could perform with my hands as she does.

I'm off to jury duty.

Love and kisses,

J

119 West 10th Street
New York
March 30, 1961

My dear Helen — [1]

I am leaving on Saturday for San Francisco and then for Portland for two or three days, because I must look in on Lucille[2] and see what goes on, as she is not terribly well. I return on the 10th and fall into a hectic round of duties before I leave on the 12th.

Tonight, Gino and I are dining with Craig and Pierre Franey,[3] and I am eagerly anticipating a superb dinner at Franey's hands.

André has opened his restaurant and got a rather stiff review from Craig, which has made him extremely angry. However, he seems to be packing them in, at fantastic prices. We had a dinner there, fifteen of us, which I considered to be extremely good.

Love and kisses,

J

---

[1] The Browns were in Madrid at this point.

[2] JB's stepsister.

[3] Chef at Le Pavillon, later in charge of the Howard Johnson kitchens and then a *New York Times* columnist.

119 West 10th Street
New York
[May 5, 1961]

Dear Philip and Helen —

I am so grateful that things have worked so you are in Germany and being taken care of.[1] Your letter was a great relief. I shall arrive at the Ritz [in Paris] on the 17th. If you can give me a telephone number, I'll call you as soon as I get there.

I have just finished the peanut girls' course as of this minute.[2] Worked as I never did before. Several of them were real grass-roots, and two of them were perfect bores. I took them to the Four Seasons for dinner, and they adored every minute of it as a rare experience in their lives. That and their joy at achieving certain things in the cookery department were more than repayment for my work. They have been on the go all week and are ready to drop in their tracks, as am I.

It's my birthday, and I talked to Mary Hamblet and to Mabelle Jeffcott early this morning. Mary couldn't sleep so she called me at 5 o'clock her time. I'm going to the Four Seasons for dinner with Paula and Gino, and tomorrow Paula, Emil Kashouty and Frank Hearne are giving me a party. And Leon [Lianides] is giving me another on Wednesday. I haven't been feted like this in years.

I sail a week from today, and oh, it isn't a minute too soon. I hope you will get a letter to me before I leave. Otherwise, have a letter waiting for me at the Ritz. I know things are going to improve and that Helen is going to feel better than ever. This must happen.

Devotedly,

J

---

[1] According to Philip Brown, Helen fell ill in Spain, with bouts of almost total paralysis. Failing to get a diagnosis in Madrid or in southern France, they continued to Rome. Their son-in-law, a doctor in the U.S. Air Force, came to the rescue and diagnosed the illness as an acute shortage of potassium. No treatment was available in Rome, so an Air Force hospital plane was summoned from Germany, by which time Helen was near death. She spent three weeks in intensive care and pulled through. JB appears not to have known how serious her illness was.

[2] Winners of the Planter's peanut oil contest.

119 West 10th Street
New York
[May 6, 1961]

My dear Philip and Helen —

I thought the enclosed recipe would make you both sit up and start cooking at once. Note the cooking time carefully. Betty Crocker's, this is.[1]

I celebrated my birthday last night in fine form with a beautiful dinner at the Four Seasons. I started with baby shrimp soyed and sautéed and served in a potato basket. Then we had a leg of baby lamb for three, rarish and wonderful, and jumbo asparagus with a

Maltaise sauce. Drank the most perfect bottle of Cheval-Blanc '47 and finished off with a birthday cake Albert Kumin, the pastry chef, dreamed up for me, with a ribbon and bow of spun sugar and two lovely roses — a delicious génoise with almond butter cream and a fondant icing. And Krug non-vintage to go with that. Now the party today and dieting till I get to France.

Our spring is just beginning to break. I have never seen such a year for cold and rain. Will you believe it, the cherry trees are just beginning to bloom, and other trees are barely in bud as yet? We are about a month behind schedule and have had practically no good days.

Hope that Helen is feeling better and continues to improve.

As ever,

J

---

[1] The recipe, which appeared in a *New York Times* article on *Betty Crocker's Outdoor Cook Book*, calls for grilling cubes of lamb 30–35 minutes. JB's and HEB's *Complete Book of Outdoor Cookery* recommends 10–16 minutes.

Hotel Central-Bellevue
Lausanne
June 7, [1961]

My dear Helen —

I have been wondering where some of the French and prac-tically all of the Swiss get the idea they are good cooks. I defy anyone to get, in ninety-eight percent of the restaurants, salad which is fit to eat. Either they put so much vinegar in it you choke, or they fill it with mustard and other things and no oil. Last night I went to what is considered and used to be the best restaurant [Grappe d'Or] in Lausanne and French Switzerland. I had eaten well there before, but they gave me beef grilled over charcoal on one side only and the other completely cold. When I complained they said, "You asked for it underdone." I replied that underdone did not mean crisp on one side and raw on the other. They very grudgingly took it back and then gave me tiny new potatoes cooked in so much fat they were hard. And salad filled with so much Savora mustard that no one could taste anything but Savora.

Monday night I bought some perfectly magnificent veal chops, white asparagus and salad greens. I did the asparagus and the salad. Alexis Lambelet, who is with Nestlé, did the chops, and I was shocked to see him ruin wonderful veal by putting them into hot butter and keeping them on high heat till they were shrunken and without flavor. White asparagus I am ready to offer to the garbage can. It cans magnificently, but I think our green and the French green is so much better as far as texture is concerned. Occasionally, as at Père Bise, you get fabulous white asparagus, but it is rare. I peeled this and cooked it so long that the green would have disintegrated and it was just barely tender. As for the chocolates and pastries in Zurich and the cheese, they can have most of it. I love their sausages and their dry beef and such, but you can't eat that three times a day.

Charles Ritz[1] was sorry not to have had dinner with you and Philip. I had dinner with him the night before I left Paris, and we ate beautifully. I started with langouste mayonnaise. Then we had a perfectly roasted chicken with a brown tarragon sauce. You tasted the tarragon in the sauce, and the chicken had its own delicious flavor. That seems to me the way to do it.

I had another version of chicken tarragon at Chez Camille, a restaurant Naomi Barry[2] told me about. A woman is the chef here, and her husband is at the front of the house. And a damned good chef she is. The chicken was called grilled, but if it was grilled it was done very far from the heat, because there was no char. It was a small chicken, tender and moist, with the most delicate taste of the grill. With it was a béarnaise, with twice as much tarragon — fresh and coarsely chopped — as usual.

I'm getting some work done. Yesterday I worked solidly for about six hours. Looking over the lake and having no distractions is a fairly good idea.

Love and kisses all round.

Toujours,

J

---

[1] Of the Hôtel Ritz.

[2] Columnist for the Paris edition of the *Herald Tribune* and author of *Paris Personal.*

Hotel Central-Bellevue
Lausanne
[June 12, 1961]

Helen, dear —

I am superstitious about reading a manuscript over before
reaching a hundred pages of type. I am near there now. I have a lot
of recipes which were Mother's, in business and later, and which I
have never used at all. I have been saving them for something like
this, and they are damned good ones. When I go home I shall have
to try them out again after all these years.

Paula writes that they had quite a time with Mapie Toulouse-
Lautrec. She went to be photographed for the *New York Times* and
announced that all the Osterizer was good for was a milk shake.
After Osterizer had spent all the money bringing her over. Craig
had Paula show her how to use it to do a hollandaise. She was
impressed. Next day she went to the *World Telegram* for an interview and said, of course, that all the Osterizer was good for was a
milk shake. Finally, I guess, the Roy Bernard Agency had to tell her
what she was being paid for. She insisted on being photographed
in the damnedest hats in the world, in the kitchen yet.

Père Bise was wonderful again yesterday. Jerry and Grace
Brody[1] had never had the Omble Chevalier with the sauce au
Porto. There were ten of us for lunch, so they had two big ones,
and they were really super-superb. Then saddles of lamb with
slices of kidney, in the fat, skewered to them for the last few
minutes of cooking. There were two saddles with the kidneys and a
great attelet, with a nest of lettuce and tomatoes and a truffle.
Looked absolutely wonderful. How horrible to come back to
Lausanne cooking after that.

Have you started making an outline for our book?

Love,

J

---

[1] Jerome Brody was president of Restaurant Associates.

Hotel Central-Bellevue
Lausanne
[June 1961]

Helen, dear —

I went back to Paris for two days this week. I had a long talk
with Alice [on the phone] and she is not well. The taxi ride from
Acqui Term to Milan was too much for her, and then she got
home and found all the pictures moved out.[1] Now there are
lawsuits, and she has to fight about the damned will. Also, she can
barely see. The one good thing is that she has written about two
hundred pages of manuscript and is determined to finish it by
September.

I feel she is determined to get this book done no matter what
happens because she wants to leave her version of Gertrude Stein
behind, after all the detrimental things have been said. This, of
course, is merely my idea and is not backed up by anything anyone
has said. At any rate, I'm happy we had the long talk, and if I get
back I shall see her. She has to write an introduction to some
cookbook with recipes of famous writers and artists, and that is
holding her up on her own book. And the lawsuit! Poor darling,
she has her hands full.

Right now I'm in such a vale of indecision that I don't know
when I'll be coming home. I may just stay on till about the 15th of
August if I can find a simple little quiet place to stay. Jerry Brody
would like to establish me in Paris for a while, but I think this is not
the place to get any work done. There are too many people and
too many telephone calls.

Love and kisses,

J

---

[1] Gertrude Stein's collection of paintings included twenty-eight Picassos.
In 1961 her sister-in-law, in the interests of her children, who were next in
line to inherit after Alice Toklas's death, procured a court order to have the
pictures taken to a bank vault, on the ground that Toklas's absence from the
apartment put them at risk.

[Hotel Central-Bellevue
Lausanne
July 10, 1961]

My dearest Helen —

I'm sick that you are back in the hospital. But it is all part of the mess, I guess, and you have to face it.

My trip with the Pecks and Grubers was heaven. The bouillabaisse at Brasserie des Catalans [in Marseille] was excellent, the Bourride superb. The bouillabaisse at the little inn in Les Saintes Maries in the Camargue [Chez Camille] was as good as that if not better. Naturally, we ate superbly at Bise — the best there is for me, still — and at Bonne Auberge Chez Ma Mère in Nice and at [the Château] Meyrargues; well, in Marseille at Catalans and New-York; well, in the Camargue and at Le Prieuré [in Villeneuve-les-Avignon]; horribly, at La Petite Auberge at Noves, the new three-star spot — and they knew it, for they presented us with a bottle of champagne with dessert, and brandies, and said they knew we didn't like it. Last night we dined chez Point [Pyramide in Vienne], and it was incredibly good. Madame Point wept when we talked of other days — she is a darling person. Today we came back here to Lausanne and lunched en route at the Hôtel de France in Nantua.

Pat Knopf has jumped at the idea for our book. Lester and Paula have read what I have written so far on my new one and like it. I feel that it is on the right path.

Tomorrow I have my speech at Nestlé on diet foods.

Love and kisses,

J

Hotel Central-Bellevue
Lausanne
July 14, 1961

Dear Helen —

Since dining chez Point on Sunday I have been giving it a lot of thought. It is the absolute end of the great traditions. Rather like a monument to things past. Since Mme Point says it is only to the memory of Fernand Point that she does this, it makes it even more dead than if she didn't think that way. No longer are there people to do the classic garnitures. Things come on a platter with little figures and such to decorate them. The fabulous mousse of foie gras en brioche is still there in its glory — the slices are a trifle thinner than they used to be. The terrine en croûte is still there and sausages en croûte. Paula and I have almost decided that there should be no more pâtés and terrines en croûte. They all get flabby and soggy. What's wrong with just having them in the terrine?

There was a choice of only two entrées for dinner on Sunday night, a guinea hen and cold boeuf à la mode in jelly. Isn't that rather surprising in itself? Paula and Lester had the guinea hen, and the rest of us ordered the beef. We had had guinea hen elsewhere about four times — this is the season for it. It was perfectly cooked and nicely served with a gratin Dauphinois, made with a custard instead of the usual milk, cream or broth. The beef was beautifully done in a bowl and cut in slices — a big eye-of-round piece and jelly, with a layer of clear aspic on top. A string bean and julienne of raw mushroom salad went with that, with a touch of onion and pepper.

Then we had cheese — a good collection — with which we drank a Romanée-Conti 1952. And the desserts were the usual Point array of petits fours and pastries. I had a superb vanilla pot de crème and some of the little pastries. But the classic quality is too overworked.

Bise doesn't attempt to be classic. He has beautiful linen, fine food, well presented, and lovely flowers, and that is the story. By the way, he does soak crumbs and add them to the crème patissière in his soufflé mixture. They hold the liqueur flavor better than I have ever had it.

The crêpes soufflé at Meyrargues were superb. And their squab with herbs were extraordinarily good, as was the loup we had there.

Madame Baudoin at Bonne Auberge has superb pastries, and of course the hors d'oeuvre parade there is fantastic. She is modern and has broken with tradition and is really great.

This has certainly been my year for three-star restaurants and two more to go. Lester insists I go to Tour d'Argent with them and to Maxim's. Last night we went to Geneva for dinner and tried a small Italian place we had been told about. Very, very good it was, too, and perfect for the mood we were in. They had bollito misto as the day's specialty, and we needed something as all-fired simple as that to give our stomachs a rest.

We were exceedingly lucky with weather for our tour. Yesterday we had horrendous rain and wind, and I gather France is even worse. They had 100-km-per-hour winds around La Rochelle. This will probably ruin what few grapes are left on the vines. Les and Cleo started out in it all to go to Dumaine, Avallon and Sens and on to Paris. They wanted me to go with them, but suddenly I had had enough going to important restaurants. There are times when one wants just a salad and some eggs.

Did I tell you to try kidneys in a tarragon cream? They are sensationally good. Much tarragon.

Last night I went to the Palace again for dinner, for they do very good table cooking. Had a steak au poivre flambé, with a dab of mustard mixed with the Armagnac when it was done. Awfully nice addition. That and melon was my dinner, and good it was. Like so many of the spots here, they have a grill with charcoal in plain view of the dining room.

> Love and kisses to one and all,
> J

Bastille Day!

Hotel Ritz
Paris
July 17, 1961

Dearest Helen —

I just wanted you to know that Alice had a bad fall and is in a cast, and no one knows when she will walk again. She had Joe Barry[1] write me a note and said she would call me while I was here. I shall see Naomi [Barry] tomorrow and find out more details.

Paris has been cold and windy and wet. The Grubers have a spot on the fifth floor of the Crillon with a terrace overlooking the Place de la Concorde and such a view as you would never believe. Paula and Jim [Peck] are at the Relais Bisson in a lousy room, for which they are paying too much. Last night we had dinner, all five of us, at Tour d'Argent — one of the three best meals of the trip. I hadn't been there for ten years, and, I must say, Claude Terrail has done a great deal to maintain the traditions. Saturday night we went to Les Marronniers, which is surely one of the best bistros in Paris.

Off to the markets with Lester and Cleo. Then antiquing with them and the Pecks this afternoon and dinner at Taillevent this evening.

Love and kidneys to all the Browns,

J

---

[1] Paris correspondent for the *New York Post*.

[Hotel Ritz
Barcelona
July 20, 1961]

Helen, dear —

Paris was divine. The good restaurants are becoming fewer and fewer. It is shocking what the Coca-Cola age has done to the world.

I didn't even get to talk to Alice. Naomi says she has been in a very temperamental mood and one day sees Joe and her and the next day not, and has been disagreeable as hell to everyone. When she fell and broke her kneecap she crawled and found a coverlet and stayed there till Madeleine came the next day. Incredible woman.

Love and all that,

J

119 West 10th Street
New York
August 19, 1961

Dear Helen —

It was fortunate you called last night when Helen was here. She is certainly determined to have her magazine go through.[1] The idea is good but I have fears about raising the money.

She also has an idea for a correspondence school of cooking. I told her I wouldn't be part of it because of my loyalty to Ruth for what she has done to build the school into its present state. Also, I am not too certain that a correspondence course in cooking would ever be an outstanding success. It is quite different from a school of writing or painting, and I cannot quite see five million students signing up for it. It would be like trying to act by mail order, and, as I told Helen, people pay to come and work with other people because they enjoy the social activity and the personality of the teacher. This is why some people prefer Dione to me and vice versa, and why some of them still want to start with Helen Worth and then graduate either to Dione or me.

I have two recipes for Quatre Épices.* One is 10 grams of bay leaf, the same of thyme and of mace, 15 grams of cinnamon, 20 of clove, 20 of nutmeg, 10 of cayenne, 10 of white pepper in grains, 10 of rosemary and 10 of basil. This should be pounded in a mortar and put through a fine sieve, or it can probably be ground in a blender. The cloves should be whole and not ground.

The other one is 70 grams of white pepper, 17 grams of ginger, 8.5 grams of nutmeg and 4.5 grams of clove. You may take your pick. Both are good.

If you want a gathering during the week you are here, please let me know which night would be preferable and who you would like to have. I can take care of twenty to twenty-four with great ease.

Love and kisses,
Jim

---

[1] Helen McCully was trying to raise money for a new magazine to be called *Food and Drink.* JB agreed to write a column for it.

* Recipe.

Pasadena
August 28, 1961

James dear,

Now — and this is important — you *have* to take it easier or
you'll crack. . . . As Alexis Lichine said in a nice note I had from
him, "Now that our friend Jim has made such a reputation for
himself it's time we got him streamlined" or words to that effect.
And I am sure he didn't mean physically. You've *got* to stop doing
so much. Decide what pays best & what you do most easily — hire a
manager, if necessary — and concentrate on *that*. . . . You are too
profligate with yourself.

H

119 West 10th Street
New York
[October 15, 1961]

Helen, dear —

Well, school is over for the first week, and I am quite pleased
with the results. We have a run on married couples this time, and it
is fun to have classes fairly evenly divided between men and
women. It gives an incentive to work, for some reason.

Elena's party was delightful — about twenty persons at small
tables, so that everyone didn't have to sit facing each other and
could visit around as they wished. Freddie Rufe outdid himself,
and we all went home sagging heavily. A delicious dinner, really,
with all sorts of embellishments.

Today I have to go to a test luncheon for the Commanderie and
then to Sam Aaron's party, where the amount of food will be
staggering, so I hear.

I think the Knopf French book[1] is wonderful until they get into the chicken and meat department. The idea of cooking a
piece of American boiling beef for four hours is insane.[2] Paula
did a pot au feu for twelve people the other night, and the beef
cooked 1½ hours and was perfection. And I think all the
chicken recipes are overcooked. Otherwise, it is a great book.

Nothing new or startling, but a good basic French cookery book.

A woman wrote me and said she had tried my summer squash casserole and the squash wouldn't get tender in 35 minutes. Come to find out, she had used unpeeled butternut squash. How she ever got it into slices is beyond me. With an axe, in all probability.

Love and kisses to all,

J

---

[1] *Mastering the Art of French Cooking* by Simone Beck, Louisette Bertholle, and Julia Child.

[2] JB's recipe for pot au feu in *The James Beard Cookbook*, published two years earlier, gives a cooking time of 2 ½ to 3 hours.

119 West 10th Street
New York
October 21, 1961

Dearest Helen —

Alice's editor is just back from Paris and has many messages from Alice, who is working like a dog and now has broken her left wrist, but you are not supposed to know this. Evidently she is resigned to not having the paintings around and is quite happy. They say that her book so far is simply sensational, and she is up to Gertrude's death. The juicy part should come now.

Craig is coming for supper tonight with his friend Henry. I have white truffles, which Albert bestowed on me yesterday, and we will have them with pasta. I am going to send you the next load in rice by air and see if they come through all right. Had some last night with potatoes.

The parade of cookbooks seems unending. I went to a luncheon for the *Larousse Gastronomique*[1] on Thursday — very elegant, at the St. Regis. Saw Charlotte Turgeon, who did most of the editorial work on it. I'll send you the menu. The veal was superb and the Billi bi the best I ever had.

Did I tell you they are going to do my hors d'oeuvre book over again?

I'm going up to Stratford [Connecticut] to try out the fare at the Mermaid Tavern.

Love and kisses,
J

---

[1] *Larousse Gastronomique* by Prosper Montagné, edited by Charlotte Turgeon and Nina Froud.

119 West 10th Street
New York
November 1, 1961

Dearest Helen —

We gave Mme Beck and Mrs. Child your name and address and told them about you. They will undoubtedly call you when they are in Pasadena. They were quite pleased with the school, and I gave them a start when I had the students putting the egg whites into the soufflés with their hands. They were dying to go home and try it. I enjoyed them for their short stay very much.

Love and kisses,
J

119 West 10th Street
New York
[November 10, 1961]

Dearest Helen —

I wasted a perfectly good day by going to the Food Forum and hearing a lot of people talk about saturated fats, atomic cookery, nuclear feeding and all the rest of the shit.

I gather by this time that Kaduson has talked to you and we can do our Seattle trip before we go to the San Francisco job. I may take off for the Orient from there. I think I can raise most of the money for a round-the-world ticket and stop in Tokyo, Hong Kong, Bangkok, Teheran and one or two other places, and come

home from Paris or London. It would be a good season for me to
go. I might as well do it before the world falls apart. I'm looking
forward to seeing you in about three weeks and having a good visit
and gossip.

I'm having Alvin Kerr and Freddie Rufe for Thanksgiving, and
maybe Isabel, for Ron will be in Yucatán. I've ordered a good
turkey from my man — who has had beautiful aged mutton lately.
I might bring some chops out with me on the plane, and we could
have them for dinner. Would you like that?

Thursday Albert and I have to give a huge game presentation
for all the Restaurant Associates managers and chefs, and have
collected more game in feather and fur than you can imagine.

The school has been most rewarding this year. The old-timers
have been marvelous and some of the new ones really
exceptional — and two lemons, of course. One chap has orga-
nized almost a whole new class for us and sent in the money. And
another student is trying to organize a class from Sarah Lawrence.

Last night we did a lobster soufflé in the shells — and grilled
pig's feet. I thought of Philip, who adores them as much as I. I have
found that if they go into the oven at 400 or 425 for twenty-five to
thirty minutes and then go under the broiling unit they are much
better than if all broiled. We made pommes frites and sauce
Diable to go with them, along with watercress. And did they eat
them with gusto!

Love,

J

119 West 10th Street
New York
[November 20, 1961]

Dearest Helen —

I have been doing some of Thanksgiving tonight. Made the shell
for the pumpkin tart and the flan ring for the mince and apple.
Used cream cheese pastry rolled in sugar for the pumpkin and my
rich pastry for the flan. Also made — and don't tell anyone —
crystallized cranberries, because Gino wanted cranberries. I'll

never live it down. Going to do a stuffing with ground-up Virginia ham, lots of green onions, parsley, crumbs and pecans.

Had the first parsnips of the season tonight. I adore them but don't dare have them too often.

Just had news that my darling Connie Wolf has broken the woman's all-time balloon record, which she was determined to do. Was up for forty hours, all alone. What a gal she is! Her husband is in the hospital, and she really did this to please him more than anything, I swear.

I've been working very hard with Restaurant Associates this year and enjoying it. There is so much in this world to learn, and I am willing to take it on anytime. Our game presentation was a sensation — three whole boars, a whole deer in fur, and all the feathered game, except grouse, ortolans and grives.

Paula's book [*The Art of Fine Baking*] is beautiful. I hope it sells and gives her joy.

You didn't answer me, so I shall bring out some mutton chops when I come. If my butcher sends them that morning, I know we can have them that night, for they will keep beautifully. Next week I'm having an editor from Dutton, the Schaffners and Kate [Titus] to dinner. Going to do deviled crab, saddle of veal, and my new love, polenta with chopped green chilies in it.

Love you both — much,

J

[119 West 10th Street
New York
December 16, 1961]

Dearest Browns —

Lunched with Julia and Paul Child and Mme Beck at the Four Seasons on Thursday, with a tasting of winter things for the new menu. They loved the cheddar cheese soup, the barbecued loin of pork and the coffee cup soufflés. I adore both women, and Paul came to life. Last night, Dione's party [for *Mastering the Art of French Cooking*], for thirty. Jeanne Owen was there and the June Platts, Avis De Voto,[1] Marya Mannes,[2] the Julius Wiles,[3] Clem,

Denise Otis[4] and the Knopf group. Dione did a sole with a white wine sauce. Julia and Simone made a braised shoulder of lamb that was delicious. There was a salad and the worst Bavarian cream I have ever eaten. Dione told me she had never done such a terrible one. She had a migraine, or so she said. It was Jeanne who had upset her. That woman . . . the look she gave me last night would have killed a weaker person. Julius Wile came to me and asked me to say something about the Bollinger '55. I said, "You have the head of the Wine and Food Society here. I have already made a toast to you to thank you for the red wines, at Paul's request. It is only fitting that Jeanne make a remark." She replied to Julius that she was too shy.

It is said that Craig has sold a vast number of copies [of *The New York Times Cook Book*]. Almost 30,000, I understand. He is going to get rich. I'm glad!

Love and kisses,

J

---

[1] Credited with finding *Mastering the Art of French Cooking* for Knopf. She was married to Bernard De Voto.

[2] Writer for *The New Yorker, The Reporter,* and other magazines; author of the essay collection *More in Anger.*

[3] Julius Wile was production manager for Julius Wile Sons & Co.

[4] Editor of Entertaining features at *House and Garden.*

119 West 10th Street
New York
[December 26, 1961]

Dearest Helen —

Yesterday's Christmas breakfast was great fun. Altogether, we were fourteen. The codfish [brandade de morue] was good, the zampone, a real beauty — looking for all the world like Mae West's thigh and leg — and the ham, delicious. Paula had sent me the biggest stollen I ever saw. So they ate well and drank champagne as if it were the end of the world.

Last night went to Freddie Shrallow's for dinner and ate goose with sauerkraut — very good. Sunday, to Albert's for cocktails and caviar and foie gras, all elegant. Then home to a capon for dinner, which turned out to be lousy.

I'm glad the holidays are almost over. I have to have a couple of people here over the weekend and then on the 6th I'm having Joe and June Platt and others for a substantial cocktail party. I've never had June here, and I like her so much that I felt it would be a pleasant thing to do.

Sam and Florence and Jack and Frieda [Aaron] gave me a fabulous present — a scrapbook of Count Sutteroth, who lived in Paris and London for years. All his menus and invitations and many letters carefully pasted into a huge volume.

Did I tell you I bought a new desk and sent my other to be sold? It is rather Brighton Pavilionish and smaller, and fits into the living room much better. You will approve, I am sure.

About the book.[1] We never did get around to making an outline, did we? What exactly do you want of me? To go through the major vineyards and tell the facts about them? Do you think we can evaluate in this book? If it is to be of service to people, telling them what to buy would certainly be best. I'm not sure about recipes. And I feel it should stay away from the social side of it all as much as possible. People want information about wines, and surely there has been too much romancing about the producers rather than the truth about the wines.

I'm glad you are going to do a buffet book, for you can tell people so many things about serving and eating a buffet which they always overlook. I lunched at the Copenhagen the other day and watched the smorgasbord patrons mess up their plates generally. God, how revolting it is! And the other night at a party I saw people who should know better heap fish, with a sauce verte, ham, salad and smoked turkey on a plate at the same time. Can you get your book out for next fall so it will have a Christmas sale?

Love. New Year's is just around the corner!

J

---

[1] HEB had proposed doing a wine and cheese book, to be published by Ward Ritchie.

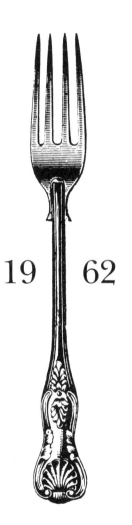

19 62

JB was dieting once more as the year opened, and he had a fall in the middle of Madison Avenue. He went to Detroit at the end of January, then Richmond, and in February and March he did food demonstrations in Florida. In May he was in Milwaukee, Chicago, Portland, Gearhart, and Seattle. In mid-month he set off from San Francisco on a world trip with Craig Claiborne, Lester and Cleo Gruber, and HEB. He was back in New York by June 25, but there is no surviving correspondence with HEB until August. At the end of September he went to Boston for two days and spent a night with Julia and Paul Child. In October he traveled for ten days to Columbus, Chicago, Seattle, Portland, and San Francisco. HEB visited New York and taught in his classes. JB and Julia Child helped produce the gala Chevaliers du Tastevin dinner in December.

119 West 10th Street
New York
[January 7, 1962]

Dearest Helen —

I'm really dieting and not drinking at all till, hope to God, I lose a few pounds and a few inches around the middle.

I had June and Joe Platt, the Soupçon girls,[1] Peggy [Lesser], Paula, the Whites and the Pedlars for a substantial cocktail party last night. It was one of the best parties I have had in ages. Everyone liked each other and they stayed and stayed and didn't leave till almost ten. Had the last of my big Hungarian foie gras, tiny shrimp done in the Provençal manner with Pernod, oil, tarragon, mustard and parsley, a roast of beef, just tepid, small tomatoes, radishes, and plenty of French bread. Lianides did the beef, just as he did for your party, and it was perfection.

In the morning the Thomas's muffin people had the finals of their high school contest here — three darling little gals, each one with an original recipe. The winner, fourteen, had adapted an old family tourtière recipe from Canada. She flavored her pork well, added crumbs from scooping out a muffin, and made a thin top with one half of it. It looked good and tasted very good. She got a thousand-dollar tuition award. The second winner made a crab-meat rarebit, which tasted good, but looked like grenadine vomit on the muffins, and the third had a delicious chicken pie idea, with crisp buttered muffins for the crust. All had really dreamed up their recipes and all seemed to love what they were doing.

John Ferrone is doing the book [*Delights and Prejudices*] with me, and we are beginning to get somewhere. I feel confident that it is going to take shape from now on. That is, if the phone ever stops. But then there are weekends.

Love and kisses,
[J]

---

[1] Owners of the kitchenware and food shop.

119 West 10th Street
New York
[January 1962]

Dearest Helen —

Did I tell you that Craig is going with me for most of the trek [around the world] and will be in San Francisco for the day or so before he flies? Do you know that his book has sold over fifty-five thousand! Nice money for him, that is.

Went to a cocktail party for the new briquets the other day, at the Tower Suite, and they had such interesting hors d'oeuvre broiled on small grills. Tiny French lamb chops all fat-trimmed. You could pick them up with your fingers. Small Pojarski cutlets with sticks. Skewered beef like they do at La Fonda. And wonderful Gulf shrimp — the bright red ones, with tails left on and served with snail holders. They passed four different sauces for them. About the briquets, I know nothing except that they are supposed to burn longer than any others.

I've been photographing like mad. Carving shots for *House and Garden* ["How to Carve Steak"] — at Caravelle, Lutèce, and Four Seasons. Also liqueur shots. And today I am supposed to be on the radio for *Larousse Gastronomique.* I would love to say what I think.

I have made up my mind that the omelet soufflé is really more delicious after dinner than the regular soufflé. I make them quite often now and have put them into the curriculum for the class. The heavy iron pans from Soupçon are perfect for them. We started the new secondary class last night, and what a bunch of eaters. We made a duck terrine and then two quick pâtés so they could have something to eat with their apéritif. We had richer than rich potatoes, steak au poivre, salad and omelet soufflés. Not a scrap of anything left.

I had brief note from Alice, saying that she was hoping she would see all of us together in June. Little does she know that we shall be far far apart in June. I shall end my world tour in England and just may go back to France for a few days before I come back here.

Lunched magnificently at André's today — really magnificently.

Love,

J

119 West 10th Street
New York
[January 1962]

Dearest Helen —

I tripped in the middle of Madison Avenue yesterday and almost did a complete somersault, landing on my belly. My identification bracelet went flying across the street, my glasses popped, and my watch got crushed, and people stood like dopes, looking. I'm sore but nothing is broken, thank God.

Since Freddie Rufe is away, Joe Baum has been working on the Fonda. As a result, the food is absolutely sensational at this point. Really, I have never had Latin food in a restaurant to equal what Joe put forth yesterday.

Do you know I am going back to iron cooking ware a great deal? And aluminum?

Love and kisses,
JB

Pasadena
February 15, 1962

James dearest —

You know, the more I think of it, the less sense this aping of hundred-year-old French cooking methods makes.

H

119 West 10th Street
New York
[February 17, 1962]

Dearest Helen —

I am glad the ham arrived safely. I haven't tried these particular ones but they should be good. I'm going to braise mine in Madeira with foil over the top for 25 minutes per pound.

I have so many people I have to entertain here this next six weeks. I start with Alexis [Lichine] and the Baums. Then I have the Jerry Aldens — he is a Portlander with great ability. Then I have Gaynor Maddox[1] and his wife. And Marcia Davenport,[2] Craig and the Franeys. I'll be broke by the time it is all done. I'm doing it mostly on Saturdays and Sundays so it doesn't eat into the weeks. I start with a clam bisque, baron of baby lamb with an anchovy sauce, a tian, and omelets soufflé — they have become my great favorites at the moment. For the Aldens I'm doing the ham, and for the Maddoxes, a complete Provençale dinner.

You'll die when you see the second batch of photos we took for *Woman's Day*. I'm complete with apron and American flag in a bandstand, with picnickery on the tables in front. Eileen Tighe is something when she gets started.

Paula is now a consultant for Restaurant Associates, doing the job on pastries and breads that I do on wines and spirits and menus. She is thrilled to pieces.

You are so right about old-fashioned methods. It occurs to me that the long specific recipe is gone for good. I read an Elizabeth David recipe and get as much sense from it as from the long and involved ones. I am amazed in class how few people really read through a recipe thoroughly before attempting to do something.

A note from Julia Child. I shall see her in a couple of weeks, for I have to go to Boston for a day.

My love to San Francisco. Tell everything.

J

---

[1] Maddox was a syndicated food columnist.

[2] Novelist and music critic; author of *Valley of Decision* and *Mozart*.

119 West 10th Street
New York
[February 21, 1962]

Dearest Helen and Phil —

I went to a big dinner party last night for the Edwin Knopfs.[1] Herb Mayes[2] was there, and I sat at the same table with him. He asked me about Helen [McCully], then said, "She was one of the few things I wanted to keep at *McCall's*, but she just wouldn't recognize that there was a new regime." Mildred Knopf said, "Well, she gave you a better food page than you have now," and I agreed. "She wanted to keep it too gourmet," said he. The man fascinated me, and he seemed to know something about everyone there — there were twenty. I like Mildred Knopf very much. She and her husband are to do an Italian book — a protest cookbook, as it were, for he hates Italian cooking in America, as don't we all.

My book for Pat Knopf may be finished in the next month. John and I have been getting along famously with it, and if Pat likes it we think we can finish it. I am doing recipes now and shall do a really intensified job on it when I get back from Florida.

I'm rewriting all the recipes for the first course of the school, too. They are too vague for some of the people, and I seem to be doing a June Platt–Julia Child job on them.

Do you ever bake kidneys in part of their fat — whole, for 20 minutes at 350, then 10 minutes at 500 — then flambé them, cut them in half and serve? Heaven.

Bill Veach has gone off his nut over Paula's book [*The Art of Fine Baking*] and is evidently baking everything in sight. He calls it the Bible of baking. Wants Paula and Jim to have lunch at Bonnetable. All he has to do is use the word "nigger" once and the lunch will end PDQ.[3]

J

---

[1] Edwin H. Knopf was a television and film producer; his wife, Mildred Knopf, author of several cookbooks.

[2] Herbert Mayes had taken over as editor of *McCall's*.

[3] Veach was a social snob, and James Peck, a labor organizer and civil-rights activist.

[119 West 10th Street
New York
February 1962]

My dear Helen —

My trip with Kate to Florida was fun but rushed. Miami Beach is something you can have all tied with heavy grosgrain ribbon and decorated with roses. It is unbelievably horrible. And to top it off, the Fontainebleau oversold the convention and sent about two hundred persons to other hotels. We landed in something you wouldn't believe called the Cadillac. When we went to check out the next morning, they forced Kate — by holding our luggage — to pay for two nights; said no one could stay only one night. We were both so furious we nearly burned the goddam place down. Then a snowstorm in New York prevented our going home, and we stayed the next night in Miami proper at the old Columbus, which is wonderful. I did two demonstrations, one at the junior college and one at the convention.

We had a glorious dinner at Joe's, of stone crab, wonderful tomatoes and their famous hashed-brown potatoes. Although stone crabs don't touch the Dungeness, they are superb, and Joe's has them only at their best.

The Governor of Kentucky's party today had some of the great-est bourbons you ever drank. They brought a lot of rare brands up, and one called Maker's Best was something to remember. Also they had Kentucky hams and beaten biscuit.

Last night in class we made the most divine aïoli, with everything — salt cod, striped bass, potatoes, hard-boiled eggs, snails, carrots, zucchini, onions and artichokes. We made one big batch in the mortar and one in the Blendor and the Kitchen Aid. They lapped it up as if it were mother's milk. Three people who said they would never touch snails downed them. One person who vowed she hated fish ended up eating both kinds. It was exciting. Did a cassonade for dessert, which somehow goes with aïoli beautifully.

Finished off our wild ducks this weekend — Glenna [McGinnis][1] had given me six. I sure am the feathered-game boy, but mostly without benefit of sauce.

Did I tell you that the French and Italian editions of my big outdoor book [*James Beard's Treasury of Outdoor Cooking*] came, and the French have given me no credit on the jacket! Mr. Robert Courtine has his name smeared all over it.[2] The Italians had the courtesy to give me credit where it was due.

Love and kisses,

J

---

[1] Food editor of *Woman's Day*.

[2] Courtine, France's best-known food writer, had written an introduction to the book.

[119 West 10th Street
New York
April 1, 1962]

Dearest Helen —

In France I am hoping we can drive around Vence, St. Paul, Monte Carlo and Biot (for pottery) if you care to, and I want to go to Bonne Auberge in Nice again. As a matter of fact I'd like to go there twice and see if the patronne won't give in on a few recipes, for I think she has some honeys. And I adore the Nice market more than most any I know. Of course there are things you will want to do. I am willing for anything in that part of the world.

In Iran I have two or three people we can look up, and if it is not too expensive we might go to Isfahan for a day. Also Beirut. I'm very curious about the food and want to get as much as possible.

Had Madame le Douzen here doing Crêpes Bretonne for two days — almost three hundred before she was through. Delicious they are when fresh from the griddle. This is one thing I will not miss buying this year — the whole works for those heavenly things.

I have decided the iron skillet I have, with the rounded sides, is the best thing for pommes Anna, with a foil cover. Start them on the range, if you want, put them into the oven, and uncover them for the last few minutes of cooking. Also did some wonderful ones in Pyrex, covered. Albert does his in iron or aluminum — whatever comes along. Of course it may be like Diat and the soufflés, when we found that because of the bake ovens being on for hours and hours they did a different job than the regular household ovens, and I still believe that. The Four Seasons soufflé oven is exactly the same as my wall ovens, and they do soufflés in a different amount of time.

I have some beautiful drip-dry shorts for the hot days in Thailand. And long socks. I'm taking lightweight clothes which are dark enough for Paris. Don't let me buy anything but some silk in Thailand, please! and a kimono for my Goddaughter McNulty! and a topcoat, if cheap, in Hong Kong.

Love and kisses,

J

119 West 10th Street
New York
[April 11, 1962]

Dearest Helen —

My television show was sensational on Monday. One woman called in for a recipe for a French sandwich which she said was sat upon, traditionally, to weight it down! Also had calls from Danny

Kaye, who seems to be a great lover of cooking and is devoted to the kitchen. And Johnny Green, the composer and conductor, was on the show — he used to be Betty Furness's husband. He does cookery and knows a great deal about it. Says we are to call him in L.A. and see him.

What students can do to knives! I can't believe it is so easy to wreck one. I spend half my pittance on them. And what different students can do to the same dish! Last night's students made the best Cuban bread I ever ate, and others make it so bad it is poison.

Love,

J

119 West 10th Street
New York
[April 21, 1962]

My dear Helen —

I had a beautiful party for Harry Waugh and George McWatters,[1] with the [Sam] Aarons, the Baums and Glenna. The deviled crab came through fabulously — I have a new recipe for it — the beef was good, the sauce Périgueux smooth and the cèpes Bordelaise excellent. I had the first decent Brie in months, and I made a coffee mousse in the freezer. Clay has learned about serving, and Gus is excellent. So it went like a dream. Today I have twenty guys for cocktails — my annual roundup — with giant garlic sausages, roast beef from Lianides, a veal and ham pâté, pizza with green chilies, Jack cheese and sesame seeds, and crudités with aïoli. Oh yes, and three dozen stuffed eggs. Easter!

Restaurant Associates is doing the restaurant in the American Gas Association building at the New York World's Fair, and I am to direct the exhibits, with famous people doing demonstrations. I shall need you for demonstrations for a couple of weeks, certainly, maybe more. Everyone spoke of you. I should like you to do some regional stuff. I want to get people who are really good showmen and can hold an audience for ten minutes, for this will be in the concourse, with no seats. It has to be done with style and dispatch — a real show of good cooking. We plan a revolving kitchen, with a chance to do two things in two different settings.

Julia and Paul went up to New Haven with me on Thursday when I spoke to the Culinary Arts Institute, and Julia came on for the question period with me. She is anxious to work all over the country doing demonstrations this year.

John Clancy is now chef for Lianides at the Coach House. Or did I tell you?

Went to Craig's for a fabulous dinner on Thursday night and met Friedeman, who is the world's greatest caviar merchant and who is to entertain us in Teheran. He makes fifty trips a year to Teheran. He brought pink caviar, called the Shah's, which, like Pink Elephants, arrives only about once or twice a decade. It was incredible. He also brought — from Iran, that day — new pressed caviar and smoked sturgeon. To complete the menu Pierre Franey made such a coulibiac of sturgeon as I have never eaten — much better than he made at Pavillon. This guy Friedeman has an eighty-five-year-old cook who is famous in Iran, so we should live high off the hog those days.

Love,

J

---

[1] Harry H. Waugh was director of John Harvey and Sons Ltd. and a wine authority. George McWatters was also an executive at Harvey's.

119 West 10th Street
New York
[August 1962]

Dearest Helen —

I must say, I cannot get back into my routine again. The weather has been wonderful and the entire picture of New York enticing and delightful, but I'm somewhere between here and Hong Kong.

I sent Simone Beck a telegram from Bonnetable[1] telling her I couldn't make a luncheon she was giving me, and it never arrived! Wow! I haven't done many thank-you letters, although I managed all the English ones from Barcelona.

A little later — I have most of the French ones done, in addition. Sam and Florence's dinner last night was fun. Paula went, and there were just the four of us. Sam did a steak on the Bartron — this should prove what you have always said, that the man's place is at the grill — and Florence did braised onions with broth and Madeira which were heavenly. We drank a '59 Bonnes Mares and a '59 Château Lascombes, which was remarkable, despite the fact that we were committing rape on the youth of Bordeaux greatness.

Love,

J

---

[1] JB was visiting Bill Veach in Bonnetable (Sarthe).

119 West 10th Street
New York
[September 30, 1962]

Dear Helen —

Went to Boston for two days. Stayed with Julia and Paul and dined with them. She has a beautiful kitchen, but yours and mine and Paula's are the best ones. I am waiting to see how she gets along in my classes while we are on the Coast. She may be fabulous for a class if they have the patience to see it through.

Came back to Paula's for New Year's — Jewish — dinner. She had made a superb gefilte fish, excellent egg barley, and a salad of black radishes, with chicken fat and salt and pepper, which was delicious. I now want to do it with a mustard dressing because I think it would outdo celery root that way. She also had chicken paprikash but forgot to turn on the oven after she had browned the chicken, so it was all but raw. And a nut sponge, a honey cake, and prunes with cinnamon.

Pat Knopf insists on more and more material for the book, but he offers more money, so I am thinking it over. He will not give it up and says he will publish it as is if I insist but begs for one or two more chapters.

Love and kisses,
J

119 West 10th Street
New York
[December 2, 1962]

Dearest Helen —

School is over finally and I think that all the new students have spent their lives making the mushroom strudel since then. That was your most popular recipe except for the beef rolls — they jumped for those, too.

The Tastevin dinner is on Monday, and I have been working on it. Julia has been here for it, too, and the whole thing, if it comes off, will be a sensation.

You know, I'm getting scared, for no meat or fowl seems to taste the way it used to. Our Thanksgiving turkey was about as interesting in flavor as soap. The chickens they sent from Maryland for the school last week looked beautiful and tasted like absolutely nothing. And you could not get them to brown in the oven. The skin would bubble but never brown. I bought a steak the other night from the butcher down here — $5.50 — tender but no beef taste or quality of aging, a complete dud.

I can't say I'm so excited about this year's cookbooks. I do not like the new *Joy of Cooking* and think the Maxim's book is awful. Most of the rest of them could just as well have stayed unwritten. Elizabeth David's [*French Provincial Cooking*] is enough for the season, and that lovely book of A. J. Liebling's [*Between Meals: An Appetite for Paris*].

Did I write you about the sourdough? That I used three or four different envelopes and it all was bad? I think there is something vitally wrong with the whole thing. Ruth and I made such perfect sourdough here and in New Canaan that I suspect making it from scratch is best.

Love and kisses,

J

119 West 10th Street
New York
[December 16, 1962]

Dearest Helen —

The great dinner is over and it was a smashing success. Everyone worked till they dropped. Julia and I sat on the desk in Albert's office during the dinner. She would creep out to see the pièces montées parade around and would come back in tears. It was perfection to the last bit — with a few "fucks" and "shits" thrown around by Albert — and with reason. The food was superb. I have never had a consommé to equal his turkey consommé, which chalked up 160 pounds of turkey when it was finished. The fish were sensational, and the pâtés, which Julia and Albert concocted, looked like beautiful pastry cushions, which they really were. It was quite a night.

The week is not too strenuous except for Thursday, when I have the Lichines, Peggy Lesser, Helen and the Beiers for dinner — clam bisque, saddle of veal with kidneys, braised fennel, cheese, and pistachio ice cream with ground cherries. Going to drink a Prieuré-Lichine '59.

Sixteen are coming for Xmas breakfast — the usual menu, with zampone, codfish, Smithfield ham, brioche and champagne. The 28th I have the Brodys, the Pedlars, Ruth Dubonnet and Peggy Harvey.

Going to Craig's New Year's Eve and to a couple of parties on New Year's Day — otherwise, quiet.

We're eating broiled squab for lunch, for they won't keep till Tuesday.

Love and kisses,

J

Living without the *New York Times* is like living without sex, only worse. Have you tried reading the Philadelphia papers? or the *Amsterdam News*?[1]

---

[1] There was a newspaper strike.

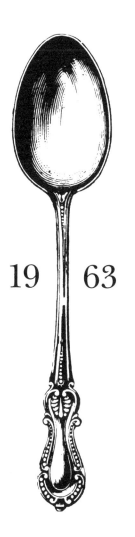

19 63

JB's first letter of the year expressed concern for HEB's health. He made appearances in Toronto and later in Davenport and Buffalo. In March he and Ruth Norman conducted the first of two sets of classes in Lancaster, Pennsylvania. On April 29 he sailed on the *Queen Elizabeth* for England, spent several exciting days in London, and arrived at his destination in St-Remy-de-Provence on May 4, the day before his birthday. There, in a rented farmhouse apartment, he worked on his memoirs and explored Provençale cooking for almost two months before returning to New York. In July he spent two nights with the Childs, and he and Julia cooked dinner together. He was in Buffalo again in August, as well as in Minneapolis, Washington, D.C., Charlottesville, and Williamsburg. In October he spent two days in San Francisco and gave another round of classes in Lancaster. He did food demonstrations in Tulsa and Rochester in November.

Dearest Helen —

I am worried about you, and really worried. You must take it easy and not try to overdo.

I feel lousy, too. But I'm not doing as much as I was, and as a consequence not earning as much as I did. But I guess I'll get through in one way or another. I definitely have the house in St-Remy for May and June, and I shall come back from that with my mind made up as to what is to follow. We have been struggling to get out of the contract for the second Dell book, but there seems no way out, so I shall have to do it.

New Year's Eve Craig did a suckling pig on the Bartron, but the skin remained tough and leathery and refused to get crisp. The flesh itself was deliciously tender and milky. But I can live without suckling pig, I'm afraid. New Year's Day, three parties — Peggy Harvey's, the most elegant, and Calvin Holt's (of Serendipity), the most fun. Had hog's head, ham, black-eyed peas and all the Southern superstitions — in a mad, mad apartment. I drank nothing but champagne, came home for a simple dinner and felt wonderfully well the next day.

Thought of you and Philip tonight as we ate the most divine saddle of mutton you ever put into your oral cavity. I served it forth with sautéed eggplant, and we finished off with pears.

I tossed away the last of the Christmas cookies tonight. I think most people who make them should desist. I received very little loot in food this year, and the presents from the commercial people were dreadful save for the liquor. How do you thank people for hideosities?

Love and kisses,

J

119 West 10th Street
New York
[January 1963]

Helen, dear —

I am glad you're back to yourself again. I am out of most of the depressed state and on the go as much as ever. When I get caught up I shall go in for a checkup and see what it's all about.

I just got notice that my revised *Hors d'Oeuvre and Canapés,* all redesigned and such, is coming in April. Yes, I still would like to do the cheese and wine book with you and Philip. And will help on the Bill Veach book, if it comes through and if you want me to. I do think your name on the book will do a lot for sales.

I sent a little note on my Christmas card to Ann Seranne, saying I really felt hurt that I never saw her and that I felt she no longer loved me. She replied that she did but that her loyalty was to her dogs now that she has been become so deeply engrossed in them, and she no longer had time for people. But she was eternally grateful to me for what I had done for her. Can you beat that?

I made Julia's garlic mashed potatoes with great success, but I think I will play with the recipe, for I don't think the cream sauce is needed. I do feel the flavor is superb, however. Had them with a steak from my neighborhood butcher and a huge endive and chicory salad, with my own vinegar — and good fresh strawberries.

Saturday night, went to an elegant dinner at the Bartos's, whom you met in class. Exquisite scallops Provençale, squab with my rice and pistachio stuffing, braised endive, and field salad. For dessert, a double crusted fruit tart with puff paste. I seem to have squab about once a week or so now and often do them crapaudine but sometimes roast them with a rice stuffing.

Made beautiful crépinettes for pictures for *House and Garden* the other day. I ran the seasoning — garlic, bay leaf, basil, cognac and whole pepper — through the blender before adding it to the pork. To some I added pistachio nuts, and some were plain. They looked so pretty when they cooked in the lacy caul.

Went to a dinner of the advanced class at the Forum on Thursday night, when Freddy Rupprecht made superb cheese soufflés for the first course and a chartreuse of partridge for the main course — wonderful flavor to the cabbage and sauce from the roast drippings and a little wine and parsley. For dessert we had the frozen oranges filled with orange and lemon sherbet, which tops off such a meal with great flair.

Love,

J

119 West 10th Street
New York
[February 12, 1963]

Dearest Helen —

Well, I can tell you that I don't care to live in Iowa. My trek to Davenport was fun, but God, what it must mean to get away from a town like that. Everyone sees the same people day in day out, and though the club where we did the demonstration is charming, it is the center for everyone's entertaining. And everyone has creamed chicken and celery ring — a good recipe, by the way.

I think our Bierstube was an event. I trained a woman chef, who is excellent, and who did a paella, a carbonnade of beef, and pork chops Alsatian with sauerkraut and beer. And we made omelets with beer. My omelet technique is improving, and I can do them now by only shaking the pan. I did four of them for the demonstration, and they all came out rolling along. I must say, Kate Titus knows how to appeal to people. There were two hundred sixty for the buffet and eighty more who came early to see the demonstration. In addition to the chef having made 240 portions of each of the dishes — not the omelets — she prepared 400 portions of fried chicken, because they were afraid people would not touch food which was different. But they ate everything and screamed for more.

The salad girl has been working there at the club for fifty-five years. I can tell you she has the sweetest, reddest French dressing you ever stumbled on, and do the Iowa gents and ladies love it. Eat it on everything which might be called a salad. A few demand another dressing, which she treats with high disdain.

Ate two of the best meals I ever had on planes going to and coming from Chicago, on United. Going out they offered drinks and their unusual idea of a first course. This one was a tiny trout, boned, cooked in a court bouillon and brushed with aspic, and with it on the plate a lovely piece of celery Victor, deftly cut, which made it fork-easy. A good sauce with this. I had fears when they brought the main course, but I was wrong. It was a broiled sirloin strip, which was hot and rare and had the grill marks on it. It was delicious with potatoes Anna and spinach, and with fresh tomato, garlic, and basil sautéed in olive oil atop it. Coming back they had a wonderful Salade Niçoise and a choice of chicken or fish. The chicken was juicy and the sauce Diable for it had green olives in it. And there was a good Linzer Torte. I tell you, I couldn't believe my taste buds.

I must say, the relationship with Ruth is much happier this year than it has ever been. We have a class in Lancaster, Pa. for three days in February and three in March. Then Standard Brand Shave have bought a class from us for July, for ten girls who are coming as contest winners.

Last night we made the most delicious steak, kidney, oyster and mushroom pie in the advanced class. Made it with two different crusts — one, a regular one, quite short, and the other a cream cheese one. Also made the easiest lobster mousse. I have taken the old fish farce recipe from Albert's stuffed salmon trout and incorporated a couple of things. It is made in the blender and cooks in 30 minutes. Want the recipe? You can also use it for stuffing fish to be served cold.

Yes, I use Elena's flan all the time. It is divinely rich. It is on our Mexican menu for the school and always brings down the house.

Love and kisses,

J

119 West 10th Street
New York
[March 1, 1963]

My dear Helen —

Restaurant Associates is having a battle to keep its head above ground because of the terrific drop in business since the first of the year and the newspaper strike. You have no idea how terrible it has been for restaurants. Much of it thanks to Rockefeller and the administration. They built up the idea of living well and now have everyone scared of using expense accounts.

Lancaster turned out to be a delightful experience — fourteen women with all the enthusiasm in the world and a pleasant gas-company kitchen with goddam gas stoves to work on. They entertained us royally and were more than kind. Ruth and I are both looking forward to the other three days.

You know, food in the hinterlands can be terrible. In Lancaster the hotel couldn't even do a good breakfast, and with all the lovely Pennsylvania Dutch sausage in the farmers' market they served commercial sausage and bacon, which like all the bacon now was adrip with water. The fassnachts for Shrove Tuesday were as tough as a whore's heart, and except for food in homes, it was a ghastly experience. We were taken to an elegant club where they had just put in as magnificent a kitchen as I have seen, and they gave us a mixed grill, supposedly rare, which was like it had been done in a greasy skillet. And a Perfection Salad, yet. And Pepperidge brown-and-serve bread. Next time we are going to Coventry Forge Inn, which is supposed to be elegant. I have decided to travel with club sandwiches, the safest diet I can think of, with an occasional frankfurter.

One woman told of her great-grandfather and great-grandmother-in-law in Lancaster. She is ninety-five and he is ninety-nine. She eats only the fat on the roast beef and butter pretzels with pounds of butter, and eats like a horse. He eats four and five sausages with eggs every morning, lives it up, and goes to the office every day. Can you beat that for high cholesterol living?

Love and kisses,

My name in Chinese character.

119 West 10th Street
New York
[March 1963]

Dearest Helen —

We were practically a sellout in Buffalo, but never speak to me about home economists. The two I had were both graduates and had never seen a leek, a scallion or a shallot, never touched or tasted lobster or artichokes — one of them, never lamb. It was absolutely shocking. I had to teach them to use a chopping knife and the basic elements of cookery.

However, Buffalo was a beautiful place to do such things. The social life nearly killed me, because that is the price you pay for being the local lecturing lion. Had some good food, though, which came from local kitchens. There was one brilliant dinner given by a man who has a fabulous cellar — done in the San Francisco fashion, stag, with the wife doing the food — a bore, I think. Interesting men, mostly doctors, all really in love with wine, and wanting no society of any kind. We had a delicious double chicken broth, with a fine old Williams and Humbert Cedro, a magnificent crabmeat omelet, with a Chevalier-Montrachet 1953 — amazingly young and great for its age — and a superb braised sweetbread dish, done with Madeira. And the wine was a Château Lafite 1943 — and nectarous. A rather blah dessert, with a Château Climens 1937, which was a delicious wine.

Another supper party had a coquille of crab, done with great flair and flavor, and piping hot, and a hostess who said, "Food is ready. Leave your drinks, and don't let the food spoil." And people heeded her.

I wish you could have seen what they sent me for a saddle of veal in Buffalo — and now I realize that in American parlance the saddle is the baron, and the saddle as we know it is the rack or double rack. But surprisingly good veal for a change. I finally had to substitute the veal roll with charcuterie for the saddle because no butcher could cut it the way I wanted. The kidneys were about the size of large lamb kidneys, the veal was so young, and tender as butter.

I shall send you a folder on the Aga, which is one of the greatest stoves in the world for slow cooking and baking, but not for brisk cookery. It is widely used in England, in the country, and in Sweden, and a few of them are here. As a matter of fact, Sheila Hibben did a booklet of recipes for them a few years ago when they were first being introduced.

I think *Cooking by the Clock*[1] is rather a bore. I hate that sort of thing. Maybe in two years we should do our correspondence cookbook, using some of our letters. We talked about this a long time ago.

Please have fun and quit dieting. I must take off some before I go to Europe.

Love,

J

---

[1] By Jean and Clarke Mattimore.

[119 West 10th Street
New York
March 23, 1963]

Helen, dear —

Julia called last night and has finished her first TV stint. Now the *Boston Globe* wants her to do a weekly column, but I told her they would probably not pay enough to interest her. She and Paul are coming down here week after next, and I shall have them to dinner. Guess I'll have Craig as well, and probably José. Craig is deep in the throes of his needlepoint and sits up in bed working on it with a special lamp and all.

I am doing a party on the 6th for the Huxtables[1] and think I shall do a choucroute the new way I like doing it — cooking each thing separately and putting a minimum of fat into the kraut. I'll add some stock to it instead. It seems much more delicate in final flavor, with stock and wine rather than goose fat or pork fat.

Lunched at Caravelle with John Ferrone and we had a paupiette of sole rolled with a tiny bit of farce, poached in a rich red wine court bouillon and served with a red wine sauce — so much better to my palate than with white wine. Gave a brilliant contrast to the sole. Also grilled sardines — did you ever try what is called the "California sardine" grilled? Caravelle is really my favorite restaurant in New York now for French food and almost my complete favorite. Everything is so pristine, if you know what I mean by that. Clean and trim, not heavy or fatty or overdone. It has the snap of perfection, which comes from constant supervision.

I have changed the book for Dell from a cooking-school book to a book of entertaining. I want to save the cooking-school book for later on.

Love to the Browns,

J

---

[1] Ada Louise Huxtable, architecture critic for the *New York Times*, and her husband.

119 West 10th Street
New York
[April 21, 1963]

Dearest Helen —

I've been somewhere for dinner every night and today go to Albert's for brunch and to the Huxtables' for supper. Yesterday, for lunch in the country, where I had the first outdoor cooked food of the season — chicken with rosemary butter, which was beautiful.

Had a lovely time with Julia. Her show is marvelous, and she is getting Boston attention if not national for it. She is a performer. We cooked dinner at her house — a lobster quiche, Chicken with Forty Pieces of Garlic, asparagus, and fruit and cheese.

Did I tell you about slowly broiling a six-inch strip steak to be rare inside and crusty outside? It is delicious. I've done three of them now, and I'm sold — except that they cost about fifteen dollars each time.

Love,

J

R.M.S. *Queen Elizabeth*
[April 28, 1963]

Dearest Browns —

Believe it or not I've stayed in bed till 11:00 a.m., had naps and have been completely relaxed. I have decided the Queens are for you next year. Probably the *Queen Mary* — but only if you get seats in the Verandah Grill, which you have to do through your travel agent, and get one like Nancy Surmain, who writes and tells how well they should treat you. The Grill only seats 148 on the Q.E. & 80 on the Q.M. But you sit high on the ship, with a view of the sea. You can order anything you want, & it's heavenly. I have had lovely Scottish beef & lamb. I dined with a gal I know the other night and had a superb rack of baby lamb, beautifully pink. Last night I dined with her again & we started with a perfect cheese soufflé, with mornay sauce and grated Parmesan, followed by a beautifully roasted chicken tarragon and grilled mushrooms.

Had a superb poached turbot the other day, with a good hollandaise. There is both fresh and smoked Scotch salmon and loads of good caviar. This morning the room steward brought me the best finnan haddie I've had for years.

Service is tops. There will never again be ships like these two, and you should have that experience while you can.

The righteous have just come from church. The British contingent is so very proper. I've not been very social. There's a group of people I know — mostly theatre folk — with whom I have had a drink a couple of times, and then there is one gal, in the fashion business in Paris, with whom I have dined, because with two you can order more interesting things in advance — and she loves food. Ordering a rack of lamb or a turbot for one a day in advance is rather precious. Otherwise I've been quite alone and very content.

I'm hoping Bettina & Mac meet me at the boat train. London will be a whirl. I leave on Saturday morning. The Fifields [William and Donna],[1] who live near St-Remy, meet me at Avignon & we dine with my landlady, Mme Baudin. Sunday I shall celebrate my birthday alone, I guess.

It's time for a couple of good stiff martinis. I think I'll send

Cunard my hors d'oeuvre book. They turn out the same ones every day.

Love,

J

---

[1] Donna Hamilton Fifield, a former film actress, was a food writer; William Fifield was a writer of fiction and nonfiction. Both were Americans.

Pasadena
May 4, 1963

James dear —

At last I have my hand in again & everything I cook seems to come out right. I think it took me a long long time to recover from my bout with death. I still think teaching isn't for me. I'd rather create and write.

H

[Lou Barcarès
St-Remy-de-Provence
May 6, 1963]

Helen and Philip —

I celebrated my birthday here in Provence by myself, had a good laugh over the stove and loved the dinner it cooked. It is the smallest two-burner and oven stove I have ever had, but I guess it will do, with the addition of a large grill, with all the twigs and vine cuttings one wants for fuel. For my birthday dinner I had a nice piece of veal braised with olive oil, garlic, thyme, black olives, red wine and a great quantity of parsley. It was delicious and festive, and with it I had fresh asparagus from the garden, good bread, Gruyère and a half bottle of Gigondas.

Monday last through Friday, in London, was a complete whirl. I had one terrible mixup, but it wasn't my fault. Joy [?] had a dinner and planned to invite the McNulties but didn't call them, and it was the same night Bettina had one. I went to Bettina's, and I hope all is forgiven by this time. Bettina had Elizabeth David, Bob Carrier,[1] and Lee and Roland Penrose,[2] who are the maddest people in the whole world. It was a nice party, and she did it beautifully, with Jambon d'Ardennes, chicken with morilles, rice, haricots verts, cheese, and a cold lemon soufflé. Very elegant and done with great charm, as only Madame McNulty can do when she has a mind to.

Had two long sessions with Elizabeth and find her a very stimulating and still quite unhappy person. She had had a bad time with Bob Carrier last fall, and Bettina's party was the first time they had seen each other since then. The reconciliation went off well. We sat in her kitchen after the dinner till almost three. She is such a darling and such a talent.

Had two superb meals at Mirabelle, a lousy one at Coq d'Or, and a very good one at a new Italian place called Tiberio, with Kiki and Bruce [Morton].[3] Lunched at the Brooks Club and ate lovely gull eggs, among other things. Simone Prunier[4] had a party, with superb turbot soufflés — individual, with hollandaise spooned into them by the waiters.

I really love this funny house. It is a typical country place and my apartment has quite a good bathroom, two bedrooms, a salon and a terrace. Furnished with all sorts of strange things. There are chickens and doves and dogs. And fresh herbs, including a huge plot of chervil right at the door. Mme Baudin sells marjoram and lavender to Germany by the acre, and sometimes rosemary. The surrounding rocks of the Alpilles range are so beautiful and the changing colors enchanting. At night, nightingales and moonlight and stars. And quiet.

The night I arrived the Fifields, who live about four miles from here, met me and had me to dinner. Do you remember them at Lascombes? Bill was working for the Lichine encyclopedia [of wines and spirits], and Donna, for the *Tribune*. Now they are both writing. Donna has a great deal to do with gastronomy. The night we dined she had just come back from the congress in Bologna and had brought a zampone. So we had a superb bollito misto — with chicken, shin of veal, the zampone, carrots, tiny artichokes, leeks, potatoes and a sauce that was a garlicky hollandaise, with capers and anchovies.

Today I go to Mme Baudin's for a lunch of cous-cous. She is a good friend of [Raymond] Thuilier at Baumanière, and I think I shall take her there next week. We are also close to Auberge de Noves, where we were so unhappy two years ago, and to the Prieuré and to Picond, and not too far from the Château Meyrargues.

May 7. Just had a baby shoulder of lamb for lunch. Not the whole thing but a part of it, roasted with fresh rosemary, and made some baby new potatoes with it. I had made a little sauce for the lamb, but it was so good without it that I couldn't bear to use it.

How funny it is to be without the convenience of home. I made mayonnaise with a fork and a saucer for the first time in years and have been using the mortar and pestle instead of the blender. Bought myself a couple of good knives this morning and a pepper mill. I'd been grinding pepper in the mortar as well.

Going to Baumanière for lunch on Friday with Mme Baudin. I want to renew my acquaintance with Thuilier, and she has known him for thirty years. Then when the Grubers and the rest of them come along we can go back. It's only three miles.

When I shop I'm shocked to see what we Americans have wrought. Everything in cans and jars, and frozen. And packaged baked goods. But the butter is divine and so is some of the cheese, although I still can't eat very much of it.

The mistral is with us today. Write often. It's kind of lonesome.

Love and kisses,

J

---

[1] Food editor of British *Vogue* and the London *Sunday Times,* and author of *Great Dishes of the World.*

[2] Lee Miller Penrose, a former model, photographer, and war correspondent for *Vogue;* Sir Roland Penrose, artist, art critic, and biographer of Man Ray, Miró, and Picasso.

[3] A reporter for CBS News.

[4] Of the family that had famous fish restaurants in London and Paris; Simone Prunier ran the one in London.

[Lou Barcarès
St-Remy-de-Provence
May 8, 1963]

Dear Helen —

I tried my outdoor grill today and it was a new experience in grilling. I bought a piece of steak — that vague thing known as steak at the butchers' in France. This was a piece of rump with no marbling at all, but, said the butcher, "It is tender." It really was, after a fashion. I made the fire with fig twigs, vine cuttings, a rosemary plant root, a great branch of dried bay, and two great plants of thyme. Such a perfume you have never had in your life. When it was down to coals or a facsimile thereof I put on the steak and added vine cuttings and thyme as it went along. I must admit, it was heavenly despite the lack of fat. With it I had a little plate of tiny new potatoes, ripe tomatoes from the garden, with chervil, and a small glass of wine.

Today was market day. There is asparagus, tiny new potatoes, artichokes, petits pois, new carrots and onions, but fruits are behind schedule and many vegetables. Our garden here and the chickens are strictly organic. Mme doesn't like artificial fertilizers. The eggs, I must say, are something you wouldn't believe for freshness and flavor. The yolks are a deep color and the whites stand alone.

Love and kisses,

J

[Lou Barcarès
St-Remy-de-Provence]
May 18, [1963]

My dear Helen —

Since I have eaten enough fresh green milky garlic spread on good pain de campagne for you to smell me all the way to Pasadena, I shall send you a whiff. Why I suddenly got so hungry for garlic I cannot tell you, but I had a loaf of yesterday's bread here and it was just right. I began rubbing a piece with garlic and then buttering it, and then another and another, till I had had five slices. Well, I had practically nothing else for supper.

It seemed to me that the bread here was getting more and more Americanized till I found this pain de campagne at my baker's. It is rough and slightly off white and has a wonderful crust — not the refined bread that everyone seems crazy for these days, which only lasts about an hour. This one is as good the second day as the first. One of the really few things about which I can rave. I bought some brandade from the charcutier today and it was awful. No garlic, and it tasted as if flour had been beaten into it. I merely tasted it and tossed it in the garbage. And the sausages around here are all too salty. Elizabeth [David] told me that. However, my butcher has a wonderful rosette de Morvan and good saucisson d'Arles, so that can keep us till we get to some Lyons sausage or Toulouse.

The other day we drove down to a little village just outside of Les Baux — not far from here — to the mill where an oilmaker lives. Good oil is very hard to find. He has about four different ones, and the one we finally picked, after tasting several, is superb — light and fruity. One could drink it as an apéritif. But my God — seven dollars a gallon right from the tap, but the local bourgeoisie think it is a fine bargain, and I guess I do too.

I've really caught up on a hell of a lot of work. I'm amazed how much ground one can cover if there is no telephone and no outside engagements to keep you running. I go to market with Madame and come home. If things get too boring we take a little foray in the car. And that is the round of living. I go to bed about ten and read and get up around seven. Have my tea on the terrace unless we have the horrendous mistral we had for two days. I haven't lived this way since the time I came out to you and no one knew where I was — remember?

We went to the Jules César in Arles yesterday for lunch. I ate a chicken Arlesienne*, and if I had closed my eyes I would have thought I was eating a beautifully made chili with a good deal of tomato in it. I adored it but it surely burned through me. Have you had any of the rice from the Camargue? It is quite different in that it is broad-kerneled and chewy. I quite like it.

I have no other gossip for you except that Cowles[1] turned down "Food and Drink" and that Helen McCully seems to think she may get the *Ladies' Home Journal* job now that they have changed editors.[2] She has certainly been the bravest person I have ever known in my life.

Do you have the Reboul *La Cuisinière Provençale?* If not, tell me, so I can send it to you.

Love,

J

---

[1] Gardner Cowles, president of Cowles Magazines, publisher of *Look.*

[2] McCully did not get the job; in 1967 she became food editor of *House Beautiful.*

* Recipe.

[Lou Barcarès
St-Remy-de-Provence]
May 26, [1963]

My dear Helen —

It was fun to return from Marseille and find your letter. The Grubers and I arrived late Monday afternoon after driving to Carry-le-Rouet for a lovely lunch at L'Escale with M. Bérot. Have you ever been there? It overlooks the sea and is quite dreamy. We ate stuffed mussels and stuffed clams, and I had a dodeline of chicken, stuffed with a chicken and chicken-liver farce and braised gently — a boneless breast with just the wing on. For dessert, a delicious lemon sherbet and such tuiles as I have never eaten. Berot is a great friend of Elizabeth and is going to be at the World's Fair next year.

Yesterday we went to Lucullus in Avignon, where the food is still superb and the prices not expensive. The best meal in a restaurant I have had.

I think you and Philip might like the other side of the house better than the place I have, because it has a bigger Provençale kitchen, living room, and bedroom, and upstairs, another bedroom if you want it. It also has a little dining spot under the trees in the garden, which is charming. You have to supply linens. Or you might make a deal with Mme for your sheets by paying a little extra, as I did. There are fresh eggs, vegetables and herbs on the place, and you have the lovely view of the Alpilles and the nearness to everything.

It's been too cold to do any grilling most of the time, but I have a great mass of rosemary and thyme ready, which I gather whenever I walk. I'm going to try a whole filet on the grill next and see what the aromatic herbs do for it.

I have actually lost a little weight since I have been here. I think I know why, too. I eat a good lunch and sometimes no dinner whatever. I feel better and look better, I am sure.

We're off to market.

Toujours,

J

[Lou Barcarès
St-Remy-de-Provence
May 31, 1963]

Dearest Helen —

Madame is having a big luncheon party today, with an aïoli, and we are going. Naomi Barry is here for a few days on her way around the South of France and is staying in the other apartment. I guess it is settled that she is to do the revised *Paris Cuisine* with me, which is to be stretched to all France. So we have been having a conference about what to include. We already have delicious recipes from Dumaine, from Lucullus and others. Do you know that out of the original sixty restaurants in *Paris Cuisine* we are keeping only thirteen and maybe six more? That is how things change.

I don't have a chauffeur. Madame Baudin suggested — because her Renault was so very uncomfortable — that I rent a 2-horse-power Citroën, and she would drive me to market in the mornings, while her son, whom she wants to get some driving experience, could drive me afternoons. This works out very well.

The little Citroën is fabulous for everything. Philip would love driving one of them.

I think it might be fun for you to have a month or so cooking in this house and shopping around. From here you have all of Provence, Lyon, Nîmes, the Camargue, Marseille, and the Massif Central within a day's trip, and you could cover a hell of a lot. It is not tout confort modern, and the decor is not *House and Garden,* but we can put up with that. The outlook is heavenly and the surroundings lovely.

Have you ever made asparagus Liegoise? Cook the asparagus and make two oeufs mollet for each person. Each then crushes the egg with fork and blends in olive oil, a bit of lemon and mustard and uses that for the sauce. We had that for dinner the other night and nothing else.

I did a thick steak this week, a contrefilet, and pan-broiled it because it was too hot to do it outside. I put butter and a good deal of salt in the skillet, peppered well, and the steak came through nicely, crusty and rare to the center. And I have found the country bread that is mine. I am still eating from a loaf bought Sunday, and this is Friday. They use the old-style yeast in it and heavy darkish flour. The rest of the bread is getting to be too Americanized, with commercial yeast, which makes it too light, and it becomes hard in no time.

The night Naomi arrived we went to the local spot in St-Remy — the Café des Arts. We had the regular menu — hors d'oeuvre, with a French cole slaw, cut very fine, a version of Salade Niçoise, tomatoes, sausages, and Salade Russe; then two excellent little lamb chops with haricots verts, a delicious salad, a choice of cheese or fruit or ice cream, a half-bottle of wine and coffee — for two dollars apiece. And very good it was. It's cheaper than living at home, almost.

I had a letter from Julia, who is doing more of her TV films. And she is doing a column for the *Boston Globe,* very amusing it is, too. She writes with great charm. I'm expecting to hear from Simone and shall plan to see her in Paris. I have sent her a couple of pupils lately, who wanted to study in Paris. Certainly L'Ecole des Trois Gourmandes[1] is preferable to the Cordon Bleu.

Rain for the first time since I've been here, and it is not welcome.

It is a thoroughly disagreeable day and bad for all the things happening this weekend, one of the biggest in the year — Pentecost. We have had tickets for the bullfights in Nîmes for weeks, and it is completely sold out. And there are all sorts of joyous things happening. But as in the United States, it always rains for holidays.

Wish you were here for the aïoli. I've found that if you keep up a steady amount of garlic you become free from smelling of it. You have to really permeate your body with it for several days and go on eating it, and no one notices.

Ta ta,

J

---

[1] The cooking school initially run by the three authors of *Mastering the Art of French Cooking.*

[Lou Barcarès
St-Remy-de-Provence
June 9, 1963]

Dearest Helen —

I have decided you should not take this place next year, for you couldn't stand the flies. You should go along the sea somewhere. And yet if you came in May perhaps it would be better, for the flies haven't started till this last week, and they are in the millions. Maybe I'm just too sensitive to them, but they drive me into a rage.

Bruce Glen, long a student and a very successful designer, comes to lunch today. I'm making hors d'oeuvre. I did onions Monagesque last night, and they are cooling, and there are lovely fresh tomatoes, a sausage, and a Salade de Museau, which my butcher does every weekend. Naturally, olives. Then roast chicken with new potatoes, a gratin of courgette, cheese and cherries.

Tomorrow John Ferrone arrives, so I'm making a daube Niçoise to have then, for the shops are all closed on Mondays, and one must get things in. I'll do it with macaroni in the Nice manner, have a simple first course of eggs in tapenade, and follow with cheese and fruit. I made a daube for the Grubers, and they loved it. The sauce, with a calf's foot or pig's foot in it, gets so thick and rich.

Tonight we are going to the neighboring village of Maillane, where a woman [Mme Fraize] has a small bistro that offers Provençale food. It is only the size of a postage stamp, and she does the cooking, so it can't be bad. It is right across the road from the Mistral home and museum. The village is about as big as a city block itself.

Last night Grandmère, Mme Baudin's mother, brought me a little dish of wild spinach, which she gathers and cooks with a béchamel, with Gruyère added, and how delicious it was. She is a really good cook and has taught me a brioche paste I never have seen before, for tarts and such. And she showed me a good clafouti, with a little yeast added to the batter, which does wonders for it. At 86 *she* is a wonder — gardens and cooks and is around the whole time.

Love and kisses,

J

[119 West 10th Street
New York
July 27, 1963]

Dearest Helen —

Tomorrow I'm having the Pedlars, Mateo Lettunich and Karl Springer, his friend, for supper — but very simple. Cold corned beef and roast beef, a bean and chick-pea salad, sliced tomatoes with fresh basil, and, of all things, a bread and butter pudding. I'm doing a pie and pudding book for December's *House and Garden,* and this is part of it. It is almost impossible to think of doing a bread and butter pudding again, but it is one of the most popular desserts at La Caravelle. I've been doing a hell of a lot of stuff — beefsteak and kidney pudding, boiled apple dumplings, cassonade. . . . I proved one thing. If you are doing a steamed pudding, foil is much better than the old pudding cloths with flour and all, and so much simpler.

Harriet Burket[1] took José Wilson and me to our annual luncheon yesterday, at Lutèce. André's chef [André Soltner] did a poached loup de mer, flown from France, with a white wine sauce with fresh tomato and mushrooms in it, that was absolutely dreamy. We all felt it had great originality and flavor. He really has the chef!

Had lunch with Craig the day before, and we surely had the other extreme. We went to Charles [French Restaurant]. Craig became furious when they gave him a commercial mayonnaise with his cold salmon and refused to eat another bite. He has bought a piece of property in East Hampton and is now planning to build a house there. I think he shouldn't do it, but he must find out for himself.

[J]

---

[1] Editor-in-chief of *House and Garden*.

[119 West 10th Street
New York
July 30, 1963]

Dearest Helen —

Somebody has sent me a manuscript to read of reconstructed and tested recipes of the Western Indians, some of which sound tremendously Mexican. I don't know whether this is a cookbook or research or what. It is fascinating, however.

Sunday supper was good. I made the salad with cannellini, kidney beans, chick-peas, olives, celery, peppers, chilies, onion and parsley and gave it a dressing with garlic and fresh basil in it. It was really awfully pretty with chicory and a garnish of hard-boiled eggs. Tonight I made hash with the leftover corned beef and cooked it down with cream till it had a marvelous crust on the bottom.

Julia is having a dinner on Friday and says we shall have to do some cooking together. I'm staying with them for two nights before I go to the Cape and then to Buffalo. Her column in the *Boston Globe* is delightful. She writes with such style and humor that the readership must be large and appreciative.

I'm invited to a luncheon to launch a new Scotch. I didn't think there were any left that had not been put on the market here.

Toujours,

J

[119 West 10th Street
New York
August 30, 1963]

Dear Helen —

I have decided Virginia Beach is the all-American low for food. With all the lovely crabmeat and fish around here, do you think you can find any? They advertise Maine lobster and lobster tails. And everything else is so bad you wouldn't believe it. It would seem that Americans outside of New York and California have no interest in food. Yet the markets teem with good things.

We did have a good dinner in Williamsburg at the King's Arms, and the plantation breakfast at the Williamsburg Inn is interesting. At the King's Arms they make the most delicious Sally Lunn bread — really good. We had a superb chicken gumbo, made with fresh okra and a rich broth, and Smithfield ham, with fried apples. And greengage plum ice cream, which I found extremely good.

The funny little college cafeteria [University] in Charlottesville, which Helen and I named as one of the outstanding places in the country, still is.[1] Sunday there was a block-long line, and few tourists. I ate the best apple pie I have ever had in a restaurant anywhere and feel they do a really excellent job of the kind of food people seem to want there.

We have seen Emil Kashouty, whom you probably remember. He lives in Hampton [Virginia]. Had dinner with him and his friend Frank Hearne the other night, and he made wonderful raw kibbee, which took me back to Beirut. He also used some of it to make those hollow balls we ate for lunch the day we went to Baalbek.

Fondly,

J

---

[1] The restaurant was given a *McCall's* award.

[119 West 10th Street
New York
October 1, 1963]

Dearest Helen —

The school is sold out. Craig's story on us ran with the wrong
telephone number and caused a day's consternation to a Jewish
woman who runs a hand laundry, but she finally transferred the
calls, because she figured every call was worth $132 to us.

Lester and Cleo are here for three days. Isabel, Craig, Paula and
I are giving them a party tomorrow night at Isabel's. She is doing
scallops in escabeche and mushrooms à la Grecque, I'm doing a
huge cassoulet, Paula is doing plum tarts, and Craig is spelling us.
We shall be fourteen.

I had a wild weekend of testing and cooking this week. I went
through my galleys [for *Delights and Prejudices*] and of course
didn't trust myself and tried about twelve or fourteen recipes, in
addition to making a new version of zuppa inglese. It was very
rewarding — the first I have really gone at it for a long time.

Love and kisses,
J

119 West 10th Street
New York
[November 1963]

Dearest Helen —

If you boil or steam your potatoes, purée them and beat
the softened butter into them — do not reheat them — it works
perfectly. The temperature will be about 85–90 degrees when
you add the butter. I spoke to Fred Rupprecht about it, and
he said this was right. The butter and potatoes are creamed together, just as a beurre blanc is creamed, without ever melting the
butter.

The thoughtful cranberry people sent me the largest collection of cranberries and by-products you have ever seen. I'd love to be able to send them to Philip, including the little sprig of cranberries on the vine. I am having the Callverts and Peggy for Thanksgiving and one or two others. I've got about six gallons of mincemeat and shall do it with a streusel topping instead of pastry. It's delicious that way. I'll add a few apples to it, for I never put apples in my mincemeat. But well over a gallon of cognac, liqueurs and such like.

Julia and Paul are back. They are bringing me a beautiful braisière, which I needed. I seem to be going to copper again. Bought two wonderful sauté pans of Swiss copper. They are lovely and cook things beautifully. I really think I'm becoming a better cook as the years go by.

Love and kisses,

J

119 West 10th Street
New York
[December 6, 1963]

Dear Helen —

With the great changes in Restaurant Associates, no one seems to know where to turn. You know that Jerry Brody is out and is starting his own chain of restaurants, Joe Baum is president, and Wechsler sold out his interests to Waldorf Cafeterias. God knows where the thing is going to end. The new restaurant, Paul Revere's Tavern in the Lexington, is doing well. In fact, every place but the Fonda seems to be making money.

I'm doing another big champagne party on Thursday — for about fifty — a project for Mumm. I'm doing a coarse pâté, beef, a Virginia ham, Polish sausages with Burgundy mustard. No time to do anything else, for I have to go out to Long Island on Wednesday for a demonstration.

The jacket of my new book is delightful.[1] I may see you for a day, for the publisher wants me to be in Portland when it comes out.

I find my taste is changing more and more all the time. I am growing fonder of the simple things and less so of heavily sauced dishes. This year I have an unholy craving for salad, for garlic, and for sausages. I have a passion for veal and chicken. Fish, I can barely get down my gullet. I can't abide the butter we get — it all tastes strong and horrid — and I am less and less interested in cheese. Fruit, I have practically given up except for melons, the only decent fruit we get anymore. Coffee, I can live without, and so it goes.

Love to you both,

J

---

[1] The jacket drawing for *Delights and Prejudices,* by Earl Thollander, portrays JB seated at a table on the beach at Gearhart, with a waiter taking his order.

119 West 10th Street
New York
[December 1963]

Dearest Helen —

I hope that you can afford to take it easy over the New Year's stretch, or are you and Philip going to have your open house on New Year's Day? I'm having the Pedlars and maybe Helen to dinner on New Year's Eve. I'm going to have smoked fish and a goose done with potatoes in the pan. I have marvelous prunes in Marsala. Then I think I'll do braised cabbage — not red. For dessert, I'm making an apple and mincemeat pudding, with streusel again. I may do a clam bisque to start instead of the fish.

Tonight Alvin Kerr is coming and I'm cooking a choucroute with Polish sausages and braised brisket, which will finish off in the kraut for an hour. I adore it that way, for the beef still tastes like beef and doesn't have too much of the cabbage flavor.

I got so much wine for Christmas — almost two cases of champagne, a lot of California wine from the Wine Institute and Advisory Board, and some of the new New York State wines from Charles Fournier, made from French varietals — and are they good! Only a tiny bit available now. Al Lessnor[1] sent me a case of his 1961 Sancerre, which is a dreamy wine. And Sam sent me a great selection of things. So I shall not be on the wagon long.

I thought most of the commercial gifts were terrible this year, and as for the Christmas cards — All this religion coming from commercial firms makes me upswallow. This must have been my Scrooge year, for I didn't like the Christmas trees and other decorations. I am in my red roses pattern again, I fear. Though there is a tree in the Four Seasons, about twenty feet tall, of poinsettias, which is beautiful, light and extremely gay.

I have so much work to do I don't know where to start, but I know you are in the same chorus line.

Love you both,

J

---

[1] An executive with Schenley Imports and later with Carillon Imports, which handled Grand Marnier.

119 West 10th Street
New York
[December 1963]

Helen —

No, I didn't tell you how happy I was with the curry book.[1] I think it is enchanting and loved what Nika Hazelton[2] had to say about it. I had a rapturous letter from Bill Veach about it as well. I think you did a remarkably good job with it and hope to God it sells, for it has such sense.

Pierre Franey gave me a pheasant last Sunday, a beauty, and I cooked it last night for Gino and me. Roasted it with plenty of salt pork at 450, in the French way, turning on all sides. Just salt and pepper with it, a few braised Brussels sprouts and a bottle of

Mumm '59. It was tender, juicy and crackly. I have two others, from John Balch[3], and those I'm taking over to Lianides and having dinner with him and his wife, Aphrodite, at the Coach House. I also have five wild ducks in the freezer, so this is my game year. Ordered a fresh-killed goose for New Year's Eve.

All love and king size,

J

---

[1] *A Book of Curries & Chutneys* by William Templeton Veach with Helen Evans Brown.

[2] Nika Standen Hazelton, contributor to the *New York Times* and numerous magazines, and author of cookbooks on Italian, Swiss, Belgian, and Scandinavian cuisines.

[3] John Balch, public relations representative for Harvey's.

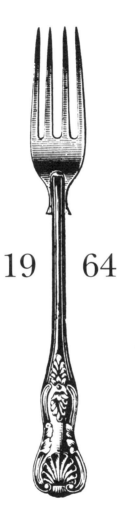

19 64

For two weeks in February, JB was in Doctors Hospital for an enforced rest and medical observation, and he was put on another diet. The next month he performed in Buffalo, Reading, Westport, and Baltimore, staying on the last occasion with a wealthy new friend, Janet Wurtzburger. In April he went to Portland to promote his newly published culinary memoirs, *Delights and Prejudices.* The same month he was at the World's Fair, working on menus for Restaurant Associates. He had invited HEB to do a star turn with him at the Fair, but she was not well enough to travel. During the next weeks he gave demonstrations in a number of cities, including Boston and Chicago. On July 20 he flew to Lisbon for a three-day stay, went on to Barcelona and then met his childhood friend Mary Hamblet in Nice. They proceeded to JB's rented apartment in a farmhouse in St-Remy-de-Provence and vacationed until mid-August. The surviving correspondence with HEB ends there. She was seriously ill by this time and had been hospitalized. JB visited her in mid-November. She died on December 4.

Dearest Helen —

I'm glad you decided to come back from Europe via New York and that you will be a star guest at the Fair. It just wouldn't have been right to have had everybody else who is important and not you, of whom we are most fond.

I still think that if you want to have old-fashioned luxury, you should book on the *Queen Elizabeth*. I shall write a note to the chef of the Verandah Grill, who is a charmer, and see that you meet him. It costs you something like two shillings a day extra, but it is so exciting to dine overlooking the water that it's worth it. Other than that, I would suggest the *United States;* and if you do take it I will write to the first-class purser. You might as well go grande luxe and have the fun of experiencing it. I know Philip will balk about dinner clothes, but he can take one of those white ones and just put on a black tie for the three nights.

You will be interested to know that California put on a tasting at the Waldorf under the slogan "California Comes to New York." It was stupendous. They lined the lobby and Peacock Alley with orange trees, flown in. All of the premium wines, many California foods, and the governor and his wife were there. The new Alma-dén blanc de blanc at $6.31 is slightly overpriced but quite a good champagne, but I think the Korbel, in that Dom Pérignon bottle, is a better one.

One thing I liked was hors d'oeuvre of fresh California dates, pitted and broiled with bacon — probably an old story but quite tart and good. They also used artichoke hearts for a fondue, which was very good.

I don't feel much better. I am going to the hospital on the 10th for a two-week regime and have a heart specialist look at me. I just may stay on a rice diet for a while. If I could manage, I would go to Duke University and join Helen and Burl Ives for a month.[1] Burl has lost fifty pounds and Helen, thirty.

I'm having the Grubers for dinner, along with Craig, who asked me not to invite anyone else. I am giving them a drunken mosaic roast of pork, which has been in a marinade for six days. I am going to stud it with pine nuts and garlic and serve it with a sauce made from the marinade, currants and additional pine nuts. It is a recipe that comes from Arles and is incredibly good. I am not going to serve the traditional rice with it but hominy, which I think will taste better, and I am making a great tian of cubed zucchini, spinach, rice and salt codfish. After that, cheese. A good healthy winter dinner.

I haven't had a drink for three days, which makes me feel much better. Maybe I was just born to be a prohibitionist.

Much love,
Jim

----

[1] The actor and his wife were on the "Rice Program" diet at Duke University Medical Center.

119 West 10th Street
New York
[January 18, 1964]

Helen, dear —

Do you have a copy of the *Somerset Club Cook Book* from Boston? Write to Alexander Williams at Little, Brown — he did it privately. It is a beautiful piece of bookmaking and a good bit of Americana for you.

Lester and Cleo have been here, as you know. I have had jury duty but have been free for lunch almost every day because of crazy cases. So I had a delicious lunch at Lutèce with them and a less than good lunch at Pavillon — in fact, shocking. Craig, Cleo and I ordered veal chops, and their veal comes from Kaufman,[1] I know. But they were so badly grilled and had stood so long on the réchaud before they were served that they were dry and practically charred on the bottom. At Lutèce they made us a perfect lobster soufflé for the first course — it baked just fifteen minutes — great chunks of lobster in it and a good sauce Américaine. Cleo had veal, and two of us had kidneys Bordelaise. The kidneys were pink, the sauce was good, and it was excellent.

I have a lovely leg of well-aged mutton in the oven. When Kaufman gets it, it is beyond belief good. Mort Clark is coming, and we shall have it with cannellini beans, sliced tomatoes, and a cold zabaglione. And I have a pâté, which we will taste before. It has spinach and olives in it.

Later. It's pretty good — needs a little more seasoning. I'll send you a recipe. Shouldn't really be called a pâté — it won't keep — but it's a delight for a buffet party, hot or cold. Looks beautiful. It's a layer of seasoned pork and veal, a layer of thin ham slices, a layer of chopped spinach, olives, and so on, so that you have three layers of meat and two of spinach. It is baked in a sealed terrine and should be weighted as it cools.

The mutton was deliciously aged but not as tender as the last piece I had. Anyway, it brought huzzahs, and I ate a piece for each of you.

Love and kisses,

J

---

[1] Of the Maryland Gourmet Market.

[Doctors Hospital
170 East End Avenue
New York]
February 17, 1964

Dearest Helen —

I am existing on a 900 to 950 calorie diet. Isn't it strange, we pay $40 a day for a room in a hospital to eat less. I must say, they are very nice about it, and the trays look and taste as well as can be expected under the circumstances. I am off salt, which is not a permanent thing. The most poisonous parts are the ersatz desserts—Sucaryl lime meringue, diet gelatin, dietetic canned fruit — so I substitute a pear or melon, which I keep here. I am so sick of juices I want to throw up. When I get home, I shall change the diet around.

Jack Sullivan called in a heart specialist named Poindexter, a delightful, hearty man, who wins one's confidence in a minute. He is putting me on a digitalis regime and is going to treat me as a special case, because I am one. My room is just lovely, with a view of the Triborough Bridge, the Hell's Gate Bridge and the mayor's mansion. I never get bored, but my ass is sore from sitting and lying.

Helen, would you mind ordering 12 cans of Fruitful Valley Nectar peaches for me? We have just run out, and they are about the only fruit Gino can eat anymore because our supply of fresh fruit is so God-awful.

I think you are entertaining too much and should call a halt. I don't know how you do it along with the rest of the work. Of course, you do have a lot of testing, and I suppose it is easier to test with people than to try a dish yourself and then throw it out.

Hope you are going to have a lovely Washington's birthday, with cherry trees, hatchets and old Martha Washington gingerbread.

> Much love,
> Jim

> 119 West 10th Street
> New York
> [April 1964]

Dearest Helen —

I have been at the Fair all this week with Joe. The Theatre of Food is off. Mr. Heinz has taken over, as threatened, and it is going to be one long commercial. However, I'm working on menus for the restaurant at the Gas Pavilion and for the Ford Pavilion private dining room. Despite all the things that have been said, the Fair is really exciting and quite fun. Some of the buildings — notably the Spanish and the New York State Pavilion — are exceptionally beautiful. The exhibits are for the most part fabulous, and the general feeling is one of great gaiety.

The restaurants, of which there are going to be 145, are promising. The Spanish one is to be run by the Jockey Club of Madrid.

Restaurant Associates is doing the Indonesian as well as my typically American one at Gas. The Swedish and Danish restaurants promise a great deal, as does the Japanese, and although the Hong Kong Pavilion is going to sell chow mein cones, it will have a good restaurant. There are to be three Mexican ones and a Thai one. New Orleans and Antoine's are doing one in the Louisiana Pavilion, Missouri will have a snack bar to celebrate the first serving of the hot dog. And so it goes, on and on.

Portland was a hell of a lot of fun and hard work as well. We all wished for you and Philip to be with us and talked about it constantly. Mary looks elegantly well and seems to increase in vitality as the years go on. People asked her to autograph books because [*Delights and Prejudices*] was dedicated to her. We sold 425 books in the sessions at Meier and Frank's. I did more radio and TV than one could possibly imagine and four demonstrations.

The beach was heavenly. Mary and I stayed at Rhoda Adams's and lunched at Marion Kingery's — a lovely house on the point overlooking the Necanicum River, Seaside, Tillamook Head and the surrounding country. Dined at Harvey Welch's. His house is built way down below Rhoda's, where it is quiet and lovely, for the moment — about 1½ miles from any other house. Sunday was a beautiful day and we drove to Canon Beach to see Bill Bingham and the damage done by the tidal wave.[1]

My sister looks wonderful but is losing her memory. She came to one of the demonstrations and to Meier and Frank's. At the Salem demonstration I sat next to the governor's wife, who is supposed to be a great cook. I'm sending her a flan ring, which seems to be the hardest thing to get in Oregon. Fell off the wagon in Portland but went back on it the day I came back. Had delicious food in homes, but certainly Portland does not boast of a good restaurant anymore.

Baltimore was also a delight. Ruth and I stayed with Mrs. [Janet] Wurtzburger, who is behind the food demonstrations. She has a beautiful house, with acres and acres, and a sculpture garden that starts with Rodin. Pieces by Henry Moore, Epstein, Maillol, and Lachaise are under the trees here and there. The house is elegantly simple, with practically no pictures on the walls, except in the bedrooms, and great sweeps of garden seen through the windows.

The demonstrations went well. You would have enjoyed all the dowagers arriving in their cars or limousines with their cooks — yes, in Baltimore they have them — and settling in for the afternoon or evening. Ruth has learned to be a fine assistant, and though we have some personality clashes, she goes a good job of organization and getting cooperation from the staff backstage. Next year we are already booked for three or four places, and have three more on the fire. Julia will be doing demonstrations in San Francisco, Ruth tells me. So perhaps it will become like the concert business — tours of cities. Get well quick, and we'll start a joint tour with fabulous fees.

Love,

J

---

[1] Rhoda Adams, Marion Kingery, Harvey Welch, and Bill Bingham were all old Portland friends of JB.

119 West 10th Street
New York
June 11, 1964

Dearest Helen —

I was so excited to talk to you the other day and to know that you are home. I hope your daily rounds have met with improvement. After all the months in the hospital just looking out on your garden must be enough to make your day.

I'm definitely leaving here on the 20th of July — going to Lisbon for three days and to Barcelona to get some shirts, and will meet Mary on the 28th in Nice and then go on to St-Remy.

Tuesday I went to Boscov's department store in Reading to do two outdoor demonstrations and had about 250 in the afternoon, when it was 90 degrees, and 500 in the evening. They had two grills going, and we broiled a leg of lamb, flank steak, herb-stuffed chicken and all sorts of appetizers. Mr. Boscov, who owns the store, gave each person a paperbound copy of *The James Beard Cookbook,* so that's at least 800 copies we can depend on having been sold. We just called out the page numbers from the stage rather than print recipes. It worked out beautifully. However, I find that two demonstrations in one day wears me down a bit.

Tomorrow I am off to the Fair. The biggest job I have is trying to get American pastry chefs to make American pie, layer cake and angel cake. It is hopeless. I am having them do little fruit pies, with crusts baked ahead of time and filled with seasonal fruits at table. Some of the berries will be lightly poached and others sugared. This was the fare I knew in Portland years ago, and I think it might be fun for an American restaurant.

Much love,

J

[Lou Barcarès
St-Remy-de-Provence
August 3, 1964]

Dearest Helen —

It was hot as hell in Nice and Cannes, but Mary and I got around. We found a silly boat that took us to Monte Carlo, where Mary won sixty francs in nothing flat. Went to Marseille on the Trans-European Express, with lunch service at your seat. Naomi Barry was in Marseille, and we were invited to the Consul General's for lunch, at a beautiful house on the sea. Yesterday Naomi came up to St-Remy and lunched with us at Baumanière.

We had Thuilier's version of pissaladière, made in a flan ring with puff paste, a coulis de tomates, anchovies and onion. Absolutely delicious. We also had poached sole with a sauce of cream and port reduced and a good deal of caviar stirred into it at the last minute — I rather think, pressed caviar.

Saturday night we went to Villeneuve-les-Avignon to a new place Naomi found on the banks of the Rhone.[1] They do beautiful grills on the outdoor fire, with vine cuttings. We had filets brushed with mustard, herbs and oil while grilling — delicious — along with plenty of watercress and eggplant Provençale. Packed with people, and we didn't arrive till nine-thirty.

This year I have Yvonne's apartment, with all her fine furniture — a dream spot, really. How I wish I could buy the house from her for all of us to have for our holidays and our old age. She is anxious to sell and get back to Périgord, for this has too many terrible memories for her, and with no one to share it with her, it is far too big.

Today is Monday, so the shops are closed. With what Naomi left behind and what I garnered from the garden, Mary and I had a pretty good lunch. I pounded fresh basil, parsley, garlic and a baby leek in the mortar with a little mayonnaise — because I lacked oil — and we ate it with leftover spaghetti and fresh tomatoes. Tonight we shall probably do a fresh egg from the hens, and that will be the day.

Everybody is grilling and barbecuing like mad here now. I don't know how my outdoor book has gone, but I get burned every time I see that jacket with Courtine's name on it — and mine only on the title page.

I can't imagine what went wrong with your socca. Perhaps the meal is too fine in the States. I thought that if you took some chickpeas and ground them in the blender, after they had been soaked, and mixed that with the meal it might do better. You make a mush of it in the double boiler, as you do with cornmeal, and then add oil, pepper and salt. Pour it into trays which are well oiled and brush with oil. We ate it again in Nice, and it is much better with a little pepper shaken on it. I shall try it again as soon as I am home.

Much love,

J

---

[1] Probably Hostellerie Provençale du Vieux Moulin.

[Lou Barcarès
St-Remy-de-Provence
August 9, 1964]

Dearest Helen —

I thought so much of Philip as I ate my kidney the other night at Auberge de Noves and of how much better he or I or any of us could have done it. I still think it is a pretty bad restaurant except for their crudités plate, which is a work of art. But that doesn't give them three stars. There were visiting firemen here, and I was asked to be nice to them. They came here for drinks and then we had to have a meal with them at this joint. The damned cook overcooked the kidney and then covered it with a béarnaise. The poor little kidney was swimming in sauce. Mary had a squab chicken, which she liked, but which I knew was cooked far too much. You would be shocked at the food in some good restaurants and the prices everywhere.

Yesterday we went over to Apt to the ceramics man [M. Bernard] I found last year. We had a lovely ride after a day of the most horrendous rains you ever saw. Shopped around and had lunch in a little restaurant [Luberon] with charming surroundings. A wonderful plate of hors d'oeuvre — Salade Russe, carrot salad, tomatoes, a barquette of pâté, a piece of toast with a slice of saucisson chaud, a tartine of rillettes, and a tiny turnover with anchovy. Then I had an andouillette — Mary had salmon trout — and a delicious veal Cordon Bleu. Salad with it and fruit. It was twelve francs apiece, with wine and coffee extra.

I have to go and put the chicken in the oven for lunch. We will have a bit of hors d'oeuvre, and I'm cooking tomatoes Provençale — slowly, slowly, slowly in oil till they caramelize.

God, it's been a long time since we had a good chat, all of us. I can hardly wait till fall when I can come and be a part of the household for a few days.

> Loads of love,
> [J]

> [Lou Barcarès
> St-Remy-de-Provence
> August 14, 1964]

Dearest Helen —

It is grand that you are recovering so much, but I understand the feeling when your legs get tired and seem to give out. I have had that happen to me several times in my life. It is so maddening and thwarting.

Yvonne is Madame Baudin, who is the owner of the place where I'm staying and who became such a good friend last year. She is a complete darling. The property is almost seven acres. The house has four apartments with baths — and gas and such. She wants about sixty thousand dollars for it all.

But Thuilier is building some houses in Paradou which promise to be most attractive and is going to let me know about them.

They will be independent of each other, with swimming pools and a year-round guardian, and will be built to suit the taste of the buyers. We might all have one built, with a huge kitchen, for ourselves and to rent. Then we could do our experimenting with French foods.

Today at Baumanière we had a guinea hen with a sauce made with morilles, cream and a bit of curry. Absolutely delicious. And I had an egg Benedictine for my hors d'oeuvre. Thuilier serves it in a patty shell filled with brandade, rather than a flat spooning of it, as I have had before. Then the egg on top and a brushing of hollandaise, and some more on the side — ravissant. Did I tell you of the terrine at Lucullus, made with thin pieces of their own cured ham, veal farce, and loads of spinach, basil and parsley? Superb. Baked in a round crock with no cover, like a meat loaf, and deliciously seasoned. A true terrine for summer.

We are having another thunderstorm, and the lights have been off for almost a half hour.

I have some introductions to write for the damned Dell book [*Menus for Entertaining*], which is finally finished, five years overdue. This is the one they contracted for when I did *The James Beard Cookbook*, and they gave me a fat advance on it. It is pretty good, I think. I didn't want to do it. But I guess it's wrong to take an advance and then settle back.

The lights are still out, and it's getting dark, so I'll send you love and kisses.

J

Recipes

Appetizers and Soups

Roquefort Spread

½ pound Roquefort cheese
¼ pound butter
¼ pound cream cheese

½ teaspoon dry mustard
2 tablespoons cognac (sherry, Madeira, or red wine may also be used)

Mash the cheese with the butter, cream cheese, and mustard, and blend together. Stir in the cognac or wine and whip until smooth. Store in small crocks or jars, and refrigerate. Will keep for several weeks.

Strathborough Paste

4 pounds beef, chuck or rump, as for a pot roast
2 or 3 leeks, trimmed and cleaned
2 carrots, peeled
1 medium onion, peeled and stuck with 2 cloves
1 teaspoon dried thyme

2 or 3 sprigs of parsley
1 teaspoon salt
8–10 anchovy fillets, pounded fine
6 tablespoons cognac (approx.)
Quatre Épices*
1½ pounds butter (approx.)
Extra melted butter

Place the meat in a deep pot with the vegetables, herbs, and salt. Add water to cover and bring to a boil. Skim off any scum that appears. Cover, reduce the heat, and simmer for 3 to 4 hours or until the meat is quite tender. Remove the meat from the broth and allow to cool. Then pound it to a paste in a mortar or blend in the food processor with a little of the strained broth. Measure the beef in cups, and for each cup add 2 teaspoons of the anchovy, 1 tablespoon of cognac, and a pinch of Quatre Épices. Turn into a

* See recipe for Quatre Épices.

saucepan and cook over moderate heat until it begins to bubble, stirring constantly. Remove from the heat, and for each cup of the meat mixture blend in 4 tablespoons of butter. Spoon into small crocks or jars, cover with melted butter, and cover tightly. Keep refrigerated, and use as a savory spread for sandwiches.

Mme Fraize's Country Pâté

2 pounds lean pork, coarsely chopped
2 pounds veal, chopped
1 pound ground pork liver
1 pound fresh pork siding or fat bacon, diced
6 garlic cloves, minced
3 eggs

½ teaspoon Quatre Épices
⅓ cup cognac
1 tablespoon dried basil
1 tablespoon salt
1 teaspoon freshly ground pepper
Salt pork slices or bacon

Combine all ingredients except for the salt pork slices. Line a straight-sided terrine, baking dish, or 2½-quart soufflé dish with the salt pork or bacon. Fill with the mixture and round the top. Arrange a few strips of salt pork or bacon over the top. Bake at 325° for 2 to 2½ hours, covered with foil for the first hour. When it begins to shrink from the sides, it is done. Remove from the oven and cool for half an hour. Then weight it down to finish cooling. Serve from the baking dish.

Quatre Épices

Mix together 1⅛ cups ground white pepper, 3½ tablespoons ground nutmeg, 3½ tablespoons ground ginger, and 1½ tablespoons ground cloves. Spoon into a jar with a lid. Keep tightly sealed, and use as needed.

Onion Sandwiches

Brioche loaf or good white bread, sliced very thin
White onions, peeled and sliced very thin

Mayonnaise, preferably homemade
Chopped parsley

Cut the brioche or bread into rounds with a biscuit cutter. Spread the rounds lightly with mayonnaise. Divide into two batches. Arrange a layer of onion slices on one batch and top with the other. Press together gently. Roll the edges in mayonnaise and then in the chopped parsley. Pile on a serving dish and refrigerate for several hours before serving.

Carnitas (Little Meats)

2 pounds lean pork, such as   *Salt and pepper*
*   boneless butt*

Cut the meat into 1-inch cubes, sprinkle with salt and pepper, and allow to stand for an hour on a rack. Transfer to a baking pan, and bake in a 300° oven for about 2 hours, pouring off any fat that is rendered. Stick a toothpick or small wooden skewer in each piece and serve with Mantequilla de Pobre.

Mantequilla de Pobre (Poor Man's Butter)

2 medium ripe avocados   *3 tablespoons red wine vinegar*
2 large ripe tomatoes, peeled and seeded   *1 tablespoon olive oil*
12 green onions, finely sliced   *Salt to taste*

Cut the avocados and tomatoes into small pieces or cubes, add the rest of the ingredients, and mix gently. Allow to mellow at room temperature for a half hour before serving.

Elena's Salsa Fria

2 cups chopped ripe tomatoes or a large   *1 tablespoon fresh coriander, chopped*
*   can solid-pack tomatoes*   *1 teaspoon oregano*
1 4-ounce can chopped green chilies   *1 tablespoon olive oil*
1 medium onion, finely chopped   *2 tablespoons wine vinegar*

1 16-ounce can tomatillas, chopped, with hulls removed

Salt and freshly ground pepper to taste
Extra chopped coriander

Thoroughly mix the ingredients together in a bowl and chill until ready to use. Serve as a condiment with hot or cold meats or fish; or use as a dip.

Crab and Clam Appetizer

1 6-ounce can crabmeat
1 6½-ounce can minced clams, drained
1 tablespoon grated onion
1 small sour pickle, chopped
1 tablespoon chopped fresh tarragon or 1 teaspoon dried

Enough mayonnaise to bind (about ½ cup)
¼ cup chopped parsley
2 tablespoons rum
Lettuce leaves

Combine all the ingredients, except for the lettuce, and let stand for an hour. Then transfer to a fine sieve to drain off excess liquid. Turn out on a plate of nicely arranged greens, and garnish with a bit more chopped parsley. Serve with toast, Melba toast, or crisp French bread.

Cream of Pumpkin Soup

2 cups clear chicken broth
1 cup cooked pumpkin purée, either fresh or canned
1 medium onion, chopped
1 cup cream, either heavy or light

Salt and freshly ground pepper to taste
Instant mashed potato, if needed
Chopped chives or parsley
Nutmeg
Optional: ¼ to ½ cup Madeira

Combine the broth, pumpkin, and onion, and a good pinch of nutmeg in a pan, and simmer for about twenty minutes. Put through a foodmill or in a food processor to purée the onion with the pumpkin. Return to the pan, stir in the cream, and reheat. Taste for seasoning. If you are using canned broth, you will probably have enough salt. Add the Madeira just before serving. Give each serving a dash of nutmeg and a sprinkling of chives or parsley. Serves 4.

Avocado Soup

1½ cups puréed ripe avocado
1½ cups heated chicken broth
1 tablespoon fresh tarragon, chopped, or
   1 teaspoon dried
¼ teaspoon Tabasco

1 tablespoon lemon juice
½ cup heavy cream
½ cup sour cream
Chopped chives

Combine the avocado with the chicken broth and stir until
smooth. Add the tarragon, Tabasco, and lemon juice, and allow to
cool. Then blend in the heavy cream and sour cream. Chill well
before serving sprinkled with chives. Serves 4.

Quick Tomato and Clam Bisque

4 pounds ripe tomatoes, peeled and
   chopped
½ teaspoon dried thyme
1 6½-ounce can minced clams

½ cup chicken broth
2 tablespoons butter
Salt and freshly ground black pepper to
   taste

Put the tomatoes in a pan and bring to a boil with the thyme and a
sprinkling of salt and pepper. Remove from heat and cool. Put
through a food mill or purée in a food processor. Pour into a bowl,
then purée the clams until creamy. Combine the tomatoes, clams,
and chicken broth, and taste for seasoning. Add a pinch more of
thyme, bring just to the boil, and stir in the butter. Serves 4 to 6.

Meats

Daube Provençale

5-pound piece of beef rump or shin
3 or 4 pieces of salt pork
2 pigs' feet or 1 calf's foot
2 bay leaves
8 garlic cloves
1 clove
1 strip orange peel

1 teaspoon dried rosemary
Several sprigs parsley
1 tablespoon salt
2 teaspoons freshly ground black pepper
1 bottle of dry red wine
1 pound macaroni

Place the beef and other meats in a deep casserole or crock with the seasonings, and pour in red wine to cover. Let marinate for 24 hours. Place in a heavy enamel braising pan or casserole and cook at no more than 200° for 6 hours or until thoroughly tender. Remove from the heat for 20 minutes or so. Then skim the fat from the sauce. Strain the sauce. Cook the macaroni in boiling salted water and drain. Serve part of the sauce with the macaroni and part with the sliced meat. This is called Macaronade.

To serve cold, let the strained sauce cool. Remove the fat. Arrange slices of the beef in a serving dish and cover with the sauce. Chill. Serves 6 to 8.

Gigot, Prieuré Style

1 small leg of lamb, about 4½ to 5
  pounds
6 to 8 potatoes, peeled and thinly sliced
Butter
1 small onion, thinly sliced

Salt and freshly ground pepper
1 cup beef broth
3 cloves of garlic, slivered
1 teaspoon rosemary
Parmesan cheese (optional)

Put the potato slices in cold water, drain, and dry thoroughly. Butter a baking dish large enough to hold the lamb. Arrange layers of potato slices in it, adding the onion after the first two layers, and dotting each layer with butter. Sprinkle with salt and pepper. Add the broth. Trim most of the fat off the lamb, make gashes in the meat, and insert the garlic slivers. Rub with the rosemary, salt, and pepper. Place the leg on a rack directly above the potatoes. Roast at 350° for about 1 to 1½ hours. The potatoes should be brown and crusty. If they are done first, remove from the oven while the lamb continues to cook (over another baking pan), sprinkle with the cheese, and return to the oven for 10 minutes to reheat. Allow the lamb to stand for 10 to 15 minutes before carving. Serves 4.

Grilled Lamb Steaks

4 lamb steaks ¾ inch to 1 inch thick
½ cup soy sauce
½ cup red wine

¼ cup grated fresh or chopped preserved ginger
2 or 3 garlic cloves, finely chopped

Mix the ingredients for the marinade, pour it over the steaks in a shallow dish or pan, and let them marinate for several hours. Drain and grill over coals or put under the broiler, brushing two or three times with the marinade, until nicely browned on both sides. Serves 6 to 8.

Near Eastern Meatballs

1½ pounds ground lamb
2 cloves garlic, minced
1 egg, lightly beaten
½ cup pine nuts

½ cup chopped parsley
Salt and freshly ground black pepper
Olive oil

Mix the meat with the garlic, egg, pine nuts, parsley, and salt (about 1½ teaspoons) and pepper. Form into small balls. Heat about 2 to 3 tablespoons of olive oil in a skillet and sauté the meatballs for a few minutes, shaking the pan to brown them uniformly. When done they should be slightly pink in the middle. Serves 3 to 4.

Marinated Loin of Pork

1 boned loin of pork, about 4 pounds
½ cup soy sauce
1 cup dry vermouth
2 tablespoons chopped fresh ginger or
* 2 teaspoons powdered ginger*

3 cloves of garlic, finely chopped
1 tablespoon fresh tarragon or 1 tea-
* spoon dried**

Mix the ingredients for the marinade, and marinate the pork for several hours, turning frequently. Drain and pat dry with paper towels. Balance on a spit and roast 20–25 minutes per pound or until it reaches an internal temperature of 165° when tested with a thermometer. During the second half of the cooking, baste the pork several times with the marinade. This can also be oven-roasted at 350°.

Carve in thickish slices and serve with the strained marinade. Serves 6.

Hawaiian Spareribs

4 pounds spareribs
½ cup soy sauce
½ cup dry or medium sherry
3 cloves garlic, finely chopped
2 tablespoons grated fresh ginger or
* chopped preserved ginger*

⅓ cup olive oil
Salt and freshly ground pepper
2 teaspoons sugar (optional)

Combine all the ingredients for the marinade, except the sugar, and let the ribs soak in it for several hours. Cut the ribs into serving sections. Either spit them or broil them. If using a spit, roast for 20 minutes and then brush with the marinade. Continue to brush from time to time until the ribs are done. If broiling, cook on one side, brush with the marinade, and turn. Do this several times until the ribs are nicely browned. To glaze, sprinkle with the sugar during the last few minutes of cooking. Serves 4.

----

* JB used "Old Man" (Southernwood) in his recipe, not easily obtainable. Tarragon belongs to the same family, Artemisia, and is suggested as a substitute.

Jambon à la Crème

6 to 8 slices cooked smoked ham
4 tablespoons butter
6 shallots, finely chopped
4 tablespoons flour
¾ cup milk, heated

¾ cup light cream, heated
2 tablespoons concentrated tomato
  purée
¼ cup dry white wine

Melt the butter in a saucepan over medium heat, and cook the shallots until softened but not browned. Stir in the flour to make a roux. Gradually stir in the milk and the cream. Continue cooking and stirring until thickened. Blend in the tomato purée and the wine. Transfer to the top of a double boiler, and simmer over hot water for 25–30 minutes. The sauce should be as thick as heavy cream.

Heat the ham slices, either sautéing lightly or placing in a moderate oven for a few minutes. Cut into strips and arrange in a serving dish. Cover with the sauce and glaze under the broiler. Serves 4.

Poultry

Chicken Calandria

4½-pound roasting chicken
1 cup white cornmeal
½ cup olive oil
3 medium onions, finely chopped
2 cloves of garlic, finely chopped
1 cup dry red wine
1 teaspoon sesame seeds

½ teaspoon caraway seeds
⅛ teaspoon mace
⅛ teaspoon marjoram
Salt
1 cup blanched almonds
1 cup pitted green olives
4 tablespoons chili powder

Cut the chicken into serving pieces and roll in the cornmeal, shaking off the excess. Save 3 tablespoons of the cornmeal. Heat the oil in a heavy braising pan, and sauté the chicken until lightly browned on all sides. Reduce the heat, add the onions and garlic, and cook until they are just softened. Add the wine, seeds, mace, marjoram, and 3 cups of boiling water. Sprinkle with salt, cover, and simmer for 10 minutes. Add the almonds, olives, and chili powder, cover, and simmer for 20 to 30 minutes more or until the chicken is tender. Remove the chicken from the pot, and skim excess fat from the cooking liquid. Mix the reserved cornmeal with ½ cup of water, and stir into the liquid. Continue stirring until thickened. Serves 4.

Poulet Arlesienne

3-to-4-pound chicken, cut into serving
    pieces, or 4 legs and thighs
4 to 5 tablespoons olive oil
2 cloves garlic, chopped
1 teaspoon salt

1 tablespoon chopped fresh basil or
    1 teaspoon dried
½ teaspoon freshly ground black pepper
⅔ cup dry white wine

For the sauce:
3 onions, finely chopped
1 clove garlic, chopped
3 tablespoons olive oil
2 cups tomato sauce, preferably
  homemade

1 hot pepper, finely chopped
¼ teaspoon Tabasco

Sauté the chicken in the olive oil in a skillet until lightly browned. Add the seasonings and one half of the wine. Simmer for about 10 minutes, turn the pieces, and cook for another 10 minutes. Meanwhile prepare the sauce: Sauté the onions and garlic in the oil until softened but not brown, add the tomato sauce, and simmer 20 to 25 minutes. Add the chopped pepper and Tabasco. Taste for salt and piquance.

Transfer the chicken to a hot platter. Remove excess fat from the pan and rinse over medium heat with the rest of the wine. Pour over the chicken. Pass the sauce separately, and serve with rice. Serves 4.

Chicken with Olives

3-to-4-pound chicken
1 cup pitted black olives
A few sprigs fresh rosemary or
  1 teaspoon dried

⅔ cup olive oil
6 to 8 garlic cloves, peeled and crushed
Salt and freshly ground black pepper

Place the chicken in a deep bowl or casserole and add the olives, rosemary, oil, and garlic. Turn to coat it well on all sides, then refrigerate for 24 hours or overnight, turning it several more times. Remove from the refrigerator and place on a rack in a roasting pan. Insert the garlic and olives in the cavity of the chicken. Sprinkle with salt and pepper. Roast at 375° for an hour or so until well browned and crisp, or roast on a spit, first closing the cavity with foil or skewers. Cut in quarters and serve with the degreased pan juices, watercress, and sautéed potatoes. Serves 4.

Mercedes' Paella

6 chicken legs and thighs
1 pound gizzards
½ cup olive oil
2 cloves of garlic, finely chopped
1 large onion, finely chopped
1½ cups rice
Pinch of saffron

1 cup dry white wine
1 cup chicken broth
½ cup chopped ripe tomatoes
12 shelled shrimp
Chorizo, thinly sliced
12 to 18 clams, well scrubbed
Pimiento strips

Cut the legs and thighs into two pieces. Heat the olive oil in a paella, and brown the chicken pieces and gizzards. Salt and pepper them. Transfer the chicken to a hot platter. Add the garlic and onion to the pan and cook for 2 to 3 minutes, then add the rice, and toss until it begins to color. Add the saffron and wine and let it cook down. Then add the broth, little by little, until the rice is nearly done. Return the chicken pieces, and add the tomatoes, shrimp, slices of chorizo, and clams. Cook until the chicken and shellfish are done and the rice is tender. Serve garnished with the pimiento. Serves 6 to 8.

Turkey Galantine

6-to-8-pound turkey, boned
Cognac
Salt
Quatre Épices
2 pounds ground ham
1 pound ground veal
3 cloves garlic, finely chopped
3 eggs

¼ teaspoon freshly ground black pepper
1 teaspoon thyme
¼ pound boiled tongue ¼ inch thick
¼ pound ham ¼ inch thick
Fresh or canned truffles, sliced (optional)
Pistachio nuts, chopped
Chicken broth

Have the butcher bone the turkey for you, removing the wings and drumsticks. Also remove the breast meat and marinate for 1 hour in cognac, 1 teaspoon salt, and a dash of Quatre Épices (see recipe). Meanwhile mix the ground meats, garlic, ½ cup of cognac, eggs, ¼ teaspoon of Quatre Épices, 1¼ teaspoons salt, and the pepper and the thyme.

To assemble, spread out the boned turkey, skin side down, and cover with meat mixture, and place the breast meat in the center. Cut the tongue and ham in ¼-inch strips and arrange with the truffle slices around the breast meat, pressing into the ground meat. Sprinkle with the chopped pistachio nuts. Roll up the turkey sausage-fashion, bring the ends of the skin together so they overlap, and sew with needle and string. Roll in a damp kitchen towel and tie the ends, leaving lengths of string. Also tie string around the middle.

Pour broth into a fish cooker until half full. Lower the galantine into the broth and tie the string at either end to the handles of the cooker. Cover tightly with a couple of layers of heavy aluminum foil. Bring to a simmer, and steam for 2 to 2½ hours, depending on the size of the bird. Remove the foil and let the turkey partially cool in the broth, then transfer to a dish and weight it down as it continues to cool. Refrigerate for 36 hours. Remove the cloth and string, and arrange on a platter or carving board. Carve in thin slices, and serve as an hors d'oeuvre or buffet dish.

Roast Duck with Honey and Curry

1 duckling, 4 to 5 pounds
Salt and freshly ground pepper
½ teaspoon dried thyme, crushed
1 onion stuck with 2 cloves

¼ cup honey
1½ tablespoons curry powder
1 tablespoon lemon juice

Rub the duckling with salt and pepper and the thyme. Put the onion in the cavity. Arrange on a rack in a roasting pan and roast in a 350° oven 1½ hours for medium rare duck and 2 hours for well done. After the first half hour prick the skin all over to release the fat, and prick several more times during cooking. Remove the fat from the pan with a bulb baster as it accumulates. Mix the honey, curry powder, and lemon juice. After the first hour brush the duck with the honey mixture, and repeat every ten minutes during the next half hour until the skin is nicely glazed. For a crisper skin increase the heat to 500° during the last 15 minutes, and reduce the total time by 5 minutes. Serves 2.

To test for doneness prick the thigh joint to see if the juices run pink (medium rare) or clear (well done). Cut into halves or quarters with poultry shears.

Pheasant with Sauerkraut

1 young pheasant
2 pounds of sauerkraut
2 cups chicken broth
1 cup white wine
8 juniper berries, crushed

½ teaspoon caraway seeds
4 tablespoons butter
1 teaspoon salt
1 teaspoon freshly ground pepper

Drain the sauerkraut and place in a casserole deep enough to accommodate the pheasant. Add the broth, wine, juniper berries, and caraway seeds. Cover and simmer for 1 hour in a 350° oven.

Meanwhile prepare the pheasant. Make sure it is well cleaned and singed. Pat dry with paper towels. Melt the butter in a skillet and brown the pheasant on all sides. Sprinkle with salt and pepper, and arrange in the casserole on the sauerkraut. Increase the oven temperature to 375°. Cover the casserole and bake 45 minutes to 1 hour, until the pheasant is tender. Arrange the bird on a platter surrounded by the sauerkraut. Serves 2.

Fish and Shellfish

Pompano en Papillote

6 Pompano fillets
Duxelles (see below)
Salt and freshly ground pepper

3 tablespoons chopped parsley
6 tablespoons butter
6 thin slices of lemon

Cut six pieces of aluminum foil or parchment into heart shapes large enough to hold a fillet when folded, with room to spare. Lay a fillet on half of each piece of foil, spread a tablespoon or so of the Duxelles over it, and sprinkle with salt and pepper and a teaspoon of chopped parsley. Dot with 1 tablespoon of butter, and top with a lemon slice. Fold the other half of the foil over the fillet, not too tightly, and crimp the edges to seal. Place on a baking sheet, and bake at 425°, allowing 10 minutes per inch of thickness of the fish, with an extra 5 minutes for the foil or paper. Serve in the foil and cut open at the table. Serves 6.

Duxelles

½ pound mushrooms
4 tablespoons butter

1 shallot, peeled and finely chopped
Salt and freshly ground black pepper

Wipe the mushrooms clean with a damp cloth and chop very fine. Melt the butter in a small heavy skillet and add the mushrooms and shallots. Mix the two together and let cook down over low heat until the moisture has evaporated and the mushrooms have become quite dark in color. They should not sauté. Sprinkle with salt and pepper. Cool slightly before spreading on the fish. Any excess can be stored in a jar in the refrigerator for about a week.

Escabeche of Flounder

2 pounds flounder or sole fillets
Lemon or lime juice (enough for dipping the fish)
Flour
4 tablespoons butter
1 clove of garlic, crushed
3 additional tablespoons lemon or lime juice
⅓ cup orange juice

⅓ cup olive oil
¼ cup minced green onions
Dash of Tabasco or cayenne pepper
Salt to taste
Optional: 1 tablespoon chopped fresh coriander
Garnish: ripe olives and quartered lemons or limes

Dip the fillets in the citrus juice and then in flour. Sauté in butter until nicely browned on both sides. This will have to be done in two batches. Transfer to a serving dish large enough to marinate the fish in one layer. Combine the garlic, 3 tablespoons of lemon or lime juice, orange juice, olive oil, green onions, Tabasco or cayenne, salt, and coriander, if using. Pour over the fish and refrigerate for at least 24 hours. Serve as a first course or buffet dish garnished with ripe olives and lemon or lime wedges. Serves 6 to 8.

Codfish Portugaise

1 pound dried salt codfish
2 cloves garlic, minced
⅓ cup heavy cream, warmed
⅔ cup olive oil, warmed

2 cloves garlic, minced
2 cups mashed potatoes
½ teaspoon freshly ground black pepper
½ cup buttered bread crumbs

Soak the codfish for at least 12 hours or overnight in cold water. Then drain and break into small pieces. Put in a pan, cover with water, and bring to a boil. Simmer for 5 minutes or until it is tender and flakes. Drain and cool. Pound in a mortar or purée in a food processor with the garlic to make a paste, while alternately adding spoonfuls of cream and oil, which should become completely absorbed. Finally add the pepper.

Thoroughly blend with the mashed potatoes, spoon into a buttered baking dish, and sprinkle with the crumbs. Bake at 350° for about 35 minutes or until hot. Serves 4 to 6.

Mussels Lucullus

2 to 3 quarts mussels
1 cup dry white wine
3 to 4 pounds fresh spinach or
    2 packages frozen
4 tablespoons olive oil
3 tablespoons butter

Salt and freshly ground black pepper
1 cup heavy cream
4 egg yolks, lightly beaten
Pinch of saffron
Bread crumbs

Put the mussels in a large heavy pan, add the wine, and cover. Steam over medium heat until the mussels open. Take them out of the shell and beard them. Strain the liquid in the pan and reserve. Cook the spinach until just done, then drain and chop. Heat with the olive oil and butter, and season with salt and pepper. Butter a gratin dish, layer in the spinach, and arrange the mussels over the top.

Reduce the mussel liquid by a third over medium heat. Make a sauce by combining the reduced liquid, heavy cream, egg yolks, and saffron, and cooking over low heat until thickened. Do not allow to boil. Pour over the mussels and spinach, sprinkle with fine bread crumbs, and bake in a 400° oven for 5 to 10 minutes to glaze. Serves 6 to 8.

Scallop Quiche

9-inch unsweetened pastry shell
1 to 1½ cups bay scallops or sea scallops
    cut into smaller pieces
1 teaspoon onion juice
1 teaspoon chopped fresh dill
2 tablespoons chopped parsley

1½ cups heavy cream
4 eggs, lightly beaten
1 egg white, lightly beaten
¾ teaspoon salt
¼ teaspoon freshly ground pepper

Line the shell with foil and fill with dried beans to keep the crust from puffing up during baking. Bake at 425° for 15 to 20 minutes to set the bottom. Remove the foil and beans, brush the shell with egg white, and return to the oven for 2 minutes to dry it and seal the crust. Remove from the oven and allow to cool. Arrange the scallops in the shell, sprinkle with onion juice, dill, and parsley. Blend the cream, whole eggs, and salt and pepper together. Pour over the scallops and bake at once in a 350° oven for about 30 minutes or until the custard is set. Serves 4 to 6.

Vegetables, Dried
Beans, and Grains

Asparagus Helen Evans Brown

Allow ½ pound of asparagus per person, before trimming. Slice on the diagonal ¼ of an inch thick, so you have pieces about 1½ inches long. Plunge into salted boiling water — you can use a deep-fry basket for this — for just two minutes, then drain and toss with butter. The asparagus should be just barely tender and crisp.

Champagne Kraut

1 medium head of cabbage, shredded
4 tablespoons bacon drippings

Salt and freshly ground black pepper
1 bottle champagne

Heat the bacon fat in a large skillet, add the cabbage, and sauté it lightly, tossing it as it cooks. Sprinkle with salt and pepper. Add the champagne, cover, and reduce the heat. Braise for 10 minutes, then uncover, toss the cabbage again, and continue cooking till it tender, with a bit of crispness. Serve with pork or ham.

Helen Evans Brown's White Cucumber Salad

For each large cucumber, peeled:
1 tablespoon grated onion

½ cup good homemade mayonnaise
Salt

Slice the cucumber very thin. Combine the onion with the mayonnaise. Arrange a layer of cucumber slices in a shallow dish, sprinkle with salt, and spread with mayonnaise. Continue making layers of cucumber, salt, and mayonnaise, ending with a topping of mayonnaise. Refrigerate for 12 to 24 hours, during which the dressing will whiten and the cucumbers will wilt.

Cecily's Fried Onion Rings

3 or 4 large Spanish onions   1 cup flour
Ice water   ½ teaspoon salt
1 egg, beaten   ½ teaspoon baking soda
1 cup buttermilk

Slice the onions about ¼ inch thick, separate them into rings, and soak in ice water for two hours. Meanwhile prepare the batter. Mix the beaten egg and buttermilk together, and stir in the flour, which has been sifted with the salt and baking soda. Drain the onions rings and dry well. Dip in the batter and deep-fry in fat or oil at 375° until nicely brown. Drain well on paper towels. Serves 4.

Disgustingly Rich Potatoes

6 large baking potatoes   1 teaspoon freshly ground black pepper
12 tablespoons butter   Extra butter
1 cup heavy cream   ¼ pound Gruyère, shredded
2 teaspoons salt

Bake the potatoes. When thoroughly done, split them and scoop out their skins into a bowl. Add the butter, cream, and seasonings, toss lightly, and transfer to a shallow baking dish. Dot well with butter, and sprinkle with the cheese. Bake at 375° for 15 minutes. Serves 6.

Potato and Carrot Casserole

4 baking potatoes, peeled and thinly   ¼ cup butter
  sliced   ½ cup parsley, finely chopped
8 carrots, peeled and thinly sliced in Salt and freshly ground black pepper
  rounds   Parsley for garnishing

Butter an oven-to-table baking dish. In it arrange layers in the following order: potatoes, carrots, parsley, potatoes, carrots, parsley, potatoes. Sprinkle with salt and pepper, and dot with butter.

Bake in a 375° oven until tender, about 35 to 40 minutes, covering with foil for the first 15 minutes. Remove from the oven, garnish with parsley sprigs, and serve from the baking dish. Serve with any roast meat or fowl. Serves 4.

Ham and Kidney Bean Tureen

3 cups dried kidney beans, cooked,
  or 7 cups canned kidney beans
1½ cups onions, finely chopped
6 tablespoons butter
1 teaspoon thyme
1 teaspoon summer savory

3 cups cooked ham, cut in ½-inch cubes
2 cups red wine
2 tablespoons tomato paste
Salt and freshly ground pepper
½ cup finely chopped green onions
¼ cup chopped parsley

If using dried beans, boil until just tender but not mushy. If using canned, simply rinse briefly. Sauté the onions in the butter until softened but not browned. Add the herbs and ham, then the wine and tomato paste. Simmer over low heat for 25 minutes. Taste for salt, adding if needed, and pepper. Combine with the beans in an ovenproof casserole, and heat in a moderate oven until good and hot. Sprinkle with the chopped green onions and parsley, and serve from the casserole or a tureen. Serves 8 to 10.

Helen Evans Brown's Black Beans

2 pounds dried black beans
1 tablespoon salt
1 medium onion, stuck with 2 cloves
1 garlic clove, peeled
1 bay leaf
1 teaspoon dried thyme
1 teaspoon summer savory

2 sprigs parsley
2 stalks of celery
A ham bone or hock
Beurre manié
½ cup of Jamaican rum
1 teaspoon of Tabasco
Sour cream

Put the beans in a pot, add water, and let them soak overnight. Drain, return to the pot, and add the salt, onion, garlic, herbs, ham bone or hock, and enough water to cover by about an inch. Cover, bring to a boil, then reduce to a simmer. Cook until the beans are just tender. Drain off the liquid and set aside. Discard the vegetables, bay leaf, and parsley. Cut the meat off the ham bone or hock and reserve. Put the liquid in a saucepan and reduce over high heat for 5 minutes. Thicken with beurre manié — about 2 tablespoons each of butter and flour kneaded together and added to the boiling liquid in bits. Taste for salt. Put the beans and ham bits in a baking dish, and add the rum, Tabasco, and enough of the liquid to barely cover. Bake at 350° until thoroughly heated — 20 to 30 minutes. Serve with cold sour cream. Serves 6 to 8.

Barley and Mushroom Casserole

1 cup pearl barley
4 to 5 tablespoons butter
1 large onion, peeled and chopped
½ pound mushrooms, cleaned and sliced

2 cups chicken broth
¼ cup toasted sliced almonds (optional)

Melt the butter in a skillet and sauté the onions and mushrooms until soft. Add the barley and stir over moderate heat until it begins to color. Transfer to a buttered casserole. Taste the broth for salt, and correct the seasoning if necessary. Pour 1 cup of the broth into the casserole, stir, and cover. Bake in a 350° oven for half an hour, then add the second cup of broth. Also add the almonds at this point, if you wish. Continue cooking until the barley is done and the broth has been absorbed, about another half hour. Serves 4.

Elena's Rice

¾ cup uncooked rice
2 cups sour cream
Salt to taste
½ pound Jack cheese or Mozzarella

1 7-ounce can peeled green chilies
Butter
Additional cheese, grated (optional)

Cook the rice in 1½ cups water and a scant teaspoon of salt for 20 minutes or until tender but still firm. Allow to cool for a few minutes and then combine with the sour cream. Taste for seasoning. Cut the cheese into rectangular pieces about ¾ of an inch wide, 1½ inches long, and ¼ inch thick. Wrap each in a strip of the chili pepper.

Butter a casserole and put in a layer of half the rice. Arrange the wrapped cheese over this, and top with the remaining rice. Dot with butter and, if you want, with additional grated cheese. Bake at 400° for about 15 minutes. Serves 4 to 6.

Breads

Brioche Mousseline

1 package dry yeast
½ cup warm (100°–115°) water
1 tablespoon sugar
5 cups all-purpose flour, sifted

½ pound slightly softened butter
1 teaspoon salt
6 eggs
⅓ cup warm milk

Dissolve the yeast and sugar in the warm water, and mix in 1 cup of flour to make a paste. Set aside in a warm place.

The next step can be by hand, with a bowl and wooden spoon or spatula, or in an electric mixer equipped with a dough hook. Combine the remaining flour with the butter and salt. Beat by hand or in the mixer at low speed until well blended, then add the eggs, one at a time. Beat until smooth. Then add the yeast mixture and beat again. Turn out into a buttered bowl, cover with a towel, and let rise in a warm place until double in bulk.

Punch down, add the warm milk, and work the dough again until smooth. Transfer to a buttered and floured Charlotte mold or loaf tin, cover with a towel, and let rise again. Bake at 375° until golden brown, about 35 to 45 minutes.

Mabelle Jeffcott's Bread

1 13-ounce can evaporated milk
2½ cups hot water
¼ cup melted butter
3 tablespoons sugar

2 tablespoons salt
2 packages active dry yeast
3 cups coarse graham flour
5 to 6 cups all-purpose flour

This recipe makes two or three firm, rather hefty loaves.

Mix the milk, hot water, butter, sugar, and salt together in a bowl and allow to cool to 100°–115°. Stir in the yeast to thoroughly dissolve. Then mix in the graham flour, a cup at a time, followed by

the white flour, using an electric mixer and dough hook or working by hand with a wooden spoon. If using a mixer, beat at slow
speed until the dough is satiny and leaves the sides of the bowl. Or
turn the dough out on a lightly floured board and knead by hand.

Place the dough in a buttered bowl, cover with a kitchen towel,
and set in a warm, draft-free spot to rise until about double in
bulk. Punch down, turn out on a lightly floured surface, and
divide into two or three portions. Form into loaves and place in
buttered bread tins. Cover and let rise again until not quite double
in bulk. Bake at 375° about 1 hour, until well browned.

Helen Evans Brown's Corn Chili Bread

3 ears of husked raw corn   *¾ cup melted butter*
1 cup yellow cornmeal   *2 eggs*
2 teaspoons salt   *¼ pound Monterey Jack cheese, diced*
3 teaspoons baking powder   *1 4-ounce can chopped green chilies*
1 cup sour cream

Cut the kernels from the corn, put into a bowl, and combine with
the rest of the ingredients. Pour into a buttered 2½-quart soufflé
dish or a 9-inch square baking dish. Bake at 350° for 1 hour. Serve
with butter.

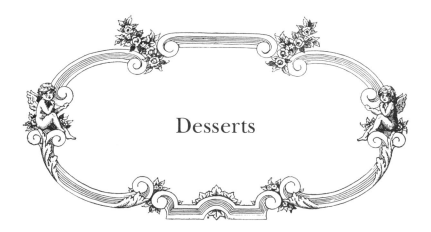

Desserts

Ginger Soufflé

6 eggs
3 tablespoons butter
3 tablespoons flour

¾ cup heated milk
½ cup sugar
½ cup finely chopped preserved ginger

Separate the eggs, setting aside one yolk for some other use. Melt the butter in a saucepan, stir in the flour, and cook over medium heat for a minute or so. Then slowly stir in the milk. Continue to stir until well thickened and smooth. Remove from the heat. Lightly beat the 5 egg yolks, stir in some of the cream sauce to warm the eggs, then add to the rest of the sauce. Mix well and then add the sugar and ginger. Beat the egg whites until just stiffened but not dry. Fold about a third of the whites into the sauce, then combine with the rest of the whites, folding gently. Pour into a buttered and sugared 1½-quart soufflé dish. Bake at 375° for 25 to 30 minutes, until nicely risen and lightly browned. Serve with sweetened whipped cream. Serves 4.

Omelet Soufflé

8 eggs, separated
½ cup sugar
¼ cup lemon juice
Grated rind of a lemon

Butter
Extra sugar
½ cup cognac or rum

Beat the egg yolks until light in texture and color, and gradually beat in the sugar. Add the lemon juice and rind. Beat the egg whites until stiff but not dry, and fold ⅓ into the egg-sugar mixture. Then fold with the rest of the whites.

Heat a 10-inch cast-aluminum or all-metal ovenproof skillet, brush well with butter, and sprinkle with sugar. Pour the soufflé mixture into the skillet, and bake at 375° for 15 minutes or until puffed and lightly browned. Remove from the oven, sprinkle with sugar, and pour the cognac over it. Carefully ignite, making sure there is nothing above it or near it to catch fire. Serve at once from the skillet. Serves 8.

Cherry Flan

8 tablespoons butter
⅓ cup sugar
5 eggs, separated
1 teaspoon vanilla
2 cups fine bread crumbs, soaked in
⅓ cup milk

1½ cup pitted Bing cherries, tossed with
1 tablespoon sugar and 1 tablespoon
kirsch or cognac
Confectioner's sugar

This recipe falls somewhere between a clafouti and a flan.

Cream the butter and sugar together, and blend in the egg yolks one by one. Press the breadcrumbs dry, and beat into the mixture. Beat the egg whites until stiff but not dry, and fold in. Pour into a buttered tart mold or flan mold, and top with the drained cherries. Bake at 375° for about 45 minutes. Serve warm or cold, sprinkled with confectioner's sugar. Serves 4.

Délice au Chocolat

1 pint milk
1½ cups sugar
½ pound unsweetened chocolate
½ pound butter
4 eggs separated

2⅓ cups sifted cake flour
2 teaspoons baking powder
Praline filling (see below)
8 ounces toasted almond halves

This is a dense, rich, almost fudgy dessert. Combine the milk, sugar, chocolate, and butter in a saucepan, and watch carefully while bringing just to a boil over medium heat. Remove from the heat and allow to cool slightly. Sift the flour and baking powder together. Stir the egg yolks and flour into the milk-chocolate mixture, and beat for 5 minutes by hand or 2 minutes in an electric mixer at medium speed until the mixture is well integrated. Beat the egg whites until beginning to stiffen; do not overbeat. Fold the whites into the chocolate mixture. Pour into a round 10-x-2-inch cake pan or deep springform pan lined with buttered parchment or wax paper. Bake at 325° for 40 to 50 minutes or until the cake is firm but still slightly soft at the center. Allow to cool thoroughly to avoid melting the filling. Then turn out on a rack and slice in half horizontally. Spread the filling on the bottom layer and reassemble. Arrange the toasted almond halves over the top. Serves 12.

Praline Filling

½ cup slightly softened butter   *¼ cup sugar*
1 cup powdered praline (see below)

Blend the butter with the praline and sugar until the mixture is light and creamy.

Praline Powder

1 cup sugar   *½ cup toasted filberts, finely chopped*
½ cup toasted almonds, finely chopped

Melt the sugar in a small heavy skillet or saucepan, and when it begins to lightly color add the chopped nuts. Pour in a shallow buttered pan, and allow to cool completely and become crisp. Then pound to a powder in a mortar or crush with a rolling pin.

Chocolate Crêpes

For the crêpes:
⅞ *cup of all-purpose flour (1 cup less 2 tablespoons)*
3 tablespoons sugar
⅛ *teaspoon salt*
3 eggs
1 to 1¼ cups of milk
4 tablespoons melted butter
2 tablespoons cognac
1 teaspoon vanilla

For the chocolate sauce:
12 ounces semisweet chocolate
2 ounces bitter chocolate
1 tablespoon instant coffee
3 tablespoons hot water
1 cup heavy cream
2 tablespoons cognac
Plus:
½ *pound semisweet chocolate, grated*
Chopped pistachio nuts
Sweetened whipped cream

To make the crêpes: Sift the flour, sugar, and salt together. Beat the eggs in a bowl or electric mixer until well integrated. Stir in the milk. Stir in the flour. Blend well, and add 2 tablespoons of melted butter and the flavorings. Beat until the batter is smooth and has the consistency of light cream. Add the rest of the milk if necessary. Cover the bowl and let the batter rest for an hour or two.

To bake: Brush a 6-inch crêpe pan well with melted butter and heat. When moderately hot pour in about 1½ tablespoons of batter, tipping the pan so it flows evenly over the entire surface. Soon after the batter has set begin lifting one edge with a spatula to see if it has lightly browned. Then turn it quickly to brown the other side.

Makes approximately 16 crêpes.

To make the chocolate sauce: Melt the chocolate in a double boiler over moderate heat. Add the coffee, dissolved in the hot water. Stir until smooth. Blend in the cream and cognac. Keep warm while preparing the crêpes.

To assemble the crêpes: As each crêpe is baked, sprinkle with a bit of grated chocolate and stack one on another until you have a pile of 14 to 16. Keep them warm as you continue to bake. When ready to serve, pour the chocolate sauce over the top. Garnish with chopped pistachio nuts. Serve in wedges with sweetened whipped cream.

Chocolate Potato Cake

12 tablespoons butter
2 cups sugar
4 eggs
1 cup unseasoned puréed potatoes
  (instant can be used)
2 ounces unsweetened chocolate
2 cups sifted cake flour
1/2 teaspoon baking soda

2 teaspoons baking powder
1/2 teaspoon salt
1 teaspoon cinnamon
1/2 teaspoon nutmeg
1/4 teaspoon cloves
1/2 cup milk
1 cup toasted, coarsely chopped walnuts

In an electric mixer, cream the butter, then cream with the sugar. Add the eggs, and beat until smooth and light. Melt the chocolate over warm water, and add to the mixture with the potatoes. Blend in well. Sift the cake flour with the baking soda and other dry ingredients, and mix in alternately with the milk. Finally add the nuts. Pour the batter into a greased and floured 10-inch tube pan. Bake in a 350° oven for about 1 hour or until the cake surface springs back when pressed lightly toward the center. Place on a rack to cool before unmolding. Serve plain as a tea cake or with sweetened whipped cream. Serves 4 to 6.

Tipsy Parson

1 8-inch sponge cake layer
2/3 cup sweet sherry
3 eggs plus two yolks
1/2 cup sugar

1/4 teaspoon salt
3 cups light cream, scalded
2 teaspoons vanilla extract
3/4 cup toasted slivered almonds

Slice the cake horizontally and douse each half with the sherry. Refrigerate to chill. Lightly beat the eggs and egg yolks and combine in the top of a double boiler with the sugar and salt. Slowly stir in the hot cream, and continue to stir over simmering water (not touching) until the mixture begins to thicken slightly and coats a metal spoon. Remove from the heat and stir in the vanilla. Cool and then refrigerate to chill thoroughly.

Butter an 8-inch springform pan and arrange the bottom layer of the sponge cake in it. Sprinkle with ½ cup of the almonds and spread with half the custard. Place the top layer over it, spread with the remaining custard, and sprinkle with the remaining almonds, which have been crushed. Refrigerate for two hours before removing from the pan to a chilled platter. Serves 6.

Blueberry Grunt

Filling:
3 cups blueberries
⅓ cup sugar
¼ teaspoon each cinnamon, nutmeg, and cloves
¼ cup molasses
2 tablespoons lemon juice

Biscuit crust:
1 cup flour
1½ teaspoons baking powder
¼ teaspoon salt
3 tablespoons butter
1 tablespoon vegetable shortening
1 egg, slightly beaten
⅓ cup milk

Pick over the berries, and wash and drain them. Spread them in a deep 9-inch baking dish or pan. Mix the sugar and spices together and sprinkle over the berries, followed by a dribbling of the molasses and then the lemon juice. Bake at 375° for 5 minutes. Remove from the oven and turn up the heat to 425°.

Prepare the crust: Sift the flour, baking powder, and salt together. Work in the butter and shortening with a fork or in an electric mixer or food processor. Then blend in the egg and just enough milk to make a quite soft dough. Drop this by spoonfuls over the berries, and smooth to cover the entire surface. Bake for 20 minutes or until the crust is nicely browned. Serve hot with heavy cream, whipped cream, or a hard sauce. Serves 6 to 8.

Viennese Nut Bars

½ pound unsalted butter
1 cup sugar

1 large egg yolk
1 to 2 tablespoons heavy cream

1 egg white, lightly beaten until slightly
    frothy
2½ cups all-purpose flour
¼ teaspoon salt

1 teaspoon cinnamon
½ cup chopped almonds or filberts
Additional sugar

This cookie has a shortbread-like texture. Cream together the butter and sugar, add the egg yolk, and thoroughly blend in the flour,
salt, and cinnamon. Roll or pat out ½ inch thick on a buttered
cookie sheet or 13¼-x-9¼-inch jelly roll pan. Brush well with the
beaten egg white. Sprinkle with the chopped nuts and additional
sugar. Bake at 350° 25 to 30 minutes until lightly browned and crisp.
Allow to cool, and cut into squares or rectangles.

Prunes, Alice B. Toklas

24 large pitted prunes
1 bottle or more of port
½ cup sugar

½ pint heavy cream, whipped
Macaroons

Put the prunes in a large bowl, cover with port, and allow to steep
for 24 hours. Drain off the port into a saucepan, add ½ more cup
of port and the sugar, and stir. Return the prunes to the port,
bring to a boil, and boil for 1 minute. Remove from the heat and
let the prunes completely cool. Refrigerate for another 24 hours.
Serve with whipped cream topped with crumbled macaroons.
Serves 6.

Coffee-Cognac Ice Cream

1 quart heavy cream
1 cup light cream
1 cup sugar
1 teaspoon vanilla

½ cup cognac
2 tablespoons instant coffee
Dash of salt

Blend the ingredients together in a bowl, and refrigerate to chill
well. Then freeze in a hand-cranked freezer packed with salt and
ice or in any of the modern electric-turned freezers,

Frozen Zabaglione

8 egg yolks
⅔ cup sugar
1 tablespoon grated lemon rind
1 cup Marsala

½ envelope gelatin dissolved in
   2 tablespoons cold water
3 tablespoons Grand Marnier
1 pint heavy cream, whipped

Place the yolks in a bowl and beat well, then beat in the sugar, lemon rind, and Marsala. Transfer to the top of a double boiler and continue beating over gently boiling water until thickened. Add the dissolved gelatin and Grand Marnier. Put the pan in a bowl of ice, and beat the mixture till cold, then fold in the whipped cream. Spoon into a serving bowl or individual dishes and put in the freezer for several hours. Serves 8.

Crystallized Cranberries

2 cups fresh cranberries
4 cups sugar
1 cup water

Pinch of cream of tartar
Small pinch of salt

Wash the cranberries and dry well. Make a hole through each berry with a thin skewer or toothpick. Combine 3 cups of the sugar with the water, cream of tartar, and salt in a 2-to-3-quart pan. Cook over medium heat until the sugar is dissolved. Increase the heat until the syrup boils, and continue boiling for about 5 minutes or until a temperature of 234°F (soft-ball stage) is reached on a candy thermometer. Remove from the heat, add the cranberries, and stir to coat them with syrup. Let them stand for at least 12 hours or overnight at room temperature.

Drain the berries over a bowl, and return the syrup to a saucepan. Bring to a boil again, and this time boil to the hard-ball stage — 250°F–255°F. Remove from the heat, add the cranberries, and stir to coat them. Then transfer them with a slotted spoon to waxed paper or parchment. Arrange in a single layer, not touching, and move individual berries to another spot if too much syrup accumulates around them. When the berries are cool enough to handle, roll a few at a time in the remaining sugar, and transfer to a clean piece of wax paper to set and cool.

General Index

Food Index